IMAGES
of America

PRESTON

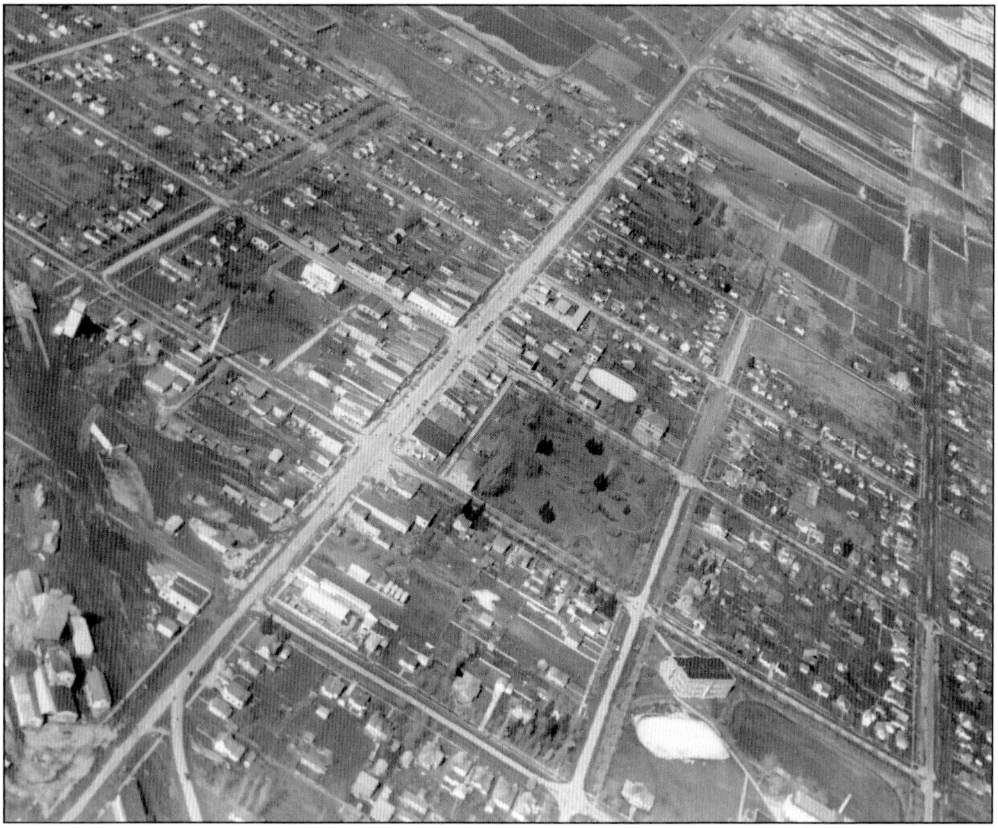

This aerial view of Preston, looking north, shows several landmarks. At lower right stand the Jefferson School (demolished in 1997), the Preston High School football field, and an iced-over skating rink. Preston's original City Park (now called Benson Park), with its circling paths and four large stands of evergreens, is at center. In the park's lower-left corner is the Opera House (torn down in 1962). On the park's north is the Central School (torn down in 1974) and Preston Post Office (built in 1939). At upper center is the original horse track that stood where today's City Park ball diamonds and playground stand. Joseph Marion Perkins deeded the property to the City of Preston during the 1940s. Former Preston City clerk Arlene Nash remembers a picture of the track that showed that it had a grandstand. (Courtesy of Myrna Fuller.)

On the Cover: Thousands of people gather along the route followed by That Famous Preston Night Rodeo Parade, as they have since 1921. This view covers the east side of State Street, from Anderson Lumber to Griggs' Cafe, run by Howard and Hulda Griggs. The couple moved from Grace, Idaho, to Preston in 1929 and opened their first café at about 40 South State Street. The census that year lists Howard as the cook and Hulda as the waitress. They had two children. The *Preston Citizen* reported that the family moved to Twin Falls, where they ran a coffee shop and motor lodge, dating this photograph to sometime between 1930 and 1938. When they left, they leased their café to Lura Newbold of Hollywood, California, who specialized in hosting parties. The newspaper reported many parties at Griggs' Cafe. (Author's collection.)

IMAGES
of America

PRESTON

Necia P. Seamons

ARCADIA
PUBLISHING

ISBN 978-1-4671-3282-4

Published by Arcadia Publishing
Charleston, South Carolina

Printed in the United States of America

Library of Congress Control Number: 2014946258

For all general information, please contact Arcadia Publishing:
Telephone 843-853-2070
Fax 843-853-0044
E-mail sales@arcadiapublishing.com
For customer service and orders:
Toll-Free 1-888-313-2665

Visit us on the Internet at www.arcadiapublishing.com

To the youth of Franklin County—may they know from whence they came, then guide their children into the future.

Contents

Acknowledgments

This book would not have been possible without the efforts of Newell Hart (1913–1983). He was Franklin County's quintessential historian, having collected vast amounts of information in his years of writing the *Cache Valley Newsletter*, *Hometown Album*, and *Hometown Sketchbook*, as well as indexing, updating, and republishing *The Trail Blazer* in 1976 (the original was published in 1930 by the Daughters of the Utah Pioneers). I never met Newell, but after visiting his wife and publishing partner, Ruth, and their granddaughter Sorel Frew at the Bloody Bucket, where they made their peacock-guarded home, I wish I had. To have met Newell would have been colorfully enlightening. I thank Hart's descendants who have passed some of his collection on to me. It is the basis from which this book has been compiled. Unless otherwise noted, the photographs in this book come from the Newell Hart collection.

Additional pictures come from Jay Burrup, Kathy Griffin, Bill Owens, Kris Beckstead (chairman of That Famous Preston Night Rodeo committee) and the history center at the Larsen-Sant Library, directed by Myrna Fuller.

Furthermore, Fuller's help in scanning large images was essential, and the book would have large holes in information if she and Allie Hansen had not lent a hand in proofreading.

Finally, thanks to my family for trying to understand my love of the people who lived out the history within these pages, and my desire to share what I have learned. My personal connection to Preston began a short 20 years ago, when my new bosses, Walt Ross and Wayne Bell, began tutoring me in public service as I wrote and edited the *Preston Citizen*. Today, I have found a much deeper tie to this place I call home: purpose.

INTRODUCTION

Although the first settlers of Preston, Idaho, began living temporarily in the city's current limits as early as the mid-1860s, it was almost 40 years before they officially incorporated the town as a formal entity on July 24, 1900, and that was for the purpose of addressing a mud fight.

With a current population of 5,145, Preston is located six miles north of the Utah-Idaho border, 28 miles north of Logan, Utah. The community sits 4,714 feet above sea level on the floor of the ancient Lake Bonneville. The millennia of silt that fell to the lake's floor has made for deep, rich soil in which local residents have built their lives as farmers, dairymen, cattlemen, and businessmen catering to the needs of the agricultural professions.

But that richness was not easy to ply from the grip of Mother Nature. Fortunately, the Mormon pioneers who set out to do just that had become used to overcoming difficulty as they fled persecution in the eastern states. Their trials had made them a determined, hardy folk, capable of taking on Gaia herself.

Preston is situated on what was once a windblown, sandy flat decorated with grass and sagebrush. Soon after building a fort at Idaho's first permanent white settlement, Franklin, in 1860, these pioneers pushed north to what they called North Meadows or Head Meadows (near Johnson Reservoir) to cut grass with a scythe and haul it back to Franklin for their cattle. Stoddard and Potter, a cattle company from Farmington, Utah, and other settlers then brought up a herd to graze a range that stretched from the east side of Glendale Reservoir to an area bordered by Winn Bottoms (on the Bear River) on the west, Worm Creek on the north, and Thomas Ditch (Lewiston Canal) on the south. That enterprise lasted but a few years, as the cattle and sheep eventually stripped the foliage that held down the sand it grew in.

By that time, a few settlers had braved leaving the safety of the fort in Franklin and were trying to build homes out of what they considered wilderness and the native residents considered their homes. William Head used squatter's rights in 1866 to claim the meadows and build a two-room home. He cut and preserved the native grasses, eventually raising 90 head of cattle, worth $6 each. His wife and children returned to the fort during the winter. There was safety in numbers there, and the children could gain an education during the cold winter months.

In 1867, John Winn built a cabin about eight blocks south of the current center of town, down by the Bear River. He used it only while grazing his cattle there, but the place became known as Winn Bottoms anyway. Other families followed, mostly on the east side of the flat, where water and grass were more plentiful. They worked together to scratch out a living, learning lessons along the way. Hyrum Jensen, who was born in 1868 in Franklin, once told local historian Newell Hart that, when he was a child herding his family's cattle out on the flat during the 1870s, the dry grass ignited a spark of curiosity in his young mind, so he touched a match to it. He thought the fire would stop at a ditch. "But boom—it spread all over the flat, for miles. There wasn't a thing left in sight. But I didn't do a bit of damage—there wasn't a single building here," he winked.

By 1877, enough settlers had come to the flat that they set up a community school in the granary of Robert M. Hull, located in the area known today as Whitney. Two years later, the community started to build a new school. Terrible winter weather forced construction to stop, and by the next spring, several residents had decided the building should be erected closer to the center of the population growing on the flat. As the area was part of the ecclesiastical unit called a stake in the Church of Jesus Christ of Latter-day Saints (Mormon Church, or LDS), and most of the settlers were of that belief, they sought a solution from the presiding leader of the Cache Valley Stake. Bishop William B. Preston decided to move the school to a location now indicated by a marker placed by the Daughters of the Utah Pioneers on the hill east of Worm Creek on Fourth South in Preston. The 16-foot-by-18-foot log structure they built there served until it was moved to the center of Preston's current city limits in 1884.

Despite the lush grasses, those first settlers barely survived the severe winters, when fruits, vegetables, and water would often freeze inside the log homes. In 1876 and 1879, the conditions were so severe that pioneers resorted to hauling hay from Smithfield for $15 per load and tearing straw from the roofing in their sheds to feed the few cattle that survived the deep snows and bitter cold.

Even the summers were difficult. Nellie Parkinson recorded that she would get up at 4:00 a.m. to wash her laundry and hang it out on the line in order to get it put away before the wind started blowing the sand dunes north at 9:00 a.m. "If I had not, we could never have found our clothes by night." By then, the wind would have blown the sand dunes back to the south "in time for the next morning's blow," she wrote. Parkinson stubbornly used her wash water to nourish tree saplings that her neighbors never thought would survive.

"I used to sit on my doorstep and cry with homesickness and think if I could just see one piece of green vegetation I would be content," she penned.

It was the ingenuity of ditch digging that saved those settlers' homesteading efforts. In 1881, they hired David Jenkins from Salt Lake City to survey a ditch. Jensen discovered that water could be brought from the larger, longer-running Cub River, around the hills, and into the area they had settled. So important was water to survival, a celebration heralded the ditch water as it crossed into the community for the first time. Men following its arrival to repair any leaks took their hats off and shouted "Hosanna!" three times. As food could be grown more efficiently, business could be conducted more readily.

Another ingredient to the success of the pioneers was pushing the railroad past Franklin to the flat in 1878. The Utah Northern Railroad brought jobs, money, more people, and goods. Eventually, a business center sprang up along the area's primary north-south street, today known as State Street. The main east-west corridor was called Oneida, honoring the name of the county to which the area belonged.

When Preston's first permanent residents arrived in 1877, they were merely an extension of Franklin, six miles to the south. But as people began to stay year-round on the flat, they developed into distinct communities. The area at the foot of the eastern foothills became Egypt. Where the school was first held became Whitney. The north side of the flat was called Poverty Flats (the name by which it was still known on the 1918 US Geological Survey). The location of the new school was Worm Creek, named after the stream winding through it.

Being settled by members of the Church of Jesus Christ of Latter-day Saints, those areas became wards (units similar to parishes) in the Cache Valley Stake. So on May 14, 1881, during a meeting of the Worm Creek Ward in the log schoolhouse constructed two years prior, Rachel Porter brought a complaint to visiting Bishop Preston. "Worm Creek" was simply not a respectable name for the community she was helping to build.

"Well, Sister Porter, what would you like your little ward called?" asked Preston.

"Let's name it Preston, after you," she replied. Apparently anyone with an opinion that counted agreed. Consequently, when the federal government granted a post office in 1882, it was to "Preston" and not "Worm Creek."

The town was officially surveyed and platted in 1888, centering on what was known as "the corner store." Legend says the store's owner moved the stake a few feet in the night because it was easier than moving the building. For that reason, say some, Preston's north-south streets are not plumb today.

But they were shady. In old photographs, one can see the fruits of the pioneers' determination to make the soil produce. Lombardy poplars line the street. "The spirit of Nellie Parkinson had spread and most of the sand stopped blowing," wrote Hart. "But most of the town's edges featured prominent dunes into my day [1913–1983]; the business section itself was crisscrossed with damp swails. As a small boy I played in the low dips of uptown Preston." A network of paths wound through sagebrush and large gaps between the businesses on the main street, Hart described.

In 1900, the town decided to cut the cord from its administrative entity, Malad City, the seat of Oneida County. The reason was mud. Once the sand was tamed, oozing mud had to be next. "Preston floats on quicksand, say the diggers," explained Hart. "It wasn't the desire to grow big, or even the natural cry to cut the umbilical cord, that caused the town to incorporate. It was the mud. And this is where Lorenzo Hansen comes in."

Hansen was the mayor of Preston from 1925 to 1935. He told Hart that, in 1900, "cattle and horses roamed the streets at will. Streets were very dirty in the summer and muddy in winter when not covered with . . . one to three feet of snow. This also included the sidewalk. You could not walk up Main [State] Street in those days of a freshet unless you had high-topped boots, and then sometimes you sunk a foot or two in the muck." Things got so bad that a public meeting was called.

A heated discussion ensued over the question of taxation. It was argued pro and con. Those who lived in Logan before moving to Preston insisted that a village or city government was a very expensive luxury, and sooner or later transient men would come to Preston and say, "let's put Preston on the map," plunging the city into debt from which it could not extricate itself. Whether the roads should be graded or graveled came in for another heated discussion. Finally, a majority decided that if some of the old reliable citizens would be named as village trustees and an extremely small levy made, that the town could get along for a few years and that a sidewalk would be laid from the center of town to the Oregon Short Line (OSL) Depot, which still stands on the corner of First South and First West.

So Preston City incorporated on July 24, 1900, "in the law offices of A.W. Hart, in the Parkinson Block, directly above today's Owl Billiards," wrote Hart. "A year later we had boardwalks—but that didn't stop the mud stories: 'Mud, mud, mud. Mud inside and mud outside, and mud everywhere! What fine school and shopping weather, you bet your rubber boots! . . . Five irrigation streams are running south past the Central School—only a good wader can cross . . . it is claimed that Preston's streets are good fishing.' "

Nevertheless, Preston prospered. In its first decade, it had two newspapers, two electric companies, two telephone companies, free band concerts once a week, and movie houses. The town just needed good water.

When the Sego Milk Plant was looking for a home, it turned down Preston due it its "yucky" well water. Following much campaigning and a deadly outbreak of typhoid fever, a bond for $75,000 passed to pipe water from Birch Springs 15 miles away in Cub River Canyon. That was accomplished by 1912. In 1913, the county was divided, and the east side, which included Preston, was called Franklin, after LDS apostle Franklin D. Richards. It is the only Franklin County in the United States *not* named after Benjamin Franklin.

The first baby born in the new county was Veda Elda, born to Alonzo and Eliza Alice Seamons just six hours and 20 minutes after the new designation. Hart captured the excitement of the community's growth:

> As 1914 dawned, Preston was abuzz with action and optimism: new Jefferson School and Nielsen Gym, 10 blocks of new cement sidewalk, Carnegie library underway, UP&L was building a new power plant in Oneida Narrows; Preston was voted the new county seat (Oxford had been); the new electric inter-urban rail line was being speeded towards town; we had exciting rumors, as always, of big developments (fur farms, hot springs resorts, gas

> wells, oil gushers) . . . and of peach orchards! (Riverdale was to become a peach grove. A corporation . . . formed . . . to raise 64,000 trees on 320 acres. Soon this would become the fruit-raising center and thousands of dollars would be left here by 'travelers who now go down to Utah.') In 1918 we built the first sewer system; in 1920 we got paved streets (we kids loved to chew tar from the many barrels)."

And so, Preston grew. People from around Cache Valley came to Preston to shop. By the 1940s, the city had 4,236 residents. The population declined to as low as 3,310 in 1970, then began growing again. In 2000, there were 4,682 residents. In 2014, there were 5,145, and the city had issued about 300 business licenses. Nevertheless, the town is considered a bedroom community to Logan, Utah. Residents joke that Preston is a town with two state capitals: Boise, Idaho, and Salt Lake City, Utah. Geographically, its residents belong to Idaho. Culturally, they identify largely with Utah.

This book draws heavily from information collected by Hart and his wife, Ruth Cutler Hart (1919–2006); the local chapters of the Daughters of the Utah Pioneers; area newspapers; and other publications. It covers the photographed history of Preston up until 1950, but by no means is it complete.

One

EDUCATION

Education was a top priority to Mormon pioneers. The first public school was organized in 1877 in the granary of Robert M. Hull that stood near the present site of the Franklin County sugar factory. Two years later, Emil Petterborg, J.O. Lawrence, and David Jensen began hauling logs for the first school building. Preston's first bishop, Nahum B. Porter, directed timbers be hewn from the hills east of Preston and stacked up to the square in the Whitney area. Then the fierce winter snows came, forcing work to stop. During those cold months, Francis Wilcox, Elam Hollingsworth, Thomas Heller, Martin Johnson, Ben Lamont, Israel West, and Erie B. Sabins (who lived on Poverty Flats) realized they wanted the building closer to their homes. A solution was sought from Bishop William B. Preston. He directed the settlers to dismantle the logs and raise them in a more central location—a hill high on the east bank of Worm Creek. The Daughters of the Utah Pioneers (DUP) placed a marker on the site on Fourth South in 1929.

In 1889, residents again deferred to church leaders to determine where to erect the Oneida Stake Academy (OSA). Mormon apostle Lorenzo Snow decided upon Preston instead of Franklin, where classes were being held at the time. Subsequently, a lot was donated where Preston High School now stands. Local craftsmen began quarrying rock from Cub River and cutting timber in Franklin Basin. It took four years to construct the elegant building, and children were educated there for over a century. The sacrifice and goal of these humble pioneers to lift the sights of their youth to greatness worked. World, national, and local leaders, as well as generations of simply good people, honed their skills within the walls of the OSA. Both Ezra Taft Benson (US secretary of agriculture) and Harold B. Lee became presidents of the worldwide Church of Jesus Christ of Latter-day Saints. Other alumni include Samuel Cowley, inducted into the FBI Hall of Fame, and E.G. Peterson, once beloved president of Utah State University (USU). The school's first football coach was Woody Romney; his great-uncle, Thomas C. Romney, was a principal there. They are both close relatives of former US presidential candidate Mitt Romney. George Nelson, one-time boxing great and namesake of the Nelson Field House at USU, coached wrestling at the OSA.

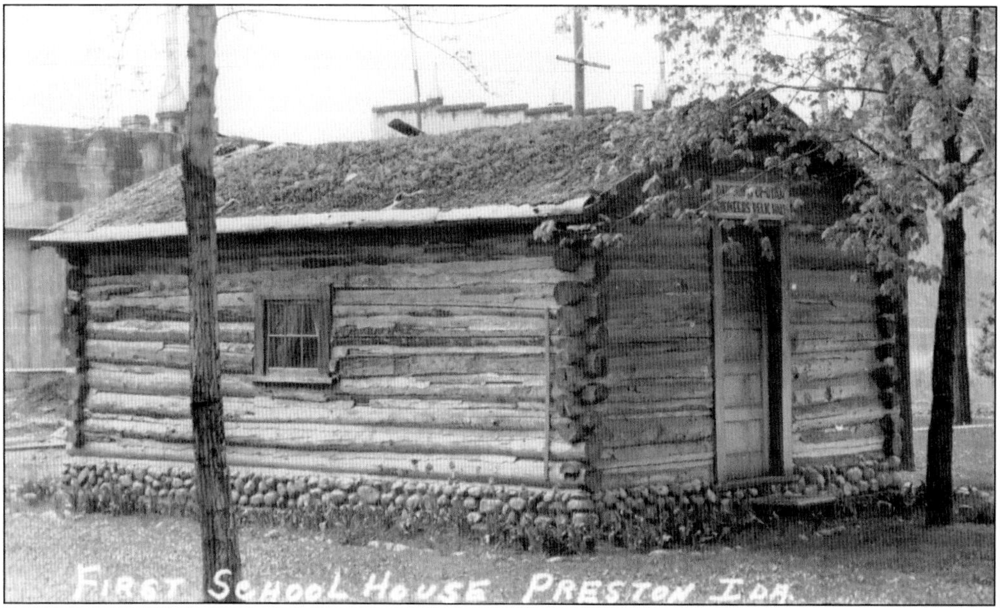

Built in 1877, this 16-by-18-foot log school also served as a church and social center. When schoolteacher Louisa Spongberg married Soren Peterson in 1882, they held their wedding dance inside. In 1884, the logs were dismantled, then raised near 70 South State Street as a chapel. They were later reassembled in Benson Park by the DUP. When the city moved the logs for a parking lot, they deteriorated. (Jay Burrup.)

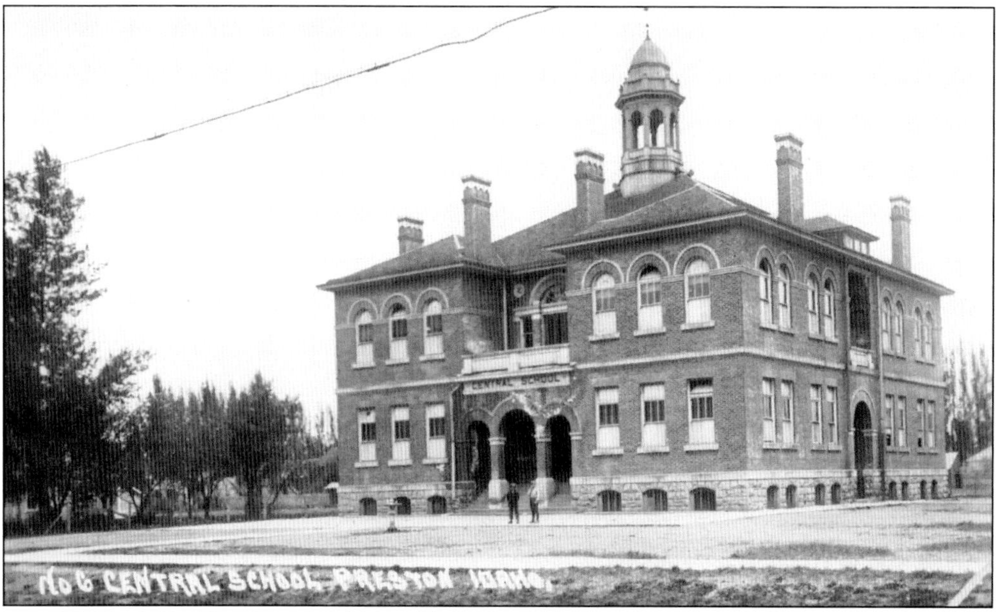

In 1885, Hugh Geddes, Peter Neilsen, and Andrew Nash operated a blacksmith shop at 85 East Oneida Street. The Central School (pictured) was built there in 1905, replacing the blacksmith shop and a frame schoolhouse next door. Its first teachers were Ella Hulet, Edna Johnson, Olive Hansen, Rae Rogers, Mary Dalley, Nellie Thomas, Mary Thomas, R. Leigh, May Eames, and Lizzie Thomas. Salaries ranged from $40 to $50 per month. The building was demolished in 1974. (Jay Burrup.)

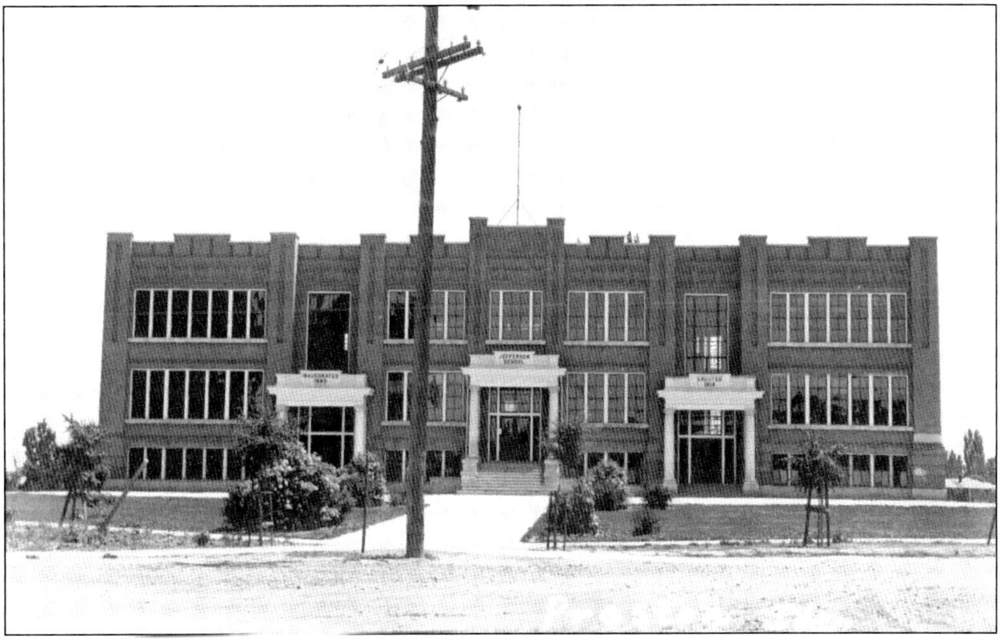

With the Central School's population doubled, the school district built the Jefferson School in 1914 on Academy Square. It was considered a modern marvel. The contents of its cornerstone box are at Utah State University. Below, a side view of the Opera House on First South Street shows the Jefferson and Nelson Gymnasium. According to a 1908 map of Preston, this was known as Millard Street. Second South Street was Academy Street, Third South Street was Cannon Street, and Fourth South Street was Canfield Street. First East Street was Preston Street, Second East Street was Whitney Street, and the First West Street was Depot or Jail Street. (Both, Jay Burrup.)

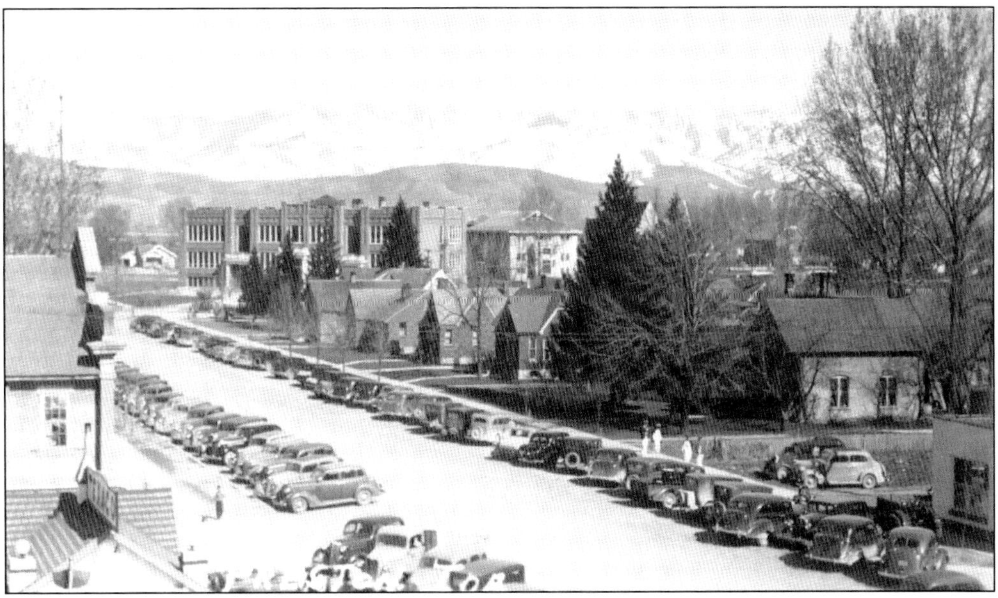

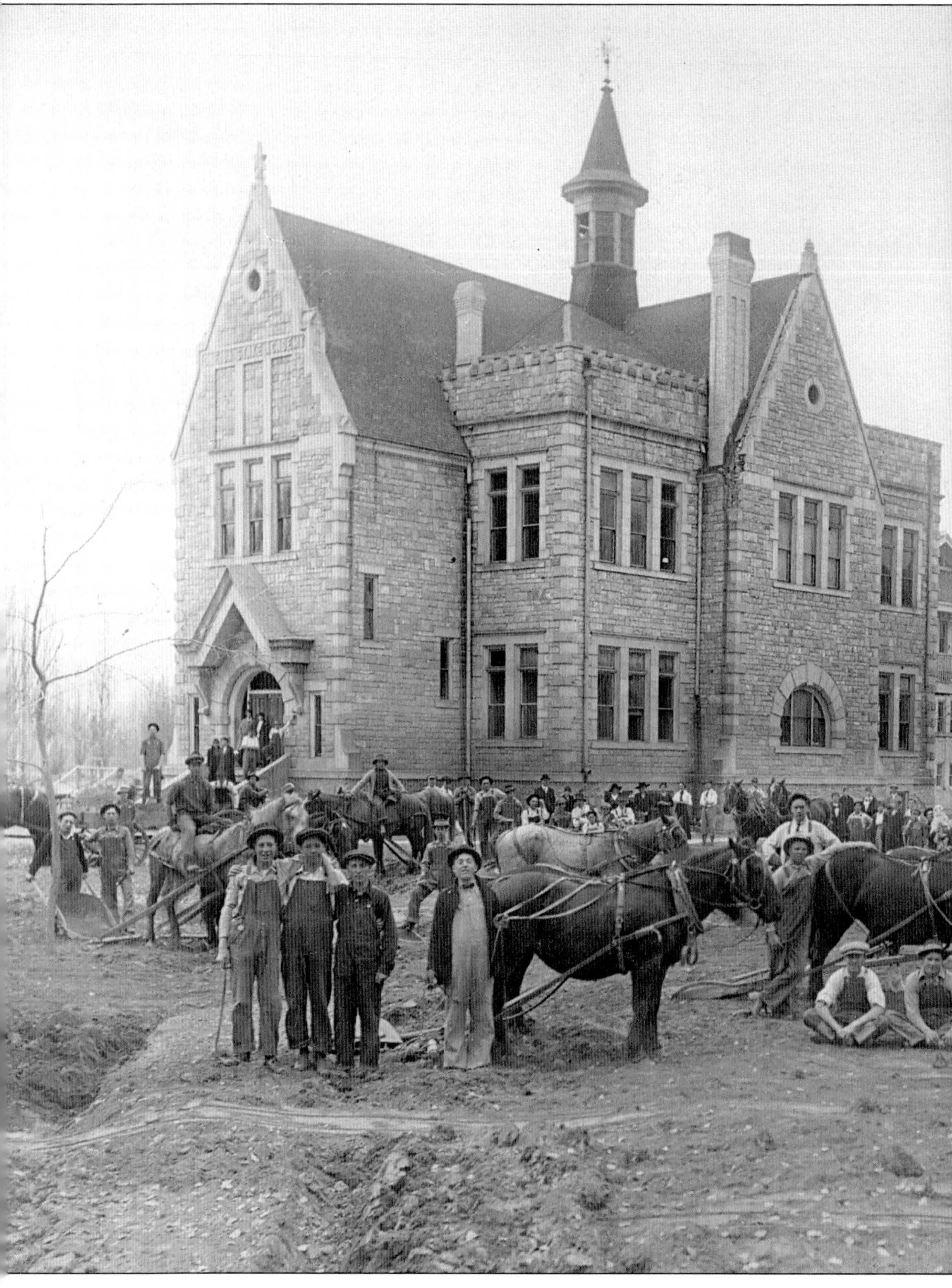

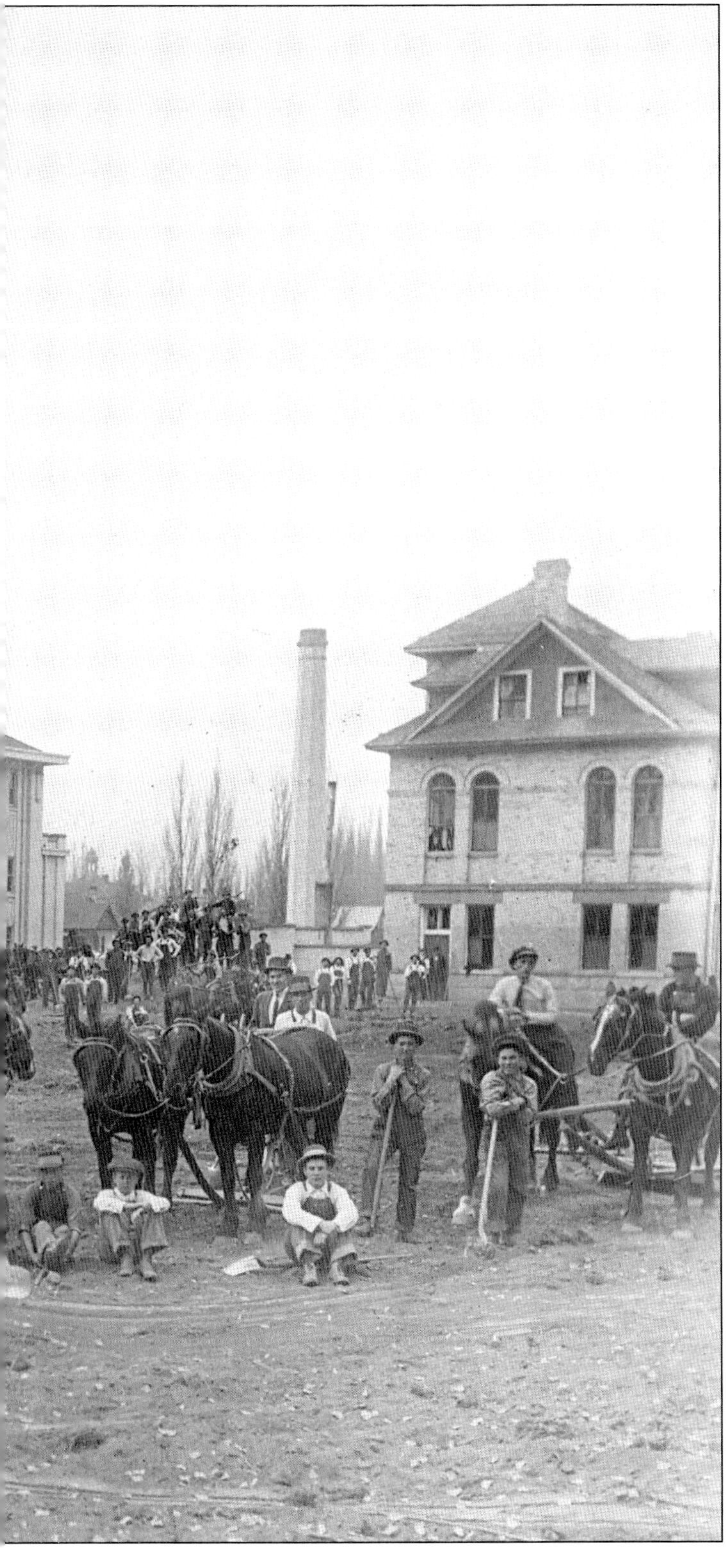

Using fresnos hitched to one- and two-horse teams, men landscape Academy Square. The Oneida Stake Academy, built between 1890 and 1894, was located at 150 North 200 South, where the current Preston High School cafeteria and library stand. The Nelson Gymnasium appears at the back left, and the Manual Arts Building is at right. The tall chimney led to a system that pumped warm water through the buildings to heat them. This picture was taken around 1914, possibly during O Day—a day students and teachers gathered to complete service projects. This building was moved to 90 East Oneida Street in 2003.

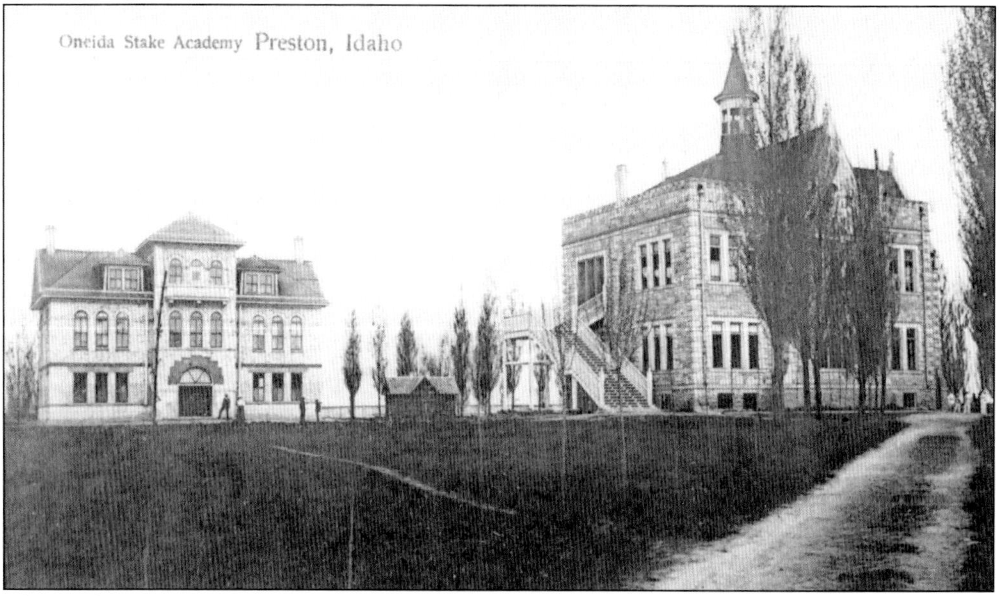

Above, this 1908 view of the OSA reveals a grand staircase. The top floor of the Manual Arts Building (left) burned on an unrecorded date. Prior to its recent demolition, this building housed arts and agriculture-related classes. The small structure at center was built in 1907 by Todd Greaves for his little sister as his senior project. A childhood disease claimed the girl, so the playhouse remained there until the Nielson Gym was built in 1914–1915. Today, it stands in the backyard of Greaves's daughter Carol Brown in Preston. Greaves went on to build/remodel houses in Preston for 50 years, according to Brown. Below, because there is no sign of electric fixtures, this picture of the shop in the basement of the OSA could have been taken as early as 1903. Oswald Christensen (standing, back left) was the carpentry teacher. (Above, Jay Burrup.)

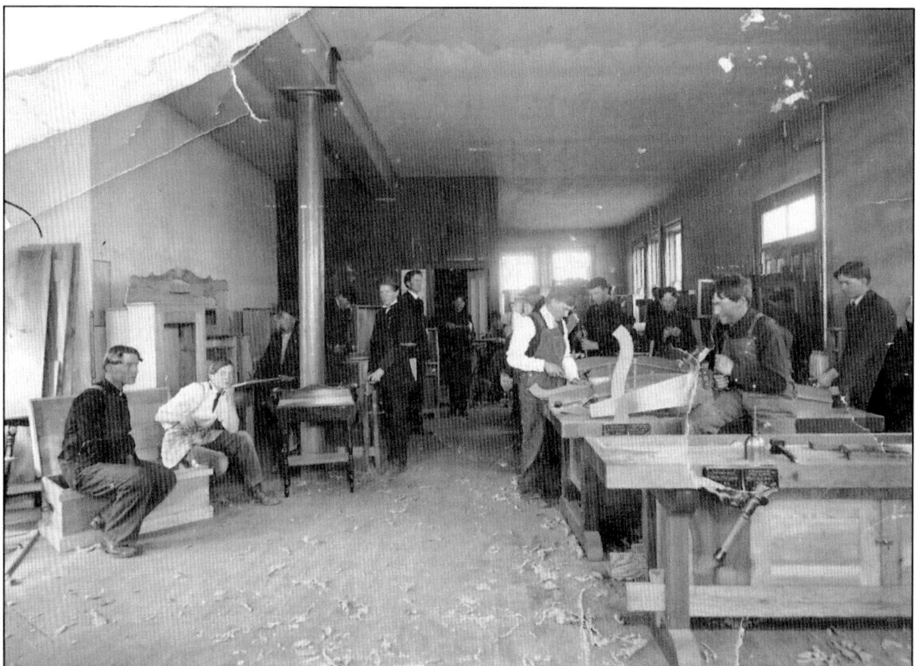

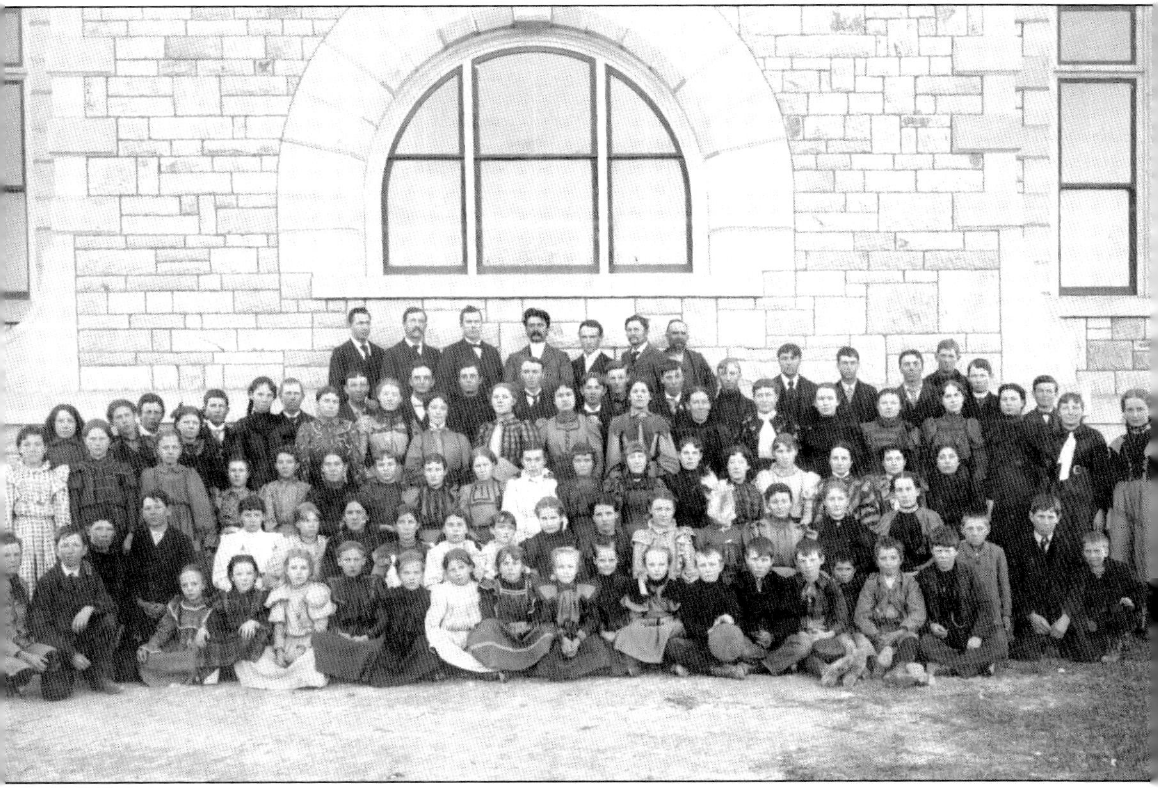

Children of all ages attended classes in the Oneida Stake Academy in 1897. Pictured are, from left to right, (first row) unidentified, Wallace Johnson, Blanche Larson, Edna Geddes Eames, unidentified, Dagmar Christiansen Anderson, two unidentified, Retta Smith Hobbs Kelley, three unidentified, Leo Parkinson, unidentified, Earl Goaslind, two unidentified, Othello Hickman, Chris Gundesen, unidentified, and Chester "Ike" Christensen; (second row) four unidentified, Erma Wilcox Hobbs, Fern Hickman, Ada Stevens, Edna Johnson Merrill, and seven unidentified; (third row) Stella Geddes Paton, unidentified, Marinda Larsen Willard, Mary Shaffer Seamons, Carrie Clausen Condie, unidentified, Carrie Gilbert Knudsen, six unidentified, Pearl Geddes Eames, and four unidentified; (fourth row) unidentified, Hazel Parkinson, two unidentified, Jim or Lawrence Johnson, two unidentified, Gertrude Griffiths, three unidentified, Linda Nelson Benson, four unidentified, Teressa Nielson Taylor, unidentified, Matilda Spongborg, and seven unidentified; (fifth row) unidentified, J.G. Nelson (professor), J.E. Hickman (principal), L.D. Edwards (music professor), unidentified, Ezra Woolley (professor), Tommy Stevenson (janitor), six unidentified, and Joseph A. Geddes.

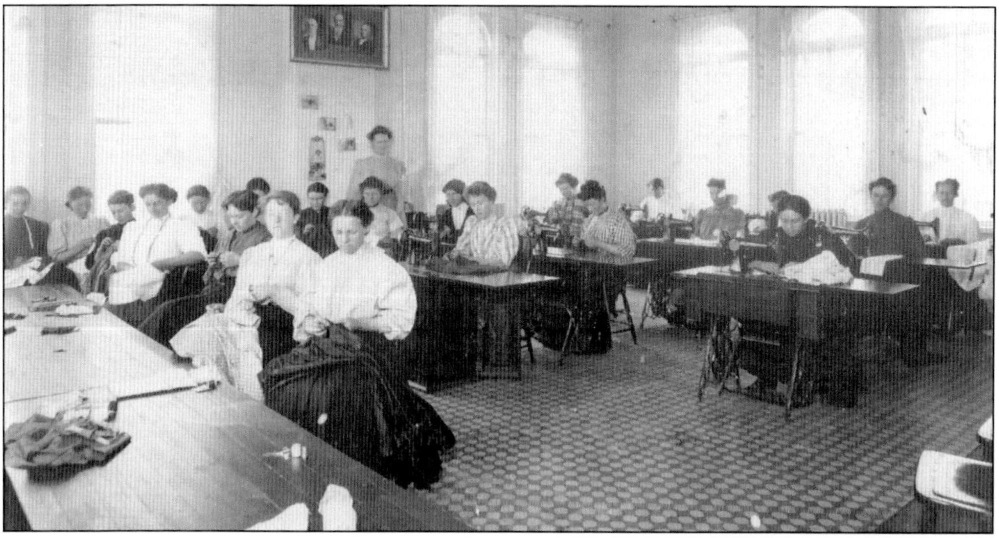

Above, this 1907 sewing class was held on the top floor of the Manual Arts Building. Registered were Della Bergquist, Edna Geddes, May Dawson, Hannah Luna, Hannah Hanson, Elva Dawson, May Moser, Valeria Larsen, Griselda Porter, Ena Peterson, Lillian George, Rachel Hoopes, Martha Steffenson, Rebecca Page, Iris Hawks, Lillie Tanner, Ida Gilbert, Mable Chapman, Florence Garner, Mary Stephens, Anna Forsgren, Myrtle Dixon, Lydia Lowe, Estella Geddes, Ethel Cutler, Hazel Garner, Luella Norton, Vinna Hale, Julia Wallgren, Charity Rasmussen, Liona Geddes, Ella Kofoed, Zoe Brimhall, Mable Wilcox, Viola Cutler, Mary Peterson, Ercil Henderson, Lola Winward, Vera Parkinson, Clara Kofoed, Bertha Petersen, Betty Nielsen, Marie Knupple, Emma Johnson, Ethel Greaves, Polly Perkins, Olive Winward, Estella Shumway, Emma Nielsen, Minnie Jensen, Lorain Smith, Carrie Nielsen, Pearlin Taylor, Laura Packer, Hannah Andreasen, Marie Christensen, Eva Larsen, Ida Egbert, Cora Page, Teanie Pearson, Gussie George, Zina Estella Woolf, and Eunice Christensen. Anna Frost (standing) was the teacher. Below, written on this picture of students standing on the OSA's staircase is, "Brother [Henry] Otte with violin. First boy to his right is Orille Neeley. Fourth girl front Allabel (Weaver Hull), #6 Ena Peterson."

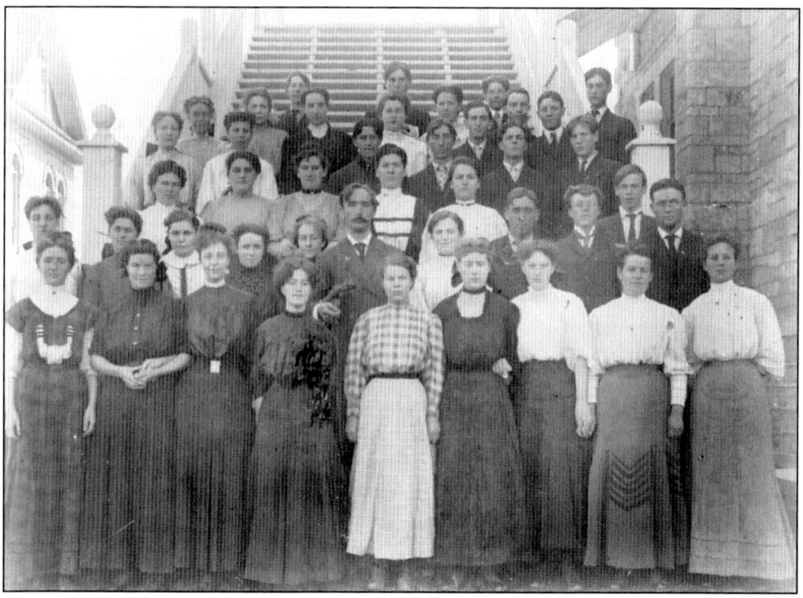

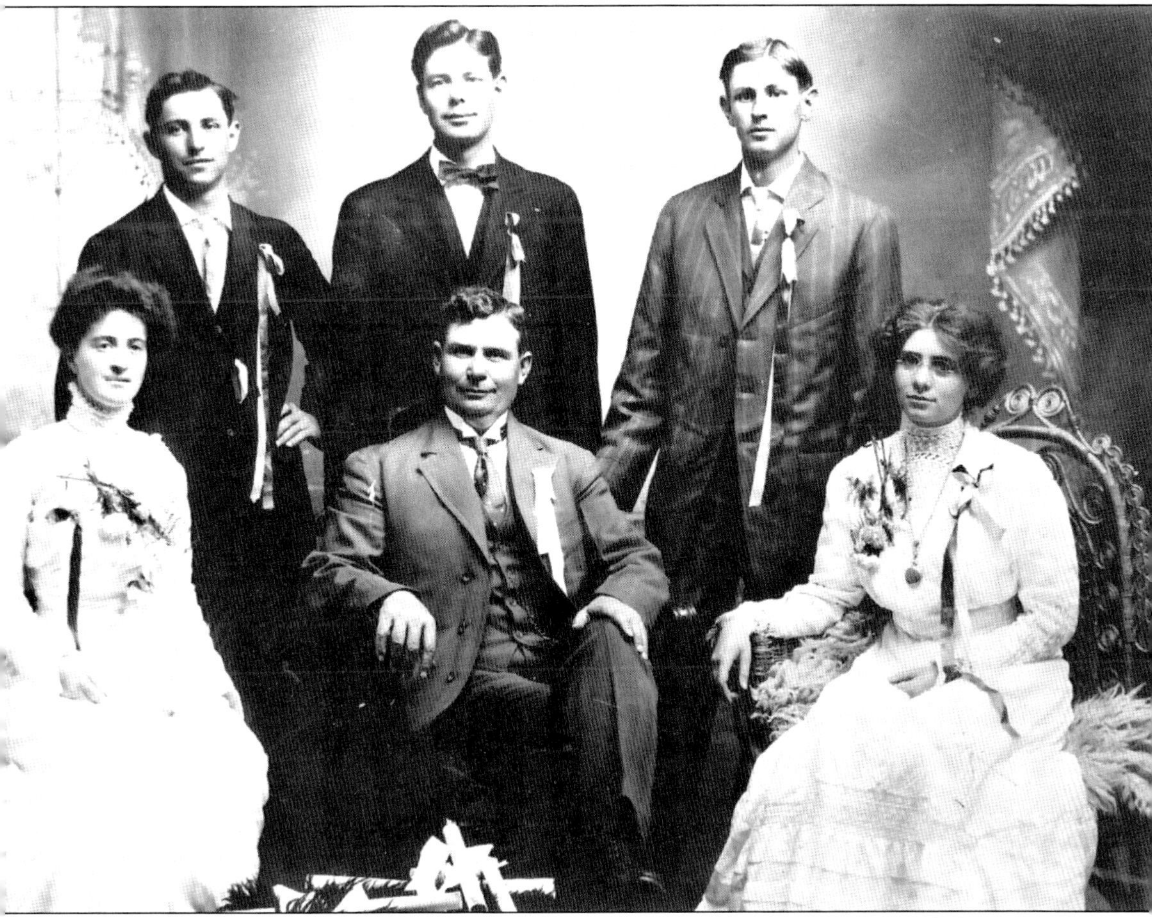

This group of four-year normal students was the first to graduate from the OSA with four years of upper education, in 1909. Pictured are, from left to right, (first row) Allabell Weaver (Hull), principal John Johnson, and Albertie Griffeth (Griffiths); (second row) Willard Nuffer, Perry Howell, and Louis Nuffer. Howell returned to the OSA as a teacher in 1914, as did Griffiths. She started sixth grade at the OSA at age 15 and attended for six years. "I graduated as a three-year normal student, in 1907. I taught school for one year at Fairview, then went back to the Academy and graduated from fourth year normal, in 1909 . . . We had been called graduates, with only three years work up to that time. . . . After graduation I taught one year at Dayton, another year at Fairview, two at Winder, one at Preston East side (called Egypt) and two at Treasureton," recorded Griffiths.

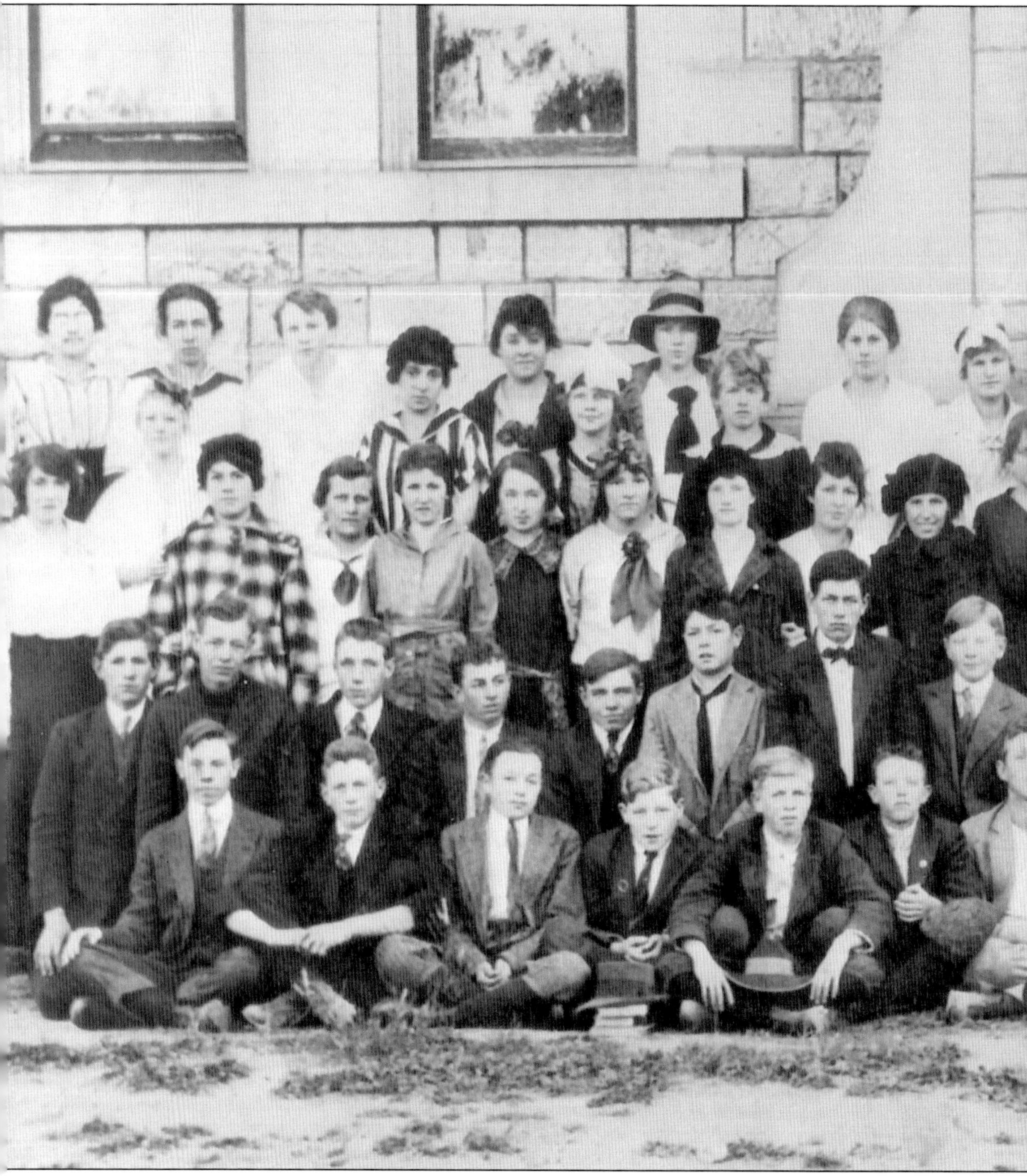

The OSA's class of 1920 is pictured here, probably as freshmen, in 1917. Identified are (first row) Platt Larsen (third from left) and Less Ballif (ninth from left); (second row) B.W. Winward (fifth from left), Elgin Campbell (seventh from left), J.W. Condie or R. Robison (eleventh from left), Elvin Cutler, Howard Swainston (fourteenth from left), and Nelson Larsen (seventeenth from left); (third row) Marguerite Pratt (fourth from left), Josie Geddes (fifth from left), Eva Packer (eighth from left), Mary Evans (eleventh from left), Lucille Ballif (sixteenth from left), and Veda Smart (eighteenth from left); (fourth row) Dora Merrill (first from left), Thelma Wooley (third from left), Veda Merrill (sixth from left), Winifred Jensen (eleventh from left), Anita Petersen

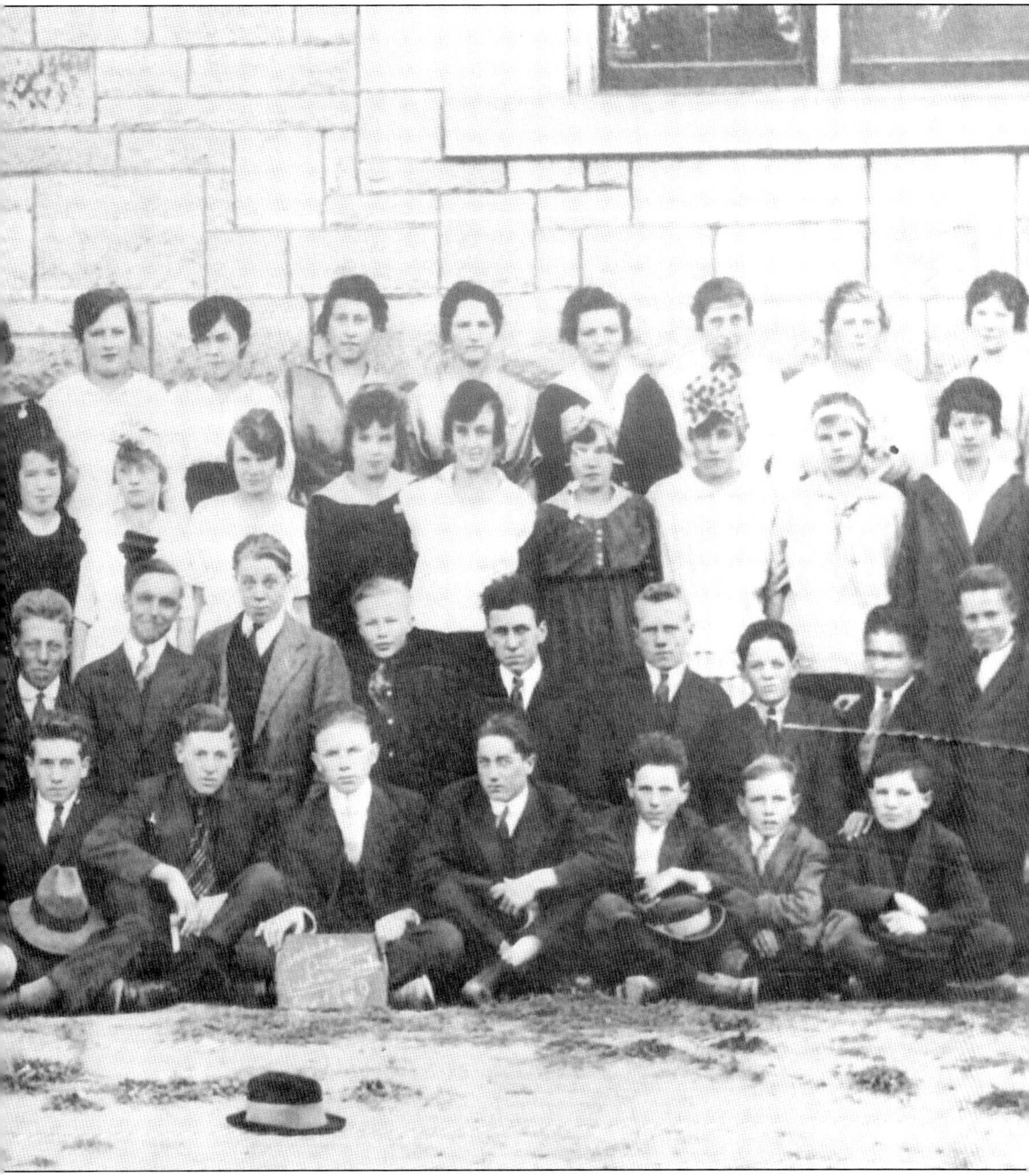

(thirteenth from left), M. Sann (seventeenth from left), and Allene Sutherland (eighteenth from left). Unidentified members of the class include Essa Bright, Florence Mitchell, Emma Foss, Earl Smith, Hazel Anderson, Asael Bell, Lila McQueen, Julia Johnson, Paul E. Hansen, Elva Crockett, Oleen Jensen, Nettie Tanner, Neva Johnson, Aneata Peterson, Christian Struve, Martha Geddes, Zola Bodily, Della Schow, Ira Sant, Earl Nelson, Lera Smith, Noama Forsgren, Herschel Neeley, Lucille Thomas, Jarold Meek, Margaret Benson, Jack Chatterton, Glen Sant, Julia Ward, Maggie Whitehead, Erma Evans, Emma Peterson, and Margaret Platt.

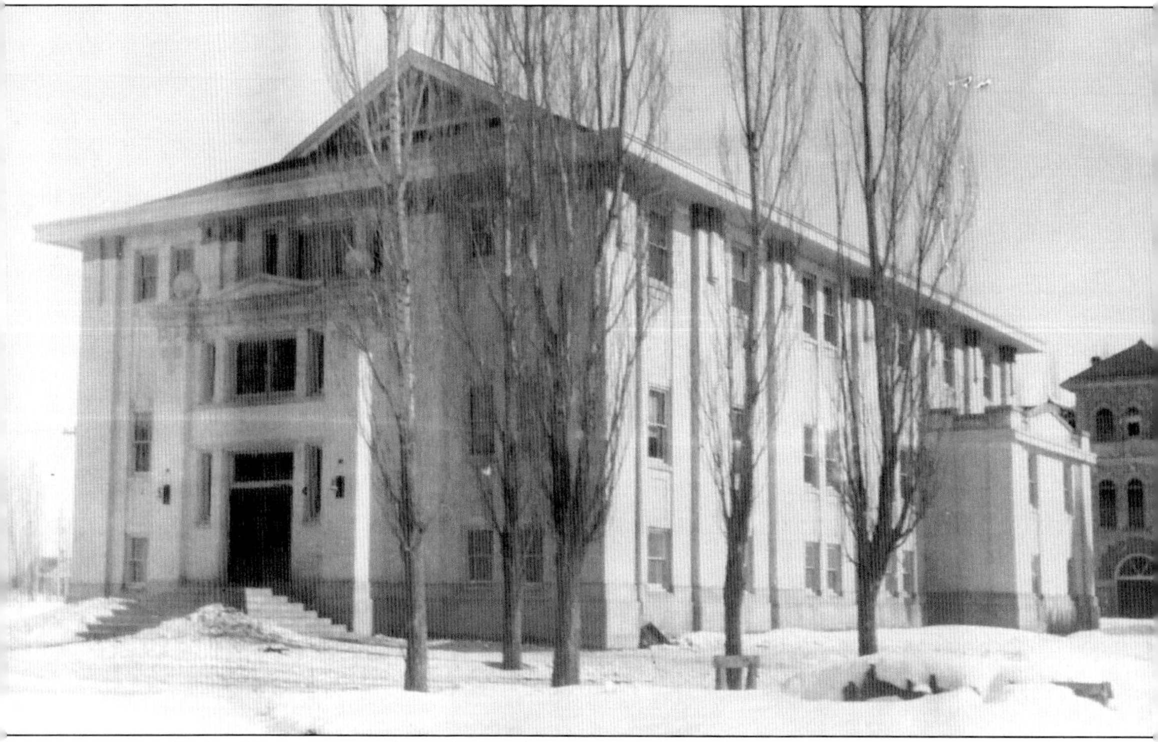

Named after Hyrum G. Nielson for his donation of the land upon which it is built, the Nielson Gymnasium was constructed in 1915 through the contributions of many. The building housed showers, a basketball court, handball courts, and a pool in the basement, which was used through the 1970s. In the 1920s, swimsuits were optional, and the pool segregated. Alumni Scott Nielson recalled that once, during the girls' turn to swim, a boy found a crack in the door. So many boys joined him that the door crashed down, alerting the janitor, who gave them the boot. A track was built above the basketball court and was later remodeled into a balcony for spectators. Professional wrestler George Nelson, namesake of the Nelson Fieldhouse at Utah State University, taught here from 1915 to 1920. Nelson was known as one of the best wrestlers of his time, with a headlock second only to Strangler Lewis. (Jay Burrup.)

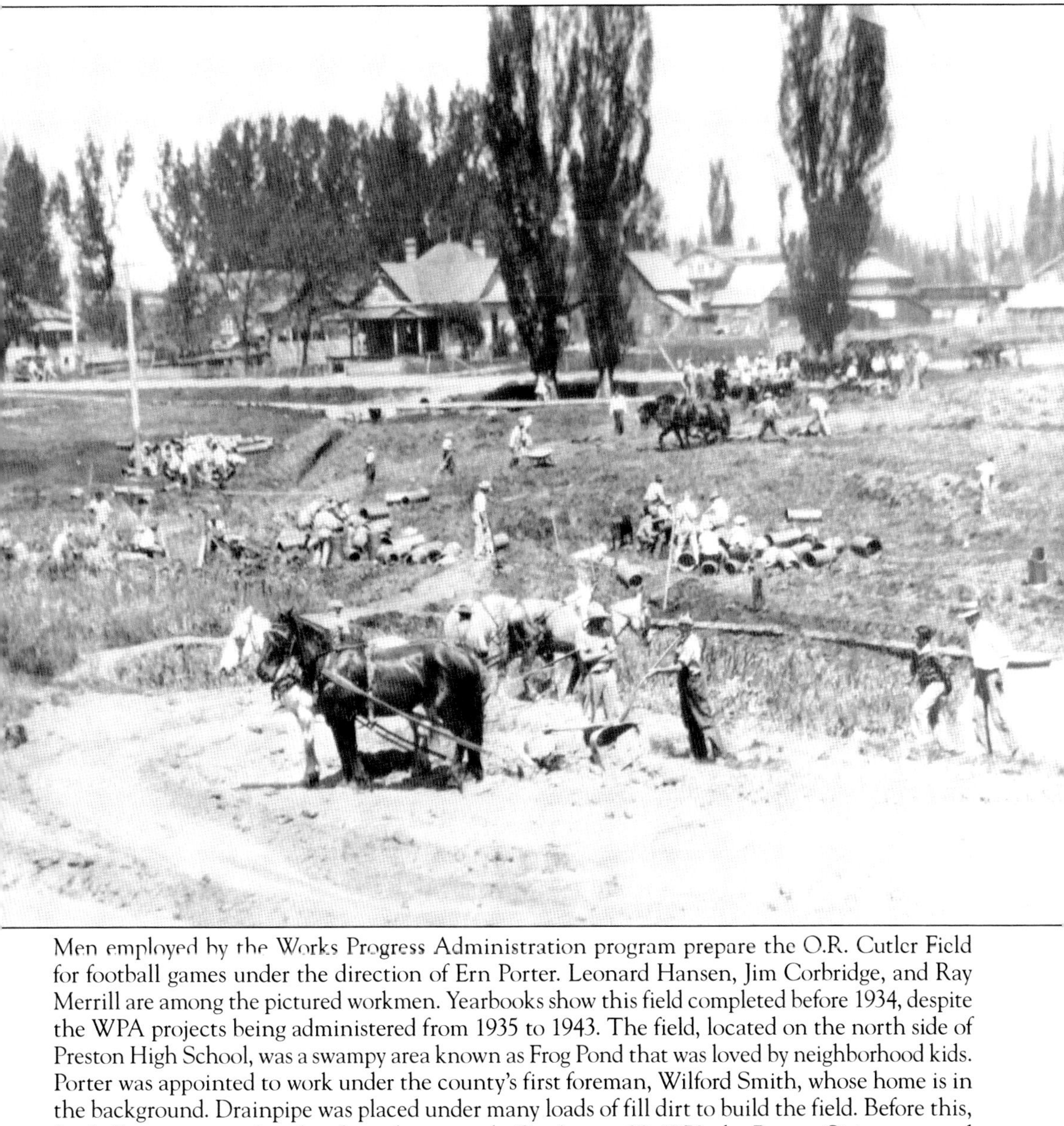

Men employed by the Works Progress Administration program prepare the O.R. Cutler Field for football games under the direction of Ern Porter. Leonard Hansen, Jim Corbridge, and Ray Merrill are among the pictured workmen. Yearbooks show this field completed before 1934, despite the WPA projects being administered from 1935 to 1943. The field, located on the north side of Preston High School, was a swampy area known as Frog Pond that was loved by neighborhood kids. Porter was appointed to work under the county's first foreman, Wilford Smith, whose home is in the background. Drainpipe was placed under many loads of fill dirt to build the field. Before this, football games were played at the rodeo grounds. On August 28, 1970, the *Preston Citizen* reported that the field was rebuilt and renamed after Dr. Orvid R. Cutler on O.R. Cutler Day. Cutler had served on the school board for many years and had played on the OSA's first football team.

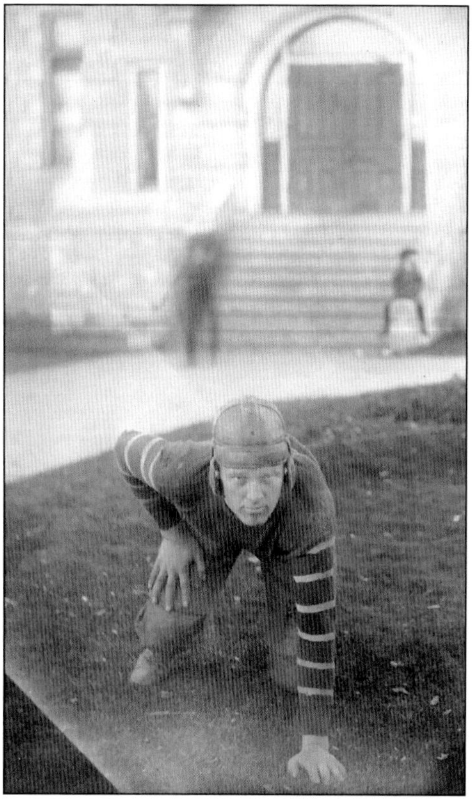

Football was introduced to Preston in 1919 by coach Woody Romney, who developed a wonderful team that "came in well-conditioned from the threshing machines." The team lost 13-3 to Logan, tied Brigham Young College 0-0, and defeated Malad 40-0. This picture of Orvid Cutler is inscribed, "Presented to Orvid Cutler V.S. Oliver Fat's Nelson December 4, 1920." Both boys were members of that first OSA football team.

In 1921, underclassmen of the last OSA football team (pictured here) became the first football team at Preston High School in 1922. From left to right are (first row) Harrison Thomas, Jerry Weaver, Oliver Nelson, Orson Pratt, Merlin Larsen, Jock Goaslind, and Veron Thomander; (second row) Theron Webster, Lowell Smith, Adolph Sorenson, Verlo Peterson, Ezra Foss, Abner Larsen, and Orvid Cutler; (third row) Halo Hart, Orval Benson, John Winward, Waldermor Degn, Helmor Jorgensen, Eugene Stockdale, and Elvin Cutler; (fourth row) Mahlon Hollingsworth, James Miller, Mourice Brimhall, and Leo Petterborg; (fifth row) Alton Spongberg, Eddie Smith, and Coach Romney.

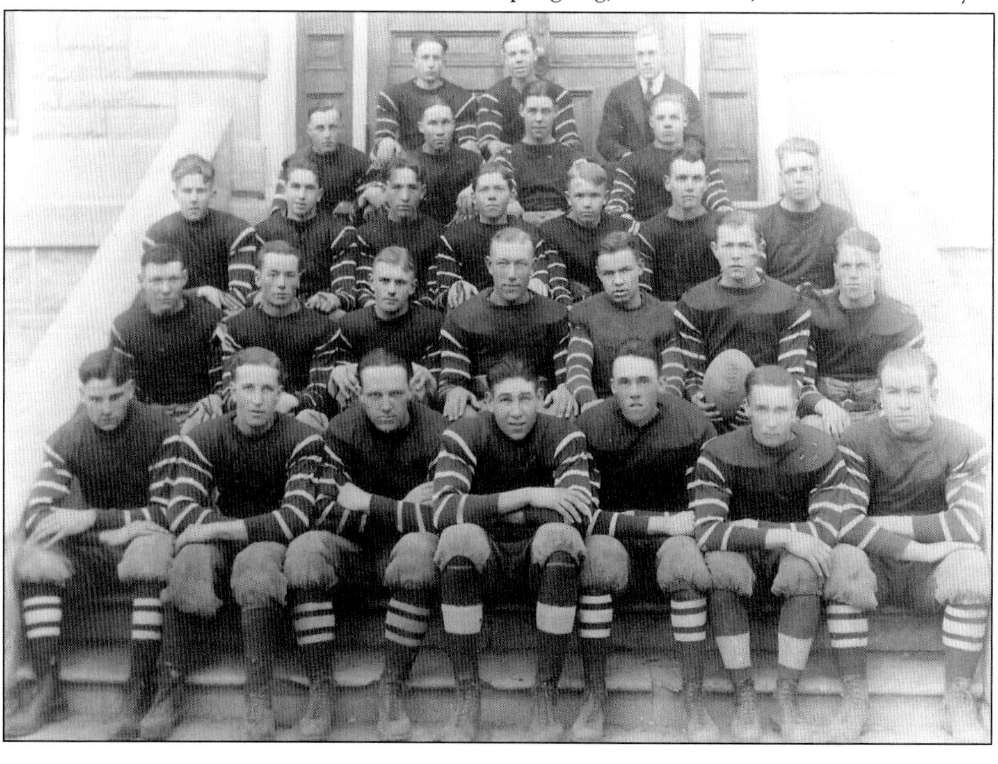

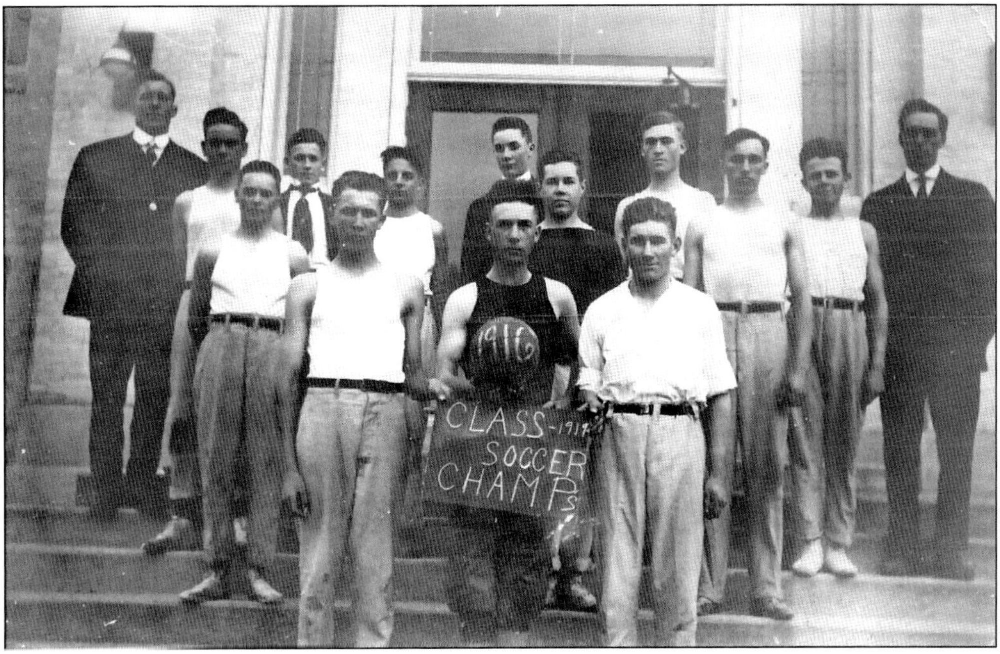

The above photograph appeared in the first OSA yearbook, the *Quiver*, published in 1917. No names were recorded, but the sign identifies them as the "soccer champs." Below, baseball was played by both the girls and the boys during the early years at the OSA. Class leagues were organized for the purpose of "creating legitimate rivalry between classes, and also to serve as tryouts for the Academy teams," according to school catalogues from 1909–1913. Skill was not the only requisite. "The players must have character and scholastic ability as well. . . . Our teams have achieved considerable success. Some of the best games seen in Preston have been played by Academy teams." According to *The Preston Booster*, a track meet in August 1912 started out with a baseball game between Cache and Oneida Stakes.

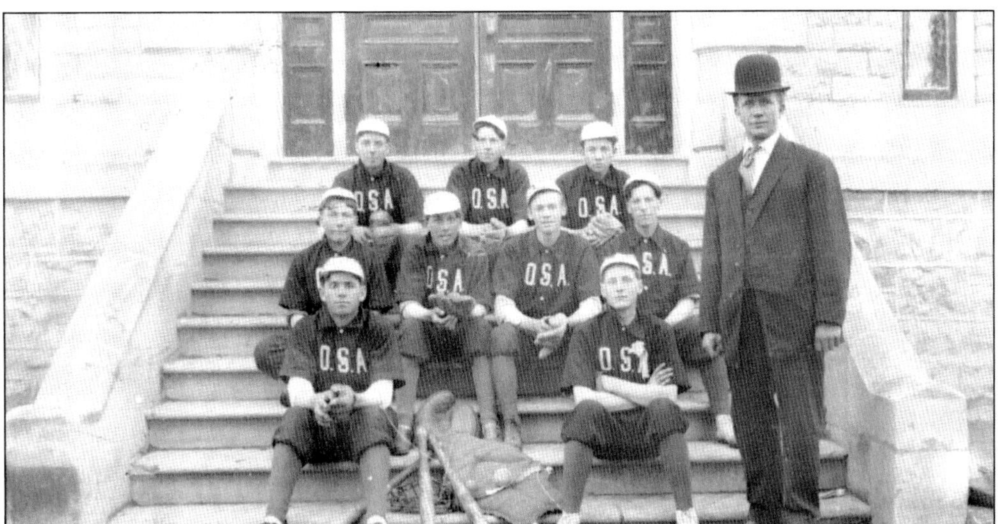

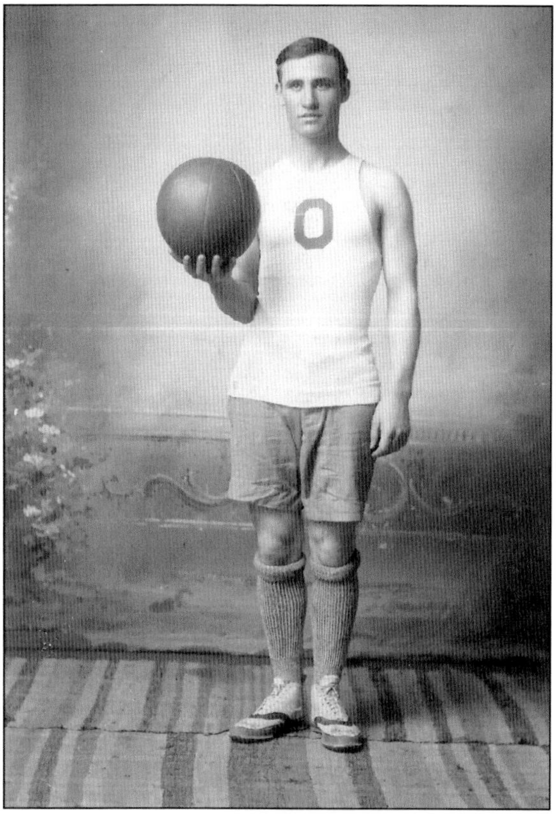

Frank Gilbert (left), son of Daniel and Amelia Hansen Gilbert of Fairview, played basketball and baseball until he graduated in 1915 from the OSA, having played under Clyde Packer. Gilbert went on to become the president of the Franklin County Farm Bureau, elected to the position for three terms. He also served as a director of the Idaho State Farm Bureau for several years. Below, 1911 OSA basketball team members are, from left to right, Herman Nuffer, Lonnie Carver, Clyde Packer, Sam Packer, and three unidentified. At the commencement services of 1907, principal John Johnson asked Clyde, a freshman, to arrange for some athletics. "We made a [basketball] court out on the ground and played a basketball game. Because of this Harrison R. Merrill called me the father [of basketball] at the Oneida Academy," stated Packer. (Below, Jay Burrup.)

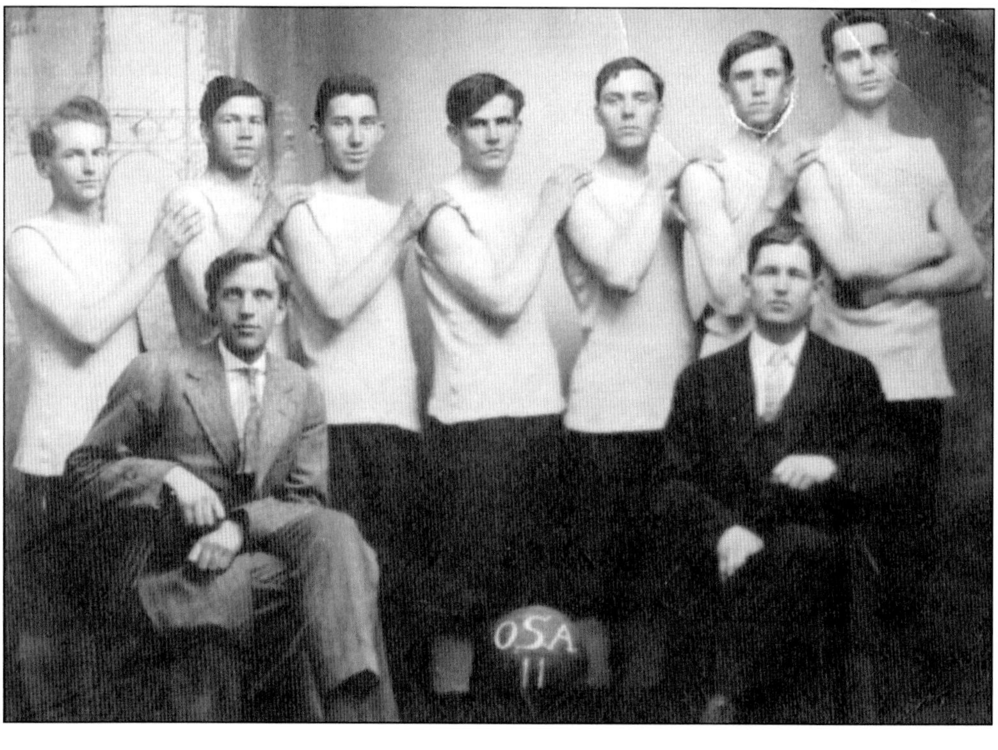

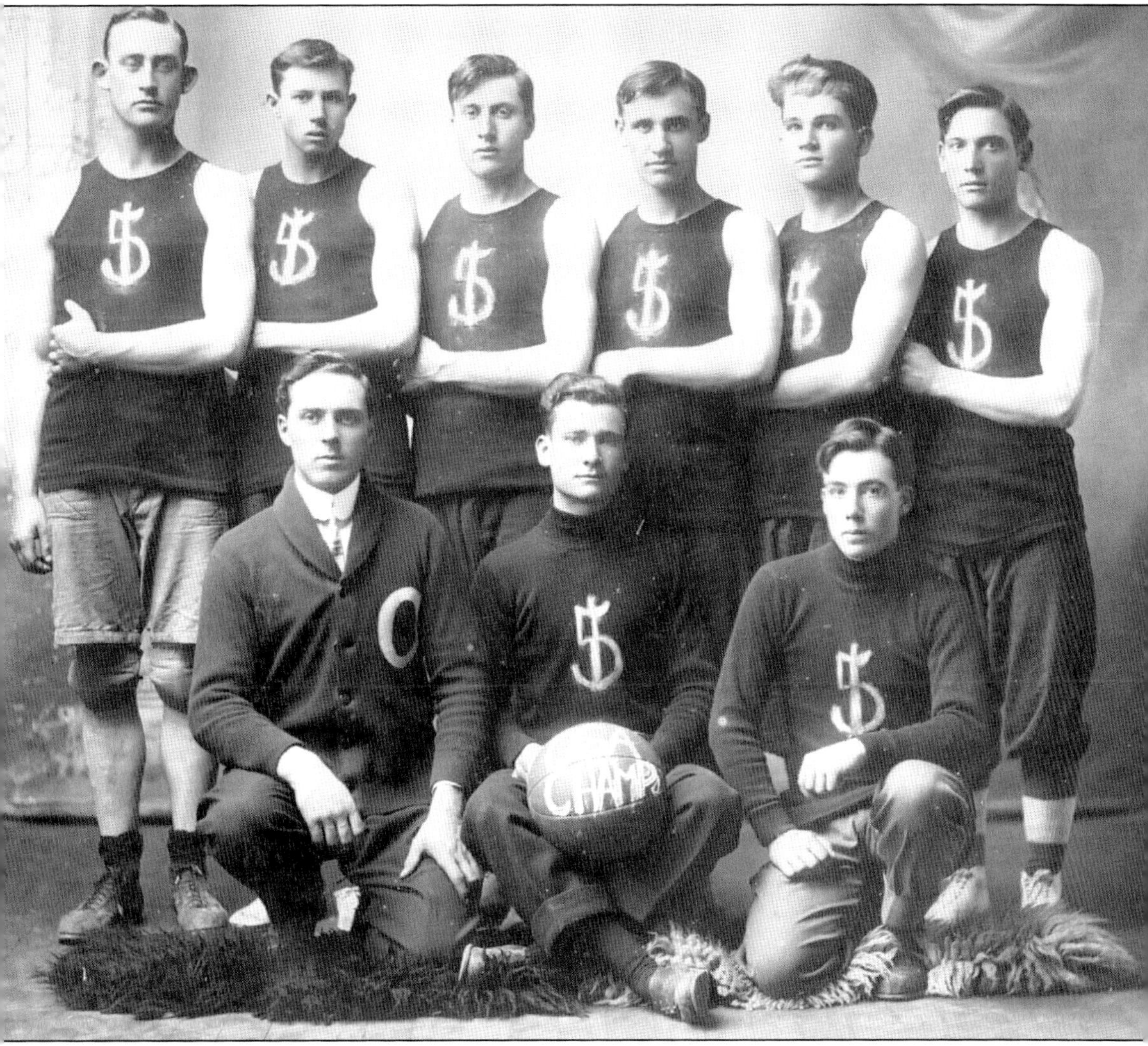

The OSA class of 1915 had won the basketball championship in 1912–1913 when this photograph was taken. Pictured are, from left to right, (first row) coach Clyde Packer, Paul Thomas, and Perry Lee; (second row) George Crockett, George Lake, Dimon Bodily, Frank Gilbert, Scott Lowe, and Elmer Choules. Coach Packer graduated from the OSA, becoming an All-American in 1916 at the Agricultural College of Logan before coaching at the OSA. During the next two seasons (1912–1914), the OSA basketball team "won the church school championship over B.Y.C., L.D.S., Weber and others," recalled Packer. "We beat the A.C. of Logan twice, the BYU right after they had won the Utah Championship." Under Packer and David Eames, the Oneida Stake boys won a $75 silver cup by beating the other three stakes in Cache Valley over three consecutive years. "Those were wonderful years and happy memories," Packer continued. "I think Ezra Taft Benson was on the squad the last year I was at the Oneida, and Harold B. Lee was the athletic manager one year." Benson and Lee became presidents of the worldwide Church of Jesus Christ of Latter-day Saints.

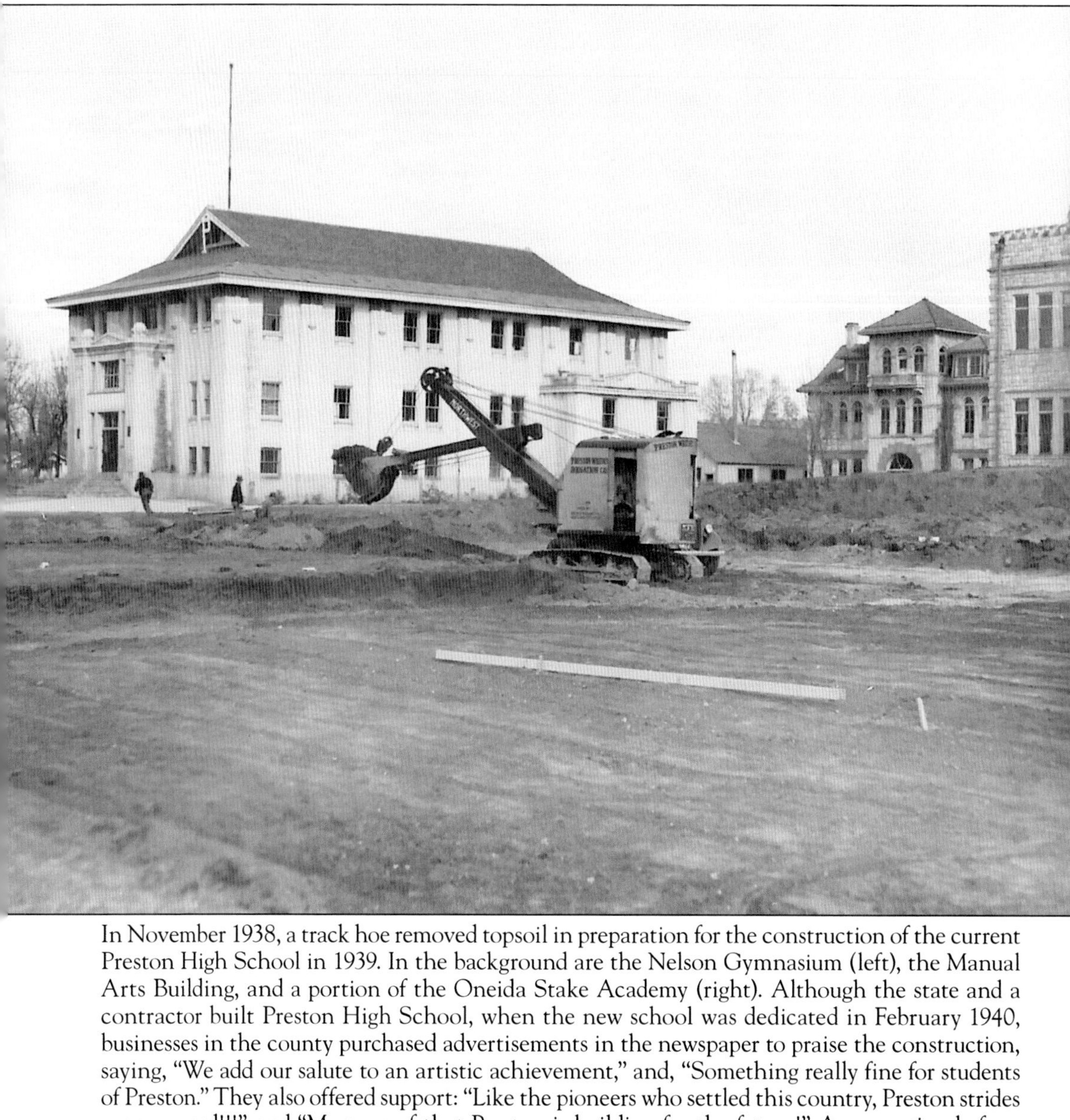

In November 1938, a track hoe removed topsoil in preparation for the construction of the current Preston High School in 1939. In the background are the Nelson Gymnasium (left), the Manual Arts Building, and a portion of the Oneida Stake Academy (right). Although the state and a contractor built Preston High School, when the new school was dedicated in February 1940, businesses in the county purchased advertisements in the newspaper to praise the construction, saying, "We add our salute to an artistic achievement," and, "Something really fine for students of Preston." They also offered support: "Like the pioneers who settled this country, Preston strides ever onward!!!" and "More proof that Preston is building for the future!" A generation before, school buildings had been built by the people themselves. At the opening of the gym in 1915, Preston mayor J.N. Larson said, "the gymnasium would be a great help to the city," and that "the people should be proud of the work of their hands." The gym was the last public building the people constructed.

Two

Arts and Entertainment

Jill Durrant, orchestra and choir teacher at Preston Junior High School, while working on her master's degree in 2012, wrote that from the beginning, there was evidence of music in the first schools:

> In the little granary school in early Preston, teacher Verena Foster, barely older than the pupils herself at only 16, would have the students sing their time tables to the tune of "Yankee Doodle." On Fridays, the best day of the week according to students, time was set aside to "speak a piece" or sing favorite songs such as "The Sword of Bunker Hill."
>
> The importance these Mormon pioneers placed on culture and the arts is evident by the fact that as they were building homes, barns and log schools they were also constructing cultural halls and opera houses, presenting plays and forming brass bands.
>
> In his book about the history of Cache County, F. Ross Peterson says, "Culture is more than what one does with his or her leisure time; but how people recreate in a frontier society is very important. People often do not have much spare time, and it is valuable when a community can come together to enjoy each other's talents. In earlier times, many country people played instruments and music was central to dancing, singing, theater, and life."
>
> The very fact that a people who had such limited time for pleasure and relaxation would choose to spend it making music says volumes. These people found time for it, however, "because the arts were not considered to be 'extras.' They were a vital part of Zion." By 1913, when the city of Preston was formally incorporated, it boasted several meetinghouses and theaters, an opera house, a music store, multiple private instructors of piano, voice, and other instruments, a central elementary school that was already too crowded, and the beloved Oneida Stake Academy.

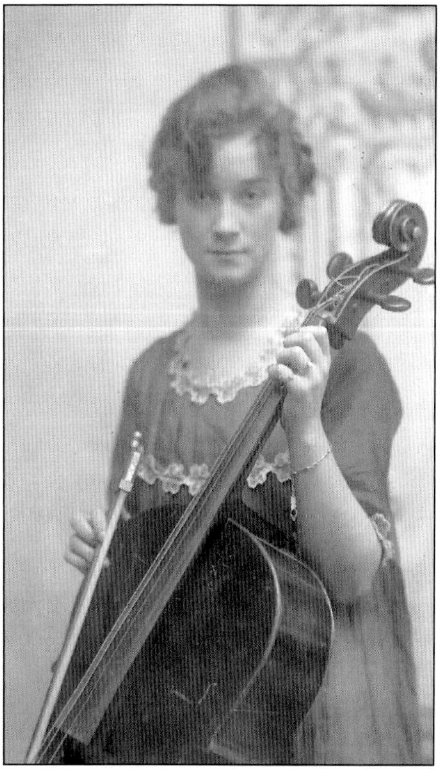

Local youth learned to play both wind and string instruments in school. In 1912, Prof. Charles J. Engar turned the music program at the OSA into something the community took great pride in. He conducted band, orchestra, choirs, and operettas. "No public high school in Idaho could claim a music program of [its] size and skill," wrote Jill Durrant. During the 1920s, school choirs sang every morning for assembly. Opal Holt (left) was a frequent performer at social functions with her sister Virginia and cousins Eva and Lillian Weaver. Below, *The Trail Blazer* credits T.A. Montague with the organization of the first brass band in Preston, in 1893. Members were Capt. D.C. Curtis, Hyrum Tippets, Harry Hurbert, E.T. Clayton, Nephi Larson, Edward Shaffer, George Shaffer, William A. Head, William A. Fellows, Peter Ericksen, James Bosworth, Phil Margetts, and Peter Jensen.

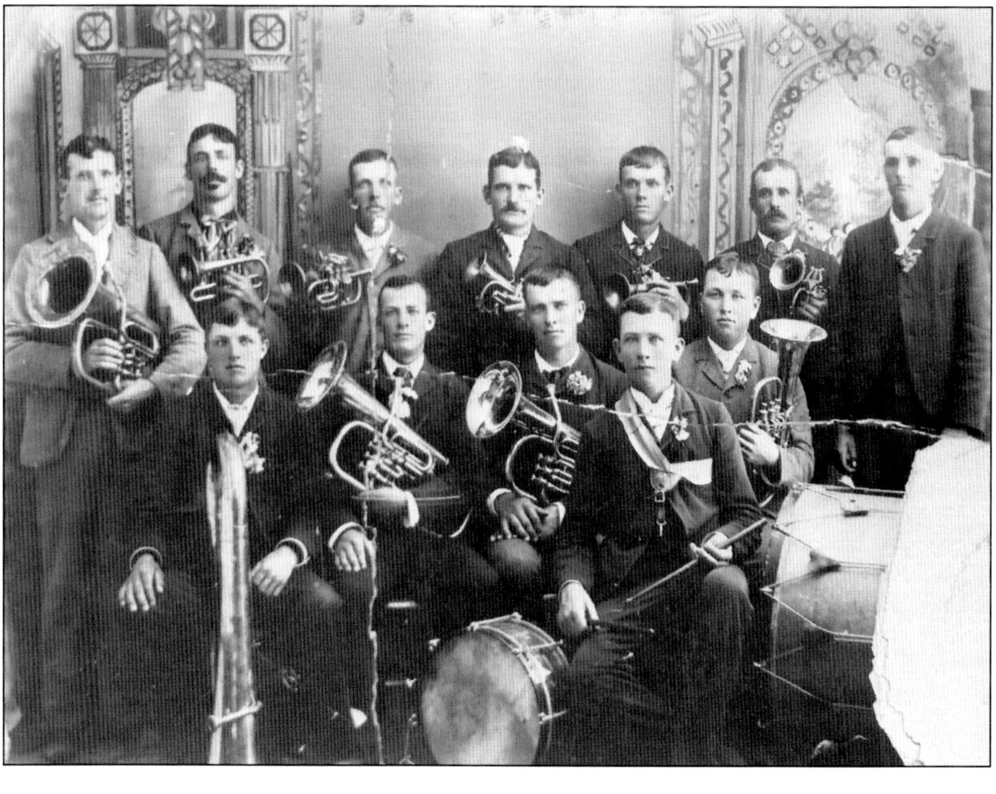

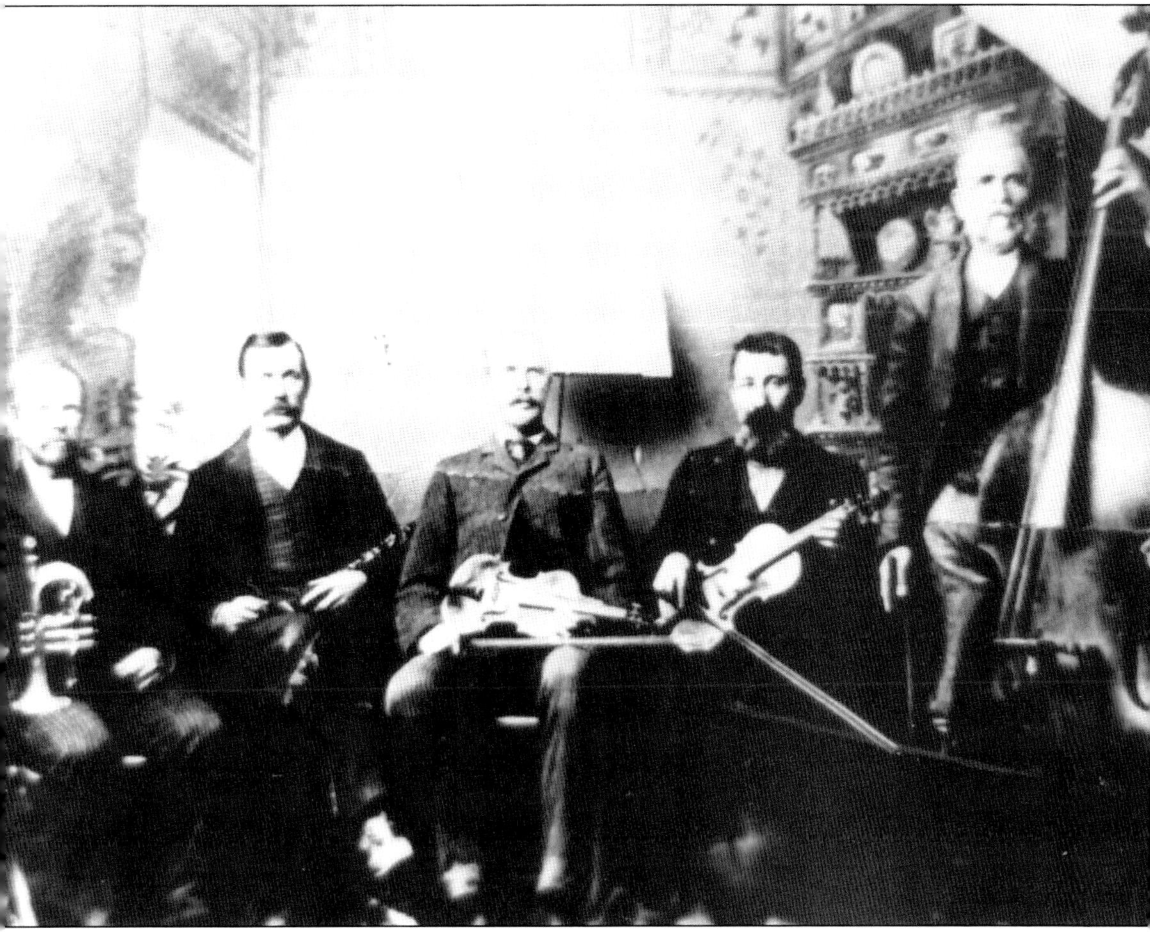

Preston's first orchestra was organized either by Alfred Kershaw (far right) in the 1880s or Phil Margetts (third from left) in the 1890s, depending on the source. Newell Hart thought Kershaw; Baltzar Peterson's papers state Margetts. Kershaw came from England in 1877, where he had performed with a sophisticated group. He and his family lived on East Oneida Street. Others in the group were, from left to right, Billy Chatterton, Axel Anderson, and John Harvey Tippets. During the early 1890s, this group performed all over the Cache and Gentile Valleys and as far away as Bear Lake. Traveling by bobsled in the winter, they performed to help raise money for the construction of the OSA building. This picture was taken on the stage of Preston's first dance and theatrical hall, the Hobbs Opera House, built in 1886 by C.R. Hobbs. It was located on State Street near Second South Street, on the east side of the road.

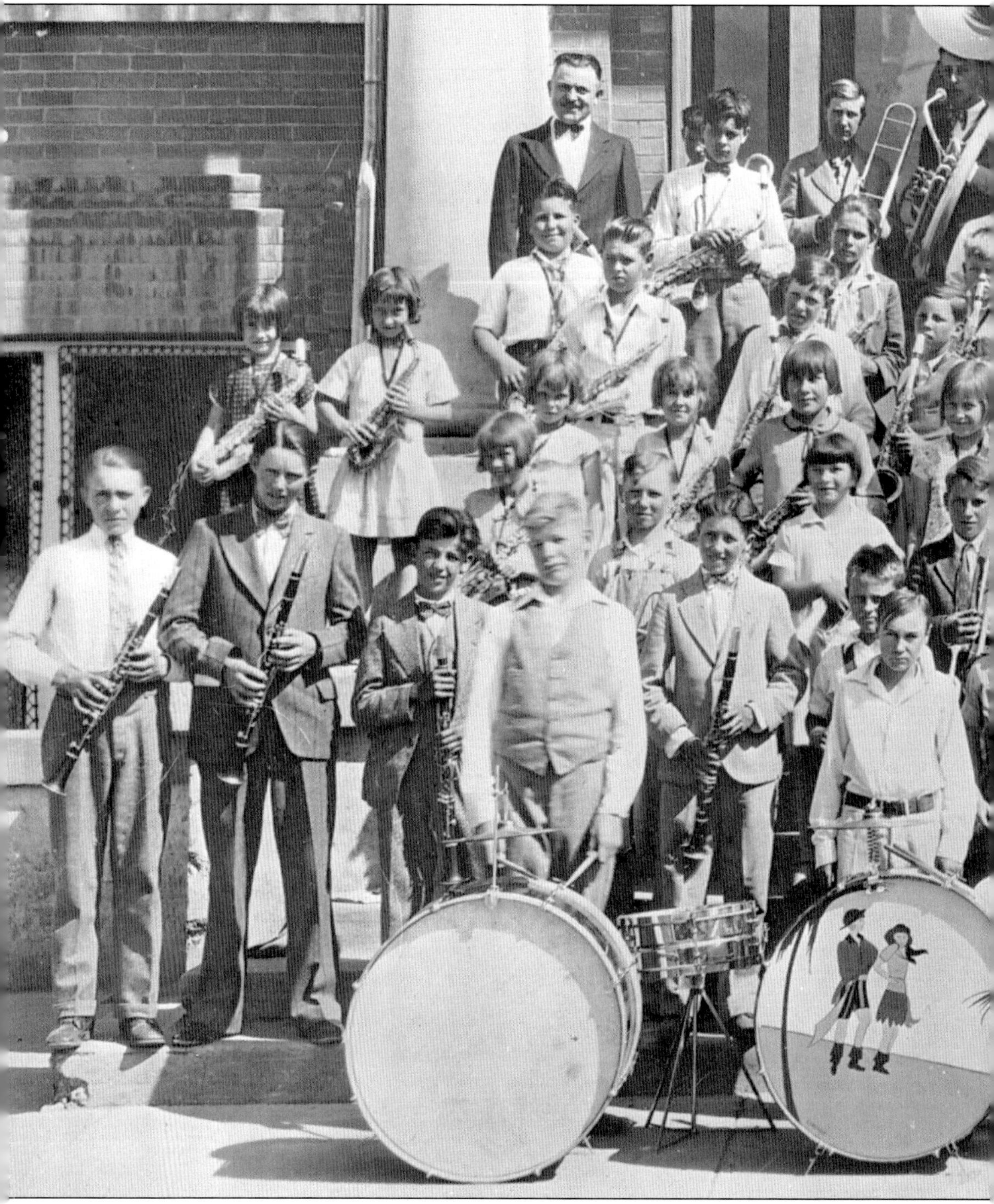

Prof. John J. Fiala, an immigrant from Bohemia, came to Preston in 1928, taught band in the schools, and played in Mickey Hart's band for several years. Stan Hawkes recalled playing with Fiala in the Persiana, then later with Fiala's band at the 1928 Preston Roundup. Fiala came to Preston from a Nebraska conservatory, where he had earned the reputation of being "one of the premier trumpet artists of the west," according an article from the July 10, 1929, edition of the

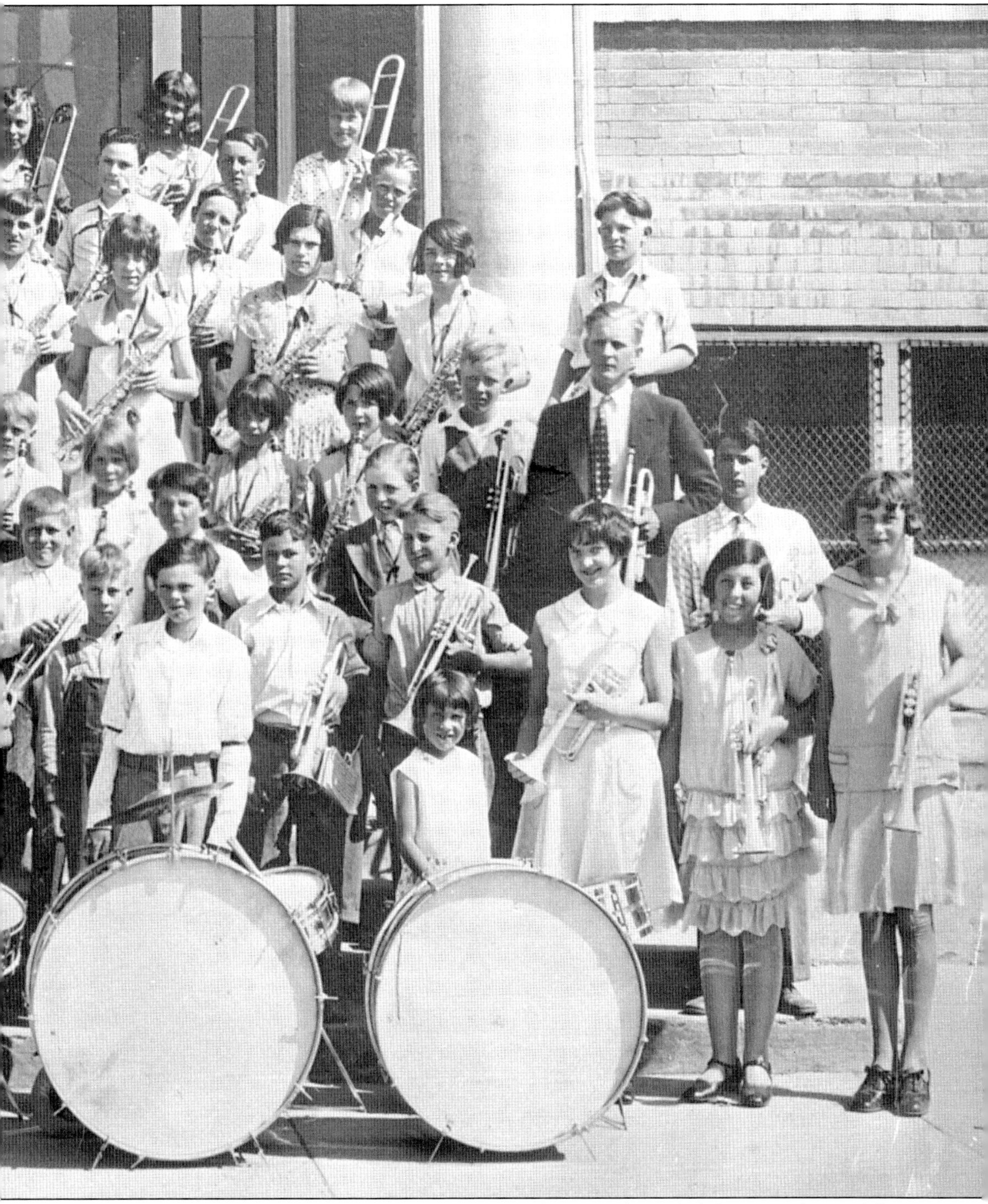

Franklin County Citizen. Hart's band specialized in the blues and traveled from Northern Idaho to California, playing at "practically every type of entertainment known to the west: weddings, receptions, balls, over the radio, in professional band concerts, street music, theatres and dance halls," according to the paper.

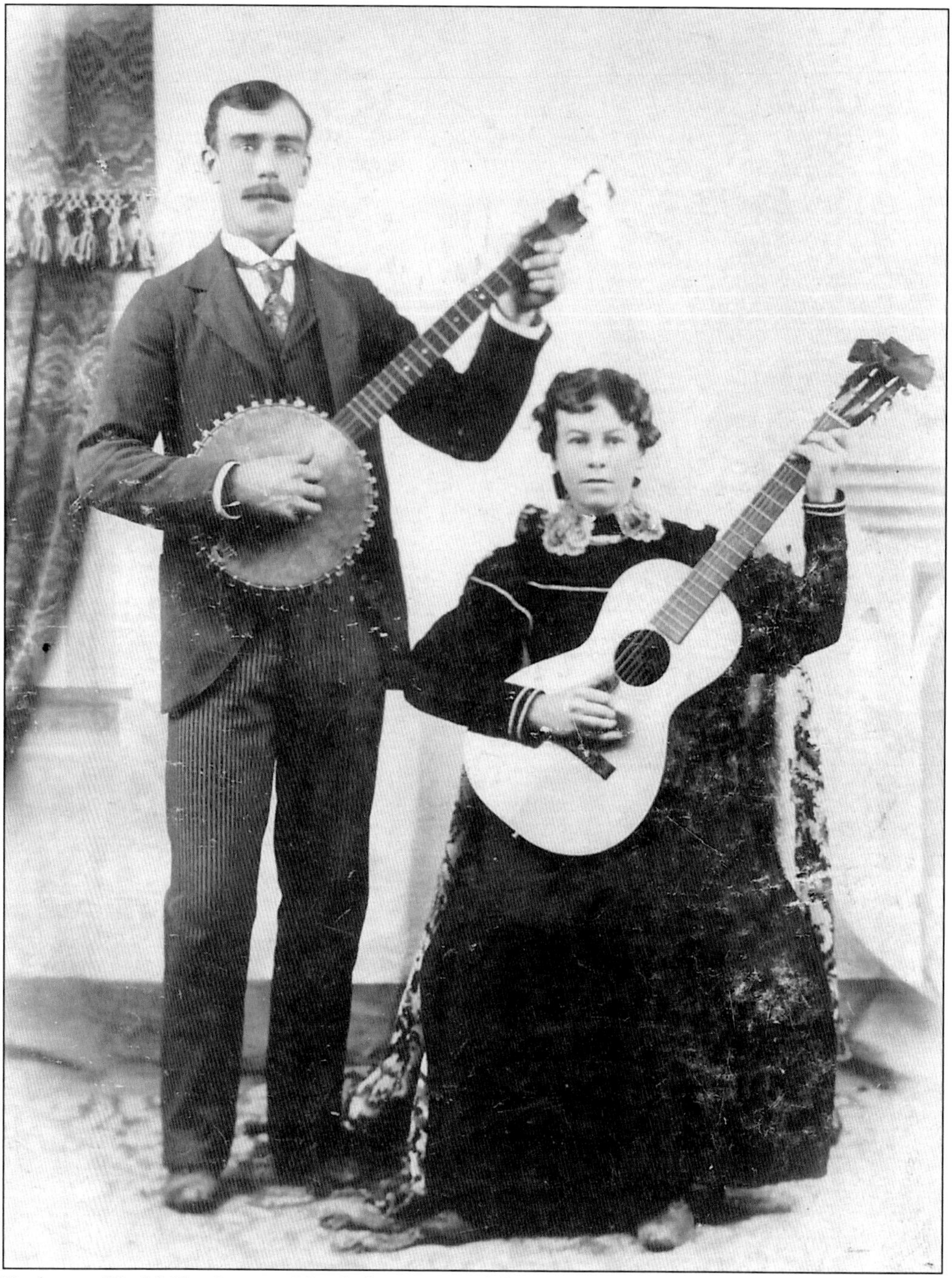

Dickesen (Dick) Kershaw and his baby sister, Adeline, were members of a musical family that immigrated to the United States in the late 1870s. Their parents, Alfred and Martha, promoted music for youth in the community, and the family helped to build the Opera House, with Alfred working to get an organ for it. Adeline was born in 1879 in Laketown, Utah. She married Martin Johnson Jr. and played both the organ and the guitar. The Kershaw family used their musical talents to entertain as well as to supplement earnings from their farm one mile east of the center of Preston. Dick and Adeline's brother Thomas raised his family in Preston.

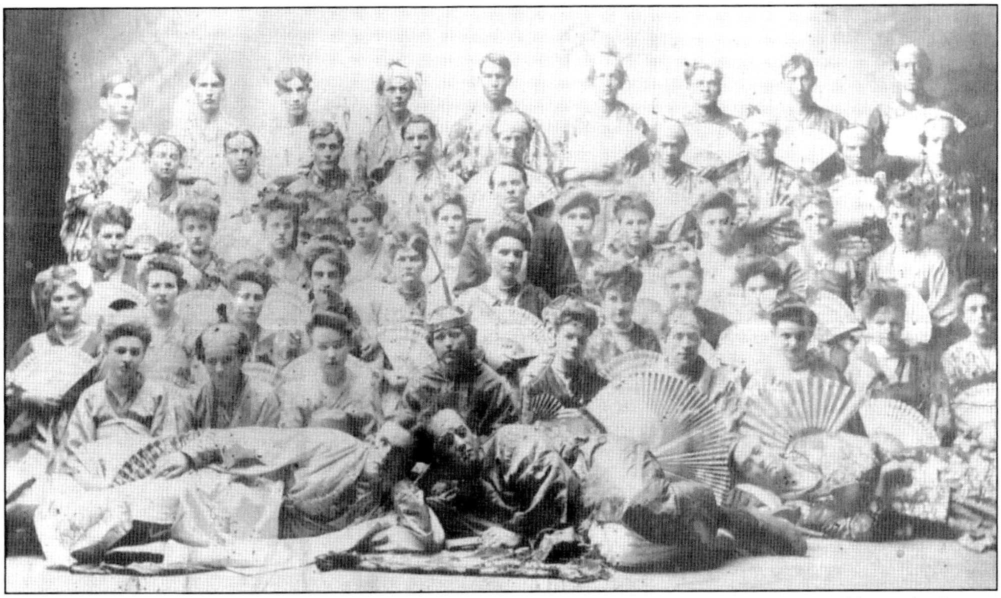

Harriet Dalley Swainston attended a play performed by the cast pictured above and brought home a fan with the following names written on the blades: Carrie Thomas, Epron Scarborough, William Miton, Mary Redford, Myron W. Robbins, K. Herd, Wesley H. Merrill, Lawrence Bailey, James J. Allen, Alonzo Wood, Scott B. Brown, Pheobe Harrison, Ezra T. Benson, Edirah Montrose, Jennie Miles, W.H. Stuart, Arthur Johnson, Lose Larsen, L.J. Shurtliff, Ruby Geddes, H.G. Wright, Lucile Jenson, Joseph Shurtliff, Florence Tarbet, Larretta Johnson, Marie Card, Nettie Bod, John Anderson, Frances, F.W. Har, Jos. A. Geddes, Mikalo, Harriet Dalley, and Alundo Ballantzore. Below, children Preston Larsen and Daisy Dean Fail participate in another play.

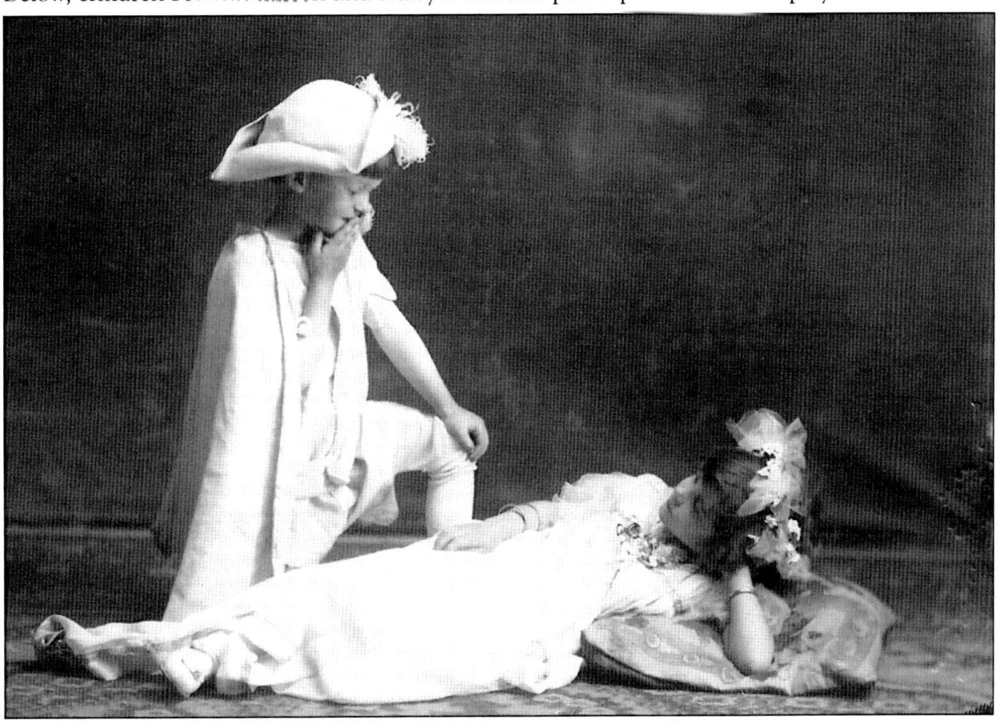

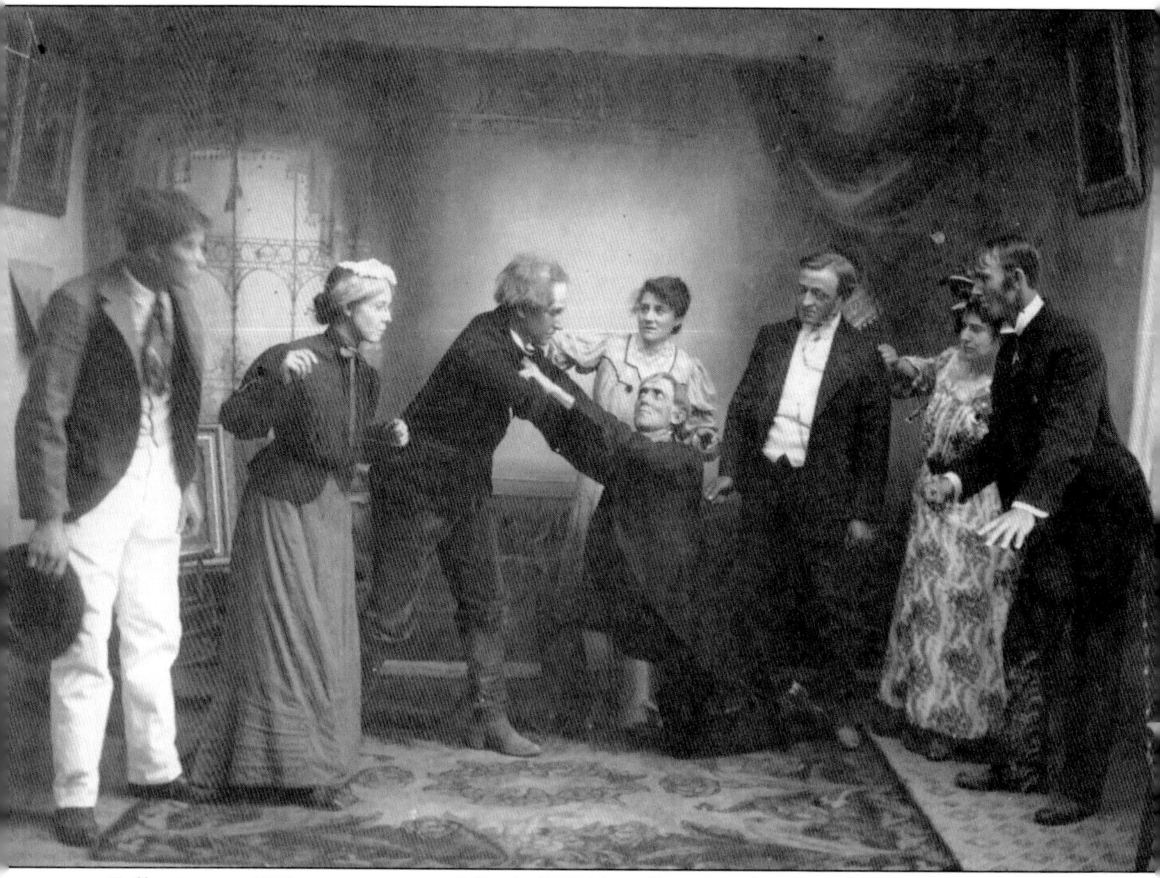

Following an 1892 presentation of *Knobs Will Turn Him Out*, local leader George C. Parkinson was so intensely impressed that he gave a short speech to the audience suggesting a building was needed to house such productions and that local dramatical talent, as pictured here, warranted such an undertaking. In 1905, work began on the large white brick structure on the north side of First South Street. The building was one large room except for the stage, dressing rooms at the north, and large balcony at the south. Audiences sat on folding chairs. The building was heavily used for stake conferences, town meetings, high school graduation exercises, and all manner of artistic purposes, such as traveling minstrels and flower shows. Operas, plays, high school musicals, lectures, and recitals rang out from the stage, and matinee dances for youth and evening dances for teens and adults kept the spring-loaded floor bouncing. Even professional boxing matches were hosted there. In 1940, the building was remodeled into a recreational center. In 1956, it became the temporary headquarters for the National Guard unit. The city tore it down in 1965. (Jay Burrup.)

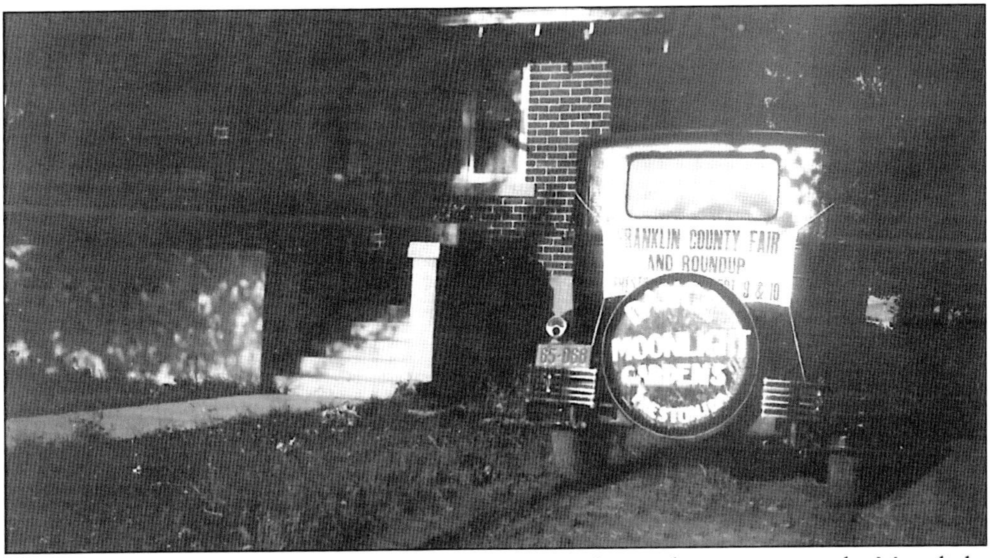

Car signs promoted the Franklin County Fair and Roundup, and an evening at the Moonlight Gardens, an open-air dance floor built in 1927 by Clarence Hansen and Baltzar Peterson and their sons Deloss Hansen and Dr. Jesse Peterson. It was on the northwest corner of State and First South Streets. Sylvia Davis was on the sidewalk on opening night when her brother called out, "Come on in and dance with me, Sylvia, maybe we can get the crowd started." Two years later, Hansen and Peterson built the Persiana at 77 South State Street. Below, August Dorigatti won a season ticket by naming the establishment. Although clever with words, he must not have been clever on his feet because he didn't use the ticket to dance; he cashed it in. Business, however, was brisk enough to bring orchestras from Salt Lake City. The Arabian Knights and Mickey Hart's band apparently caused many female hearts to flutter.

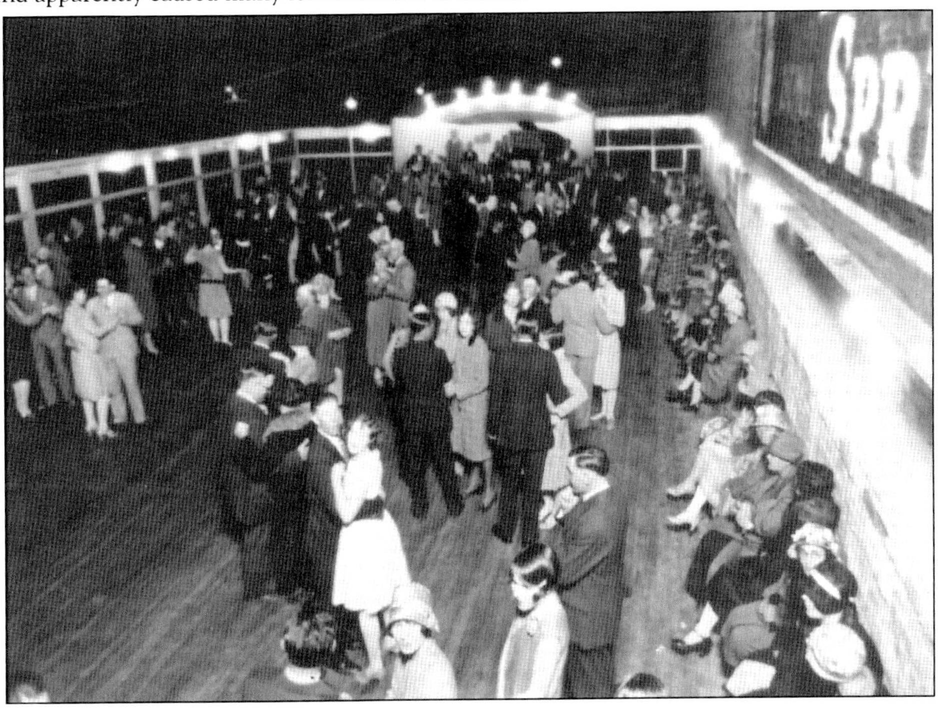

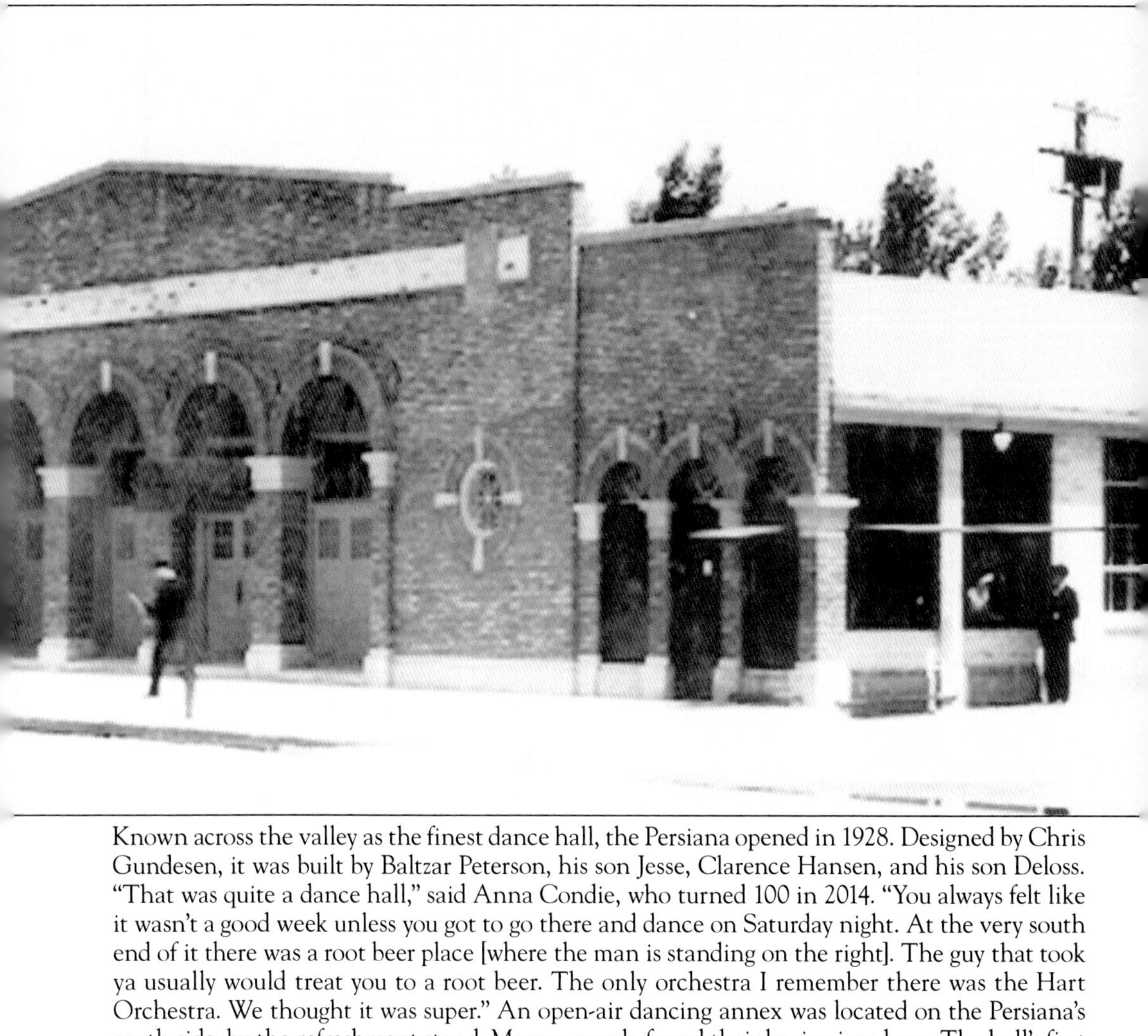

Known across the valley as the finest dance hall, the Persiana opened in 1928. Designed by Chris Gundesen, it was built by Baltzar Peterson, his son Jesse, Clarence Hansen, and his son Deloss. "That was quite a dance hall," said Anna Condie, who turned 100 in 2014. "You always felt like it wasn't a good week unless you got to go there and dance on Saturday night. At the very south end of it there was a root beer place [where the man is standing on the right]. The guy that took ya usually would treat you to a root beer. The only orchestra I remember there was the Hart Orchestra. We thought it was super." An open-air dancing annex was located on the Persiana's south side, by the refreshment stand. Many a couple found their beginnings here. The hall's first band comprised Paul Larsen, Al Greenhalgh, Reed Hart, John Fiala, Earl Laurence, Stan Hawkes, Mickey Hart, and Mark Hart. (Kathy Griffin.)

Three

That Famous Preston Night Rodeo

The first organized rodeo in Preston was called the "Great Roundup" and was held at the ballpark at 11:00 a.m., September 1–2, 1921, as part of the Franklin County Fair and Horse Show. Billed as the "only real wild west show presented this year" in the August 24, 1921, edition of the *Franklin County Citizen*, it promised "horse racing, roping and tying wild steers—bronco busting, expert lassoing, all showing life on the frontier in the early days." Under the direction of the local chamber of commerce, the Preston City Park was "fixed-up," and "Indians and whites alike" were expected to participate.

Bill Head, Franklin County sheriff, traveled to Fort Hall to recruit Indians to take part. They were great entertainers, appearing in the parade, bareback horseracing, dancing, and participating in events. Part of their wages were paid in beef, which they would butcher and process at the rodeo grounds. "They made jerky out of it, hang it all along the board fence," recalled Stan Hawkes in the *Cache Valley News*. Other features of the event included bulldogging, auto racing and "auto polo," a Roman chariot race, and Indian bareback pony racing. Anyone interested in earning a $25 cash prize was invited to bring their wild horses and "see how easily they [could] be subdued."

The rodeo was followed up with a "big free street dance," as described by the *Franklin County Citizen*. "No formal affair this. Dance in your clothes, your wife's clothes or anybody else's clothes." Lawmen reportedly looked the other direction when the rodeo's organizers tried to make the event solvent by bringing in slot machines. According to Gary Rawlings, former *Preston Citizen* editor, there were slots in the beer halls and at the hitching posts in the streets. "Those were the days of spontaneous action, when any spectator in the bleachers might become part of the action." A wheel once came off a polo jitney, and Theo Petterborg, mounting a saddle horse, raced toward the fence trying to lasso it. Although he did not succeed, he got a hearty cheer from appreciative fans.

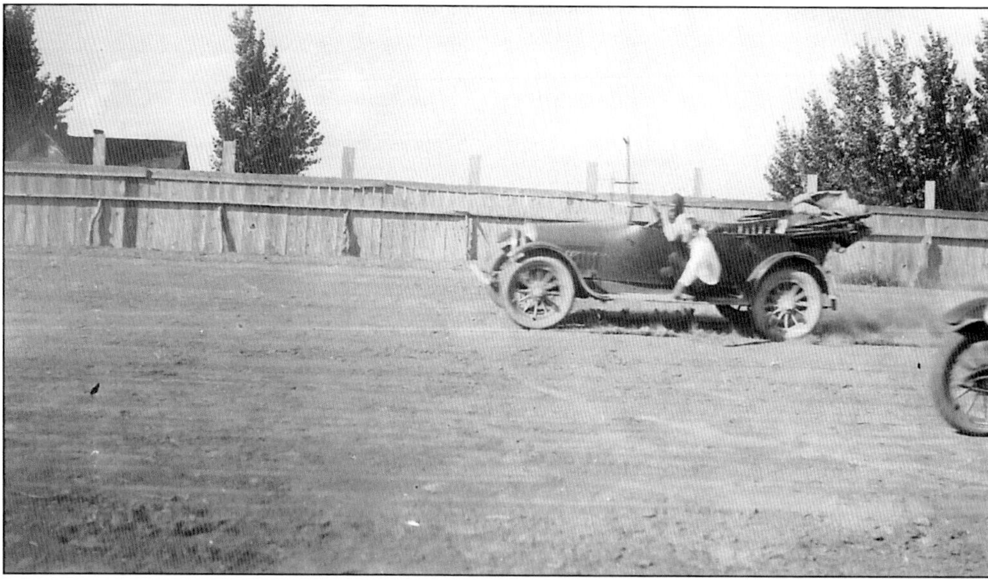

Newell Hart once wrote, "Old Model T Fords never died—they got made into bugs or polo cars" for competition at the rodeo. Roller bars were mounted on the cars for protection if the car rolled. Each auto polo team (as pictured above) had one driver and a mallet swinger. They chased a soccer-sized ball. As teams became more competitive, they eliminated seats, doors, floorboards, fenders, and brakes. Two foot-pedals controlled forward and reverse, starts and stops. The driver sat strapped to the gas tank. Below, Golden Romney is pictured in an old bug he and his gang built to race in the 1921 roundup. Golden lived in Preston while his father, Thomas C. Romney, was the principal at the OSA.

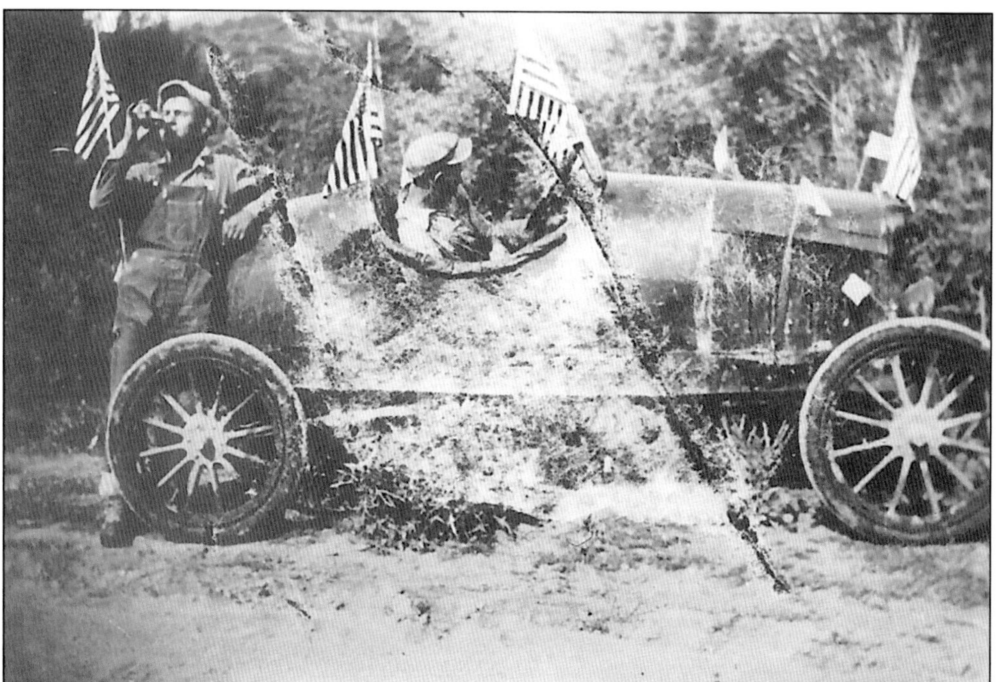

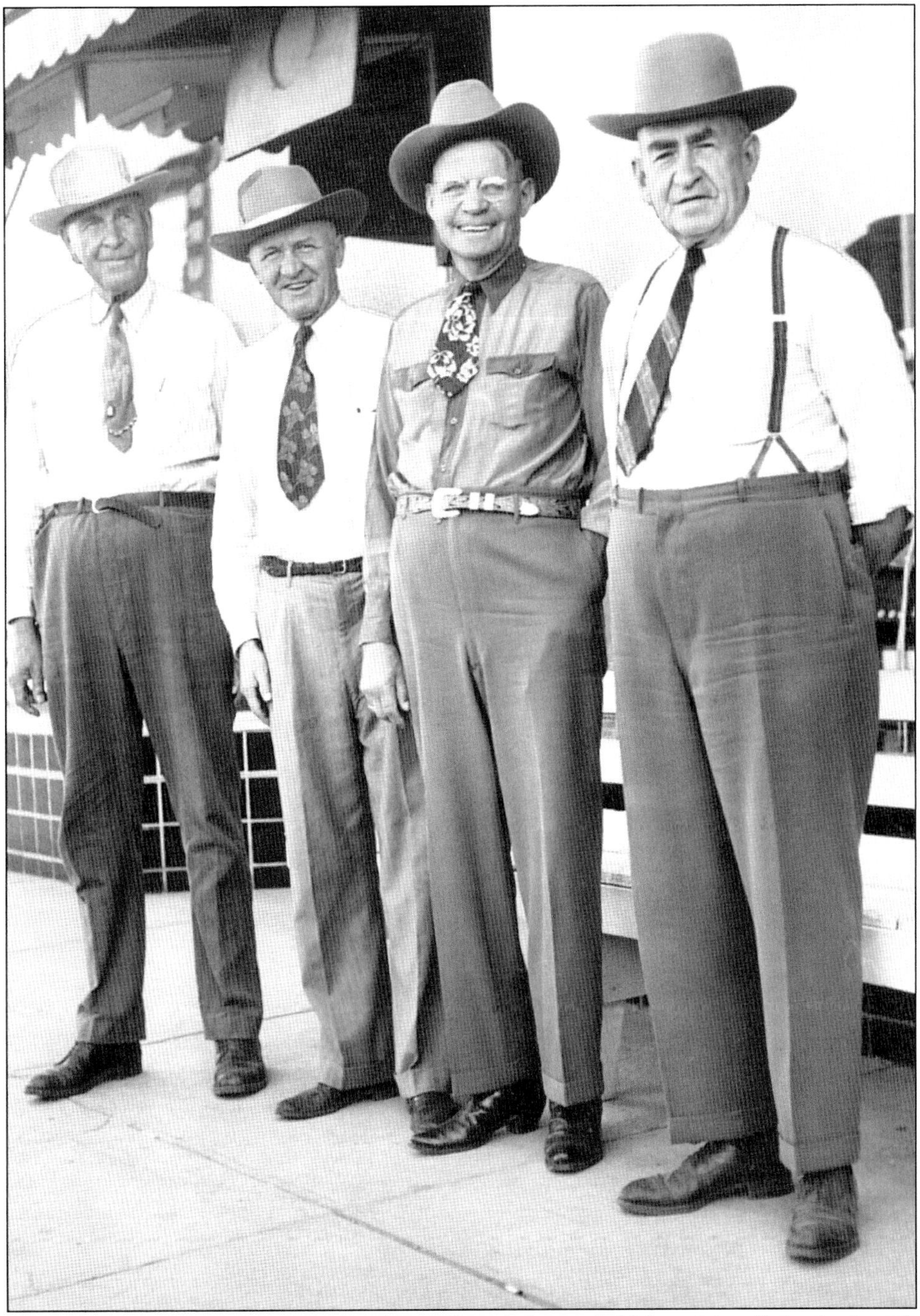

The Trail Blazer credits Preston's first rodeo to (from left to right) Elmer Merrill, Joe Luthy, Theo Petterborg, Tom Boyle, and G.T. Mitchell (not pictured). Like 3,000 other people, these men attended the Henry Stampede that year. Unlike others, they came home with the determination to create a similar event in Preston. Their idea stuck. Boyle was on the chamber of commerce and was able to get the community's backing for the Preston Stampede. That first rodeo netted $5,800, and the promoters "barely came out on top," states information for this picture recorded on the Larsen-Sant Library's Franklin County digital archives.

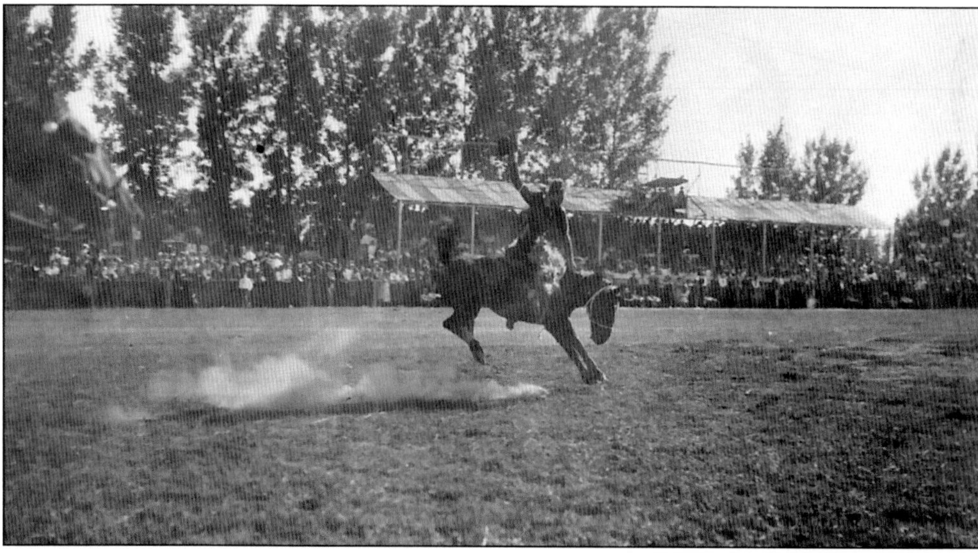

Pictured above, the wild bronc Gravedigger terrified and mesmerized many young roundup fans. As the animal circled and bucked, it dug a hole, earning the dreadful name. Pictured below is the 1945 rodeo queen court. From left to right are attendant Shirley Whitehead, queen Joyce Keller (Parkinson), and attendant Harriet Gilbert. The first recorded queen of That Famous Preston Night Rodeo was Dorothy Maughan in 1936. Other queens were Edna Palmer in 1937, Bertha Bergquist in 1938, Ida Winward in 1939, Letha Bronson in 1940, Ardis Hansen in 1941, (no rodeo was held in 1942 because of the war), Carma Oliverson in 1943, Christie Bastian in 1944, Shirley Whitehead in 1946, Conna Beth Oliverson in 1947, Mary Eleanor Swainston in 1948, Sergene Andra in 1949, and Vaunda Oliverson in 1950. This photograph was in a box with several others at an old chamber of commerce office. As they were being thrown away, Fred Titensor salvaged them.

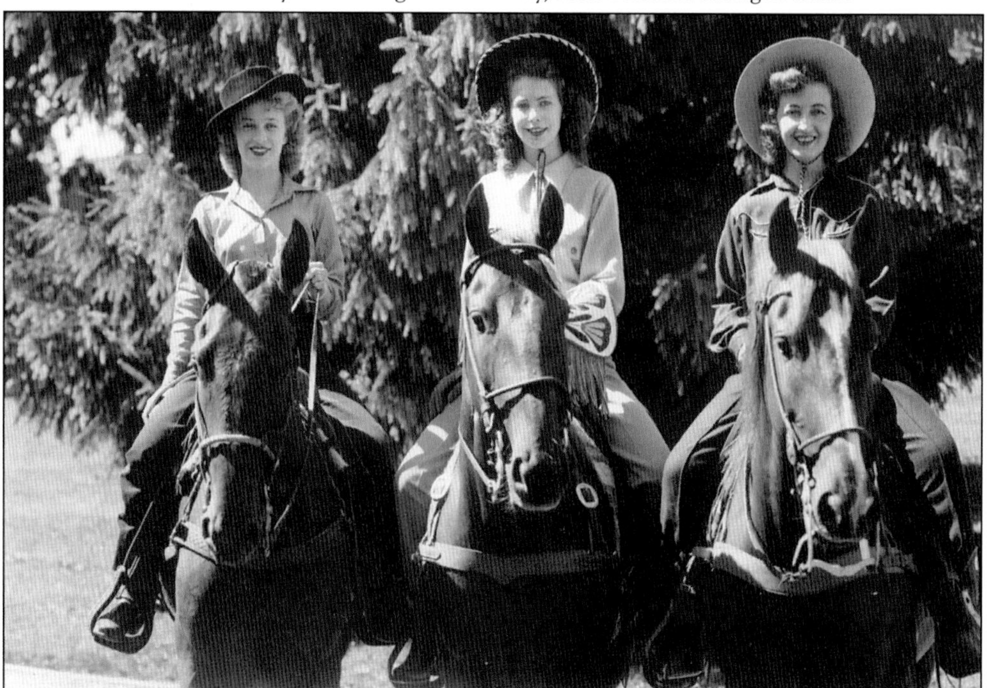

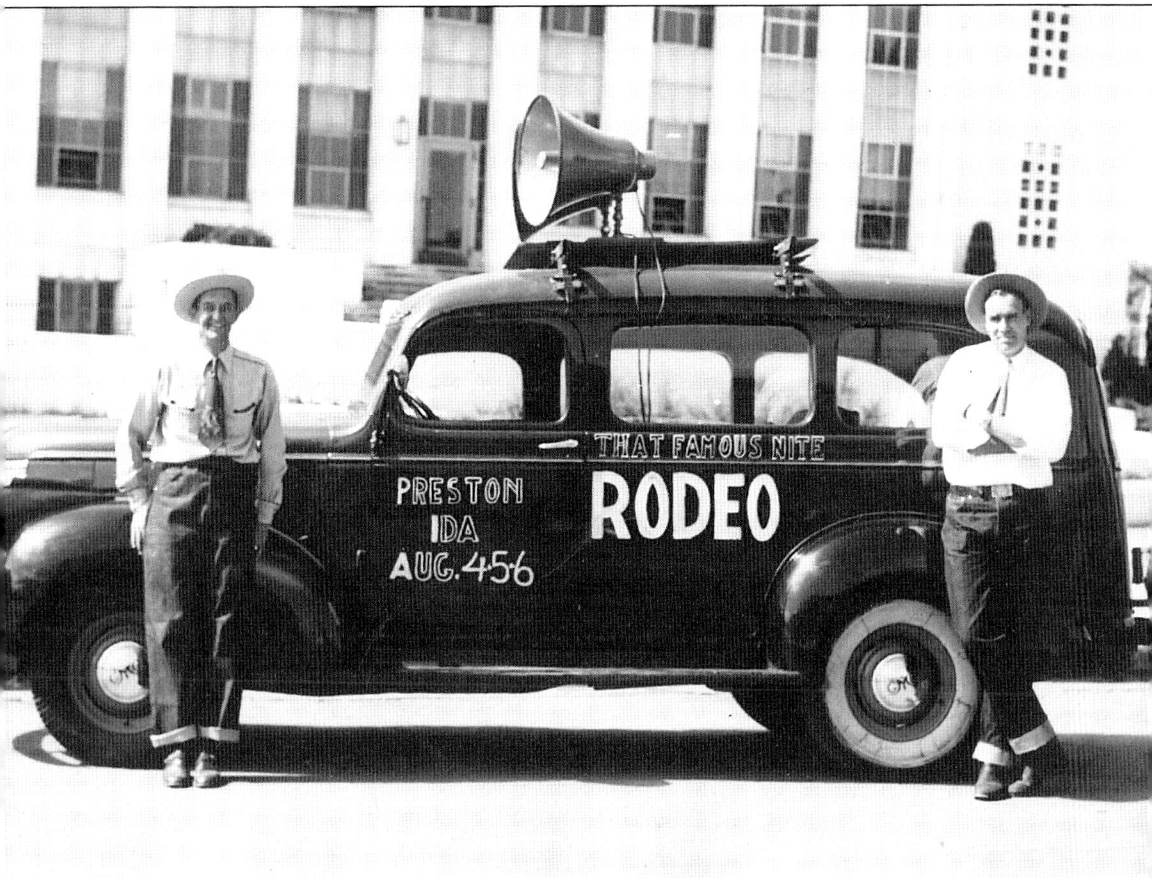

In 1935, the roundup took on a new name, That Famous Preston Night Rodeo. "Famous" because the organizers called it so, and "night" because the rodeo was changed from daytime to nighttime. Chamber president Dick Bowden, along with Ed Crockett and Theo Petterborg, had attended one of the hottest, dustiest rodeos ever, just to be turned down by the organizers of the Henry Stampede on the idea of rotating the stampede with the Preston roundup on an every-other-year basis. "Coming back in the car that evening, I suggested that we start a night rodeo to get out of the hot, dusty afternoon," recalled Bowden in the 1975 rodeo program. "I told them I'd talk to the power company and see what they could do." Utah Power and Light officials agreed to put up the lights, and the country's first night rodeo was born. Apparently, no one knew they were the first to organize a night rodeo, but the claim has stood for 80 years, giving credence to the "famous" moniker.

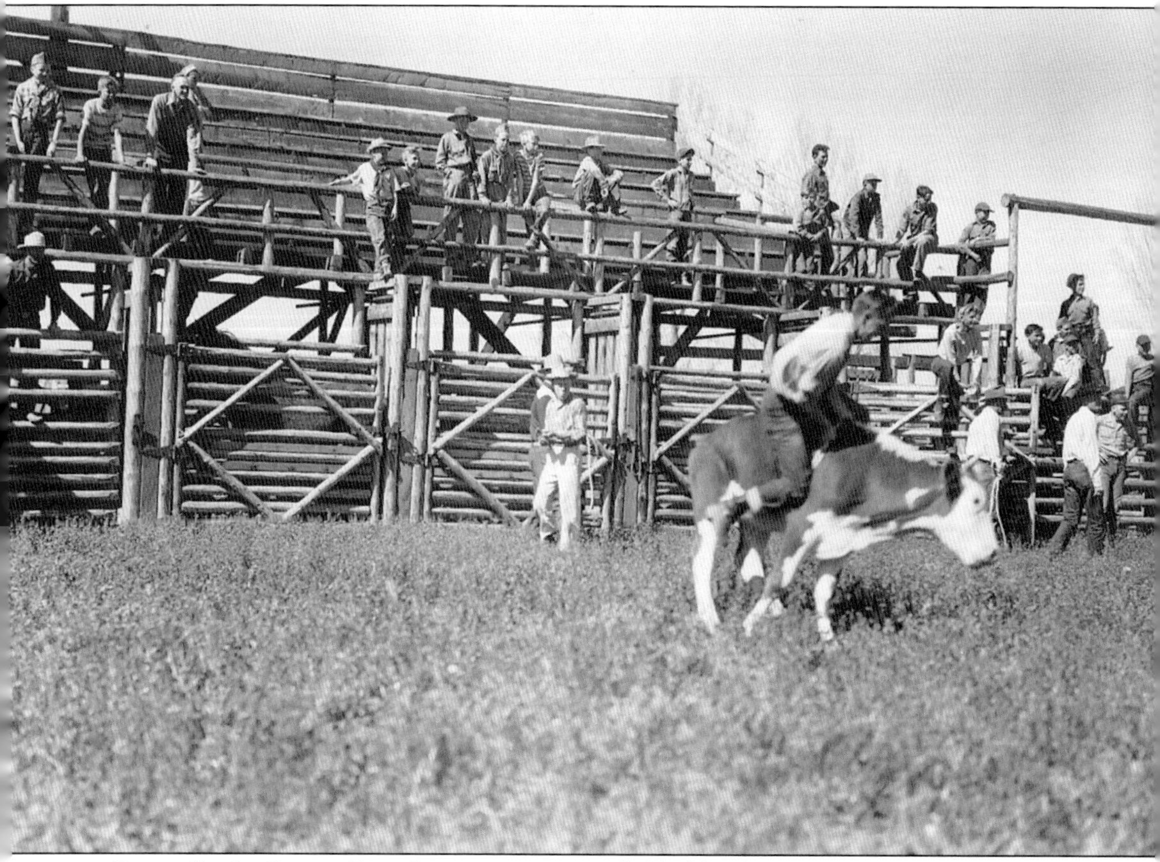

Originally, the Preston Roundup arena was encircled by bleachers roped off from the riding area. Proceeds of $14,000 from the first three years were used to build a pole arena, according to the 1975 rodeo program. Earl J. McClurg, secretary for the chamber of commerce in 1935, told Newell Hart that he, Jack Fershner, and Emil Petterborg built the first chutes for the night rodeo. Others on the board helping with the new night rodeo were Edwin Crockett (president), Harold Swift, Theo Petterborg, Andrew Nash, Laud Wright, Jim Bullock, and Tom Heath. The poles were replaced with steel one section at a time, including the chutes and holding pens. The Franklin County Commission leased the grounds to the chamber in 1938 with an option to buy, on the stipulation that the property be kept in good repair. Eventually, the grounds were purchased. The first stock came off the range, then Parley Hall and Earl Sorenson started bringing stock intended for rodeo. They were followed by several producers until Swanney Kerby, whose company currently produces stock for the rodeo, was hired.

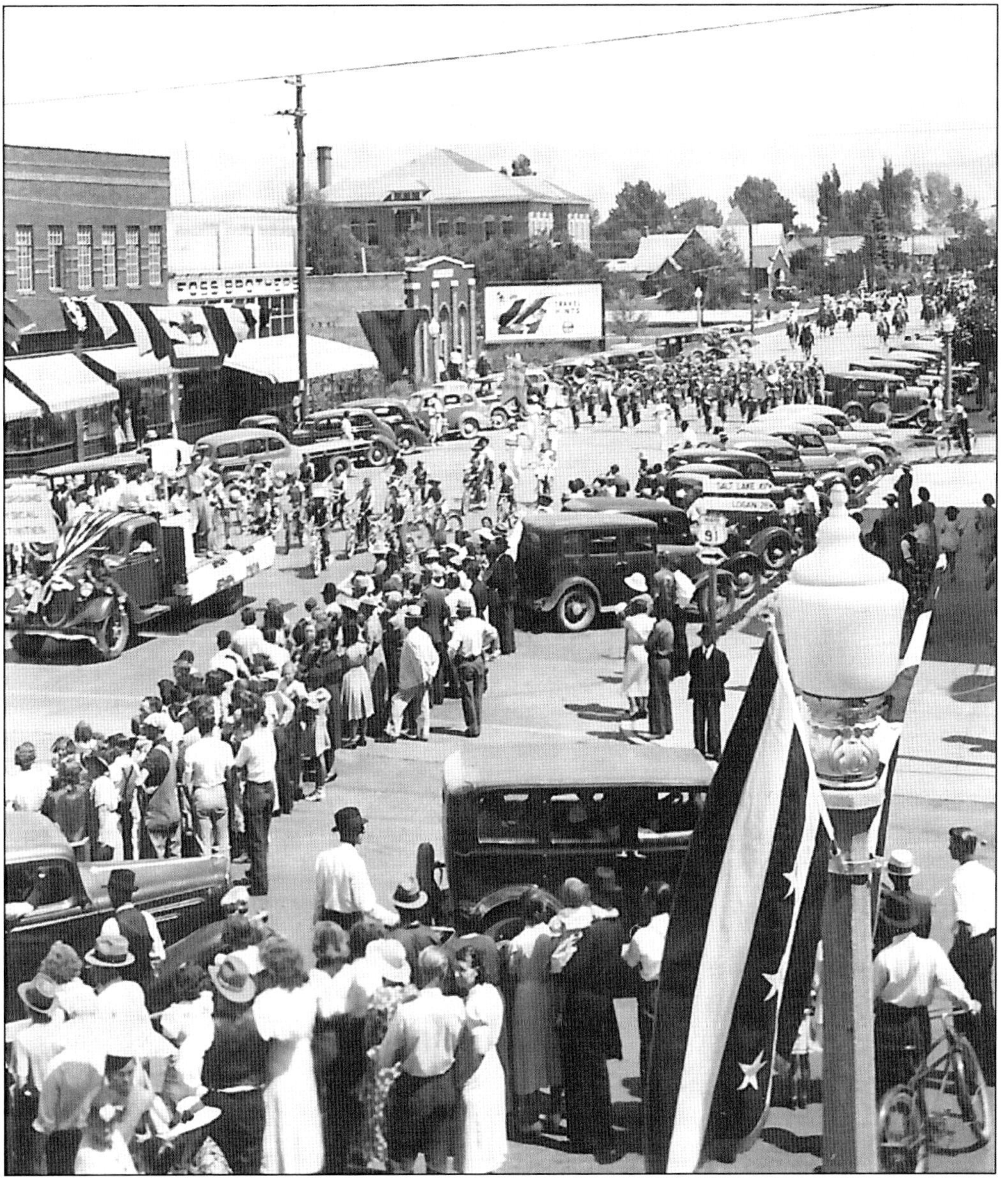

A parade has always been attached to the rodeo in Preston. In 1921, it preceded the event, starting at 11:00 a.m. When the rodeo was moved to nighttime, the parade was likewise rescheduled. In this picture, the parade is heading west on Oneida Street. The Central School is visible in the background, but the post office is not, dating this photograph to before 1939. According to the *Hometown Album*, the Foss Brothers building (second from left), erected in 1907, sported a "legendary metal canopy" over the sidewalk, which "intrigued a generation of kids; when street dances were held out front the band played beneath its cover. The canopy was removed a few years before the facade was tiled in 1948." The building to its right, with arches, was constructed in 1930 as a clinic for Drs. Cutler, Evans, and Worley; they sold it to the Huntingtons in 1951, and it was remodeled into Preston Cleaners.

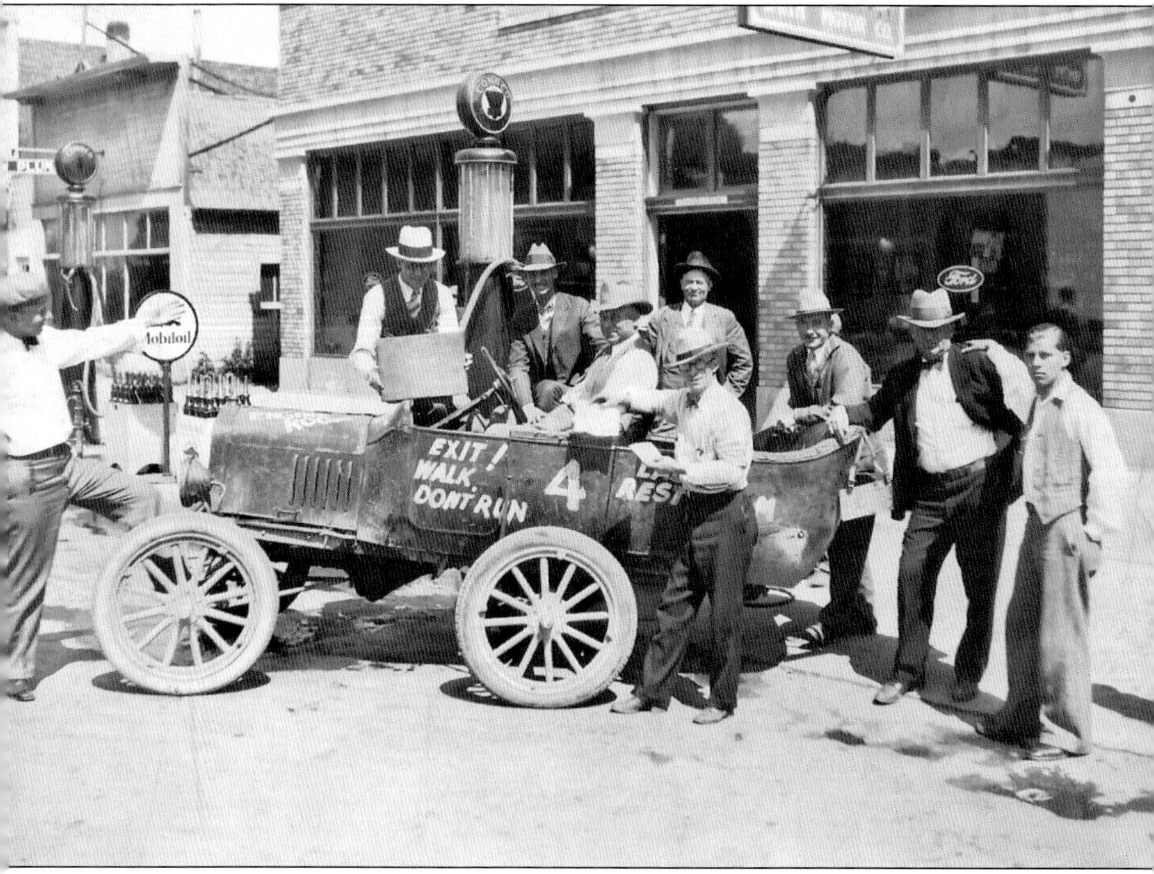

There is no record of who built this trick car, but it was usually driven in parades by Wilf Smith or Harold "Tiny" Jensen. The car had a shortened drive shaft and could tip backwards and circle. Pictured with it are, from left to right, Charley Eline, unidentified, Earl Goasling, Bill Smith, Tiny Jensen (white hat), unidentified (above Tiny), Nowlin Hale, Ern Porter, and Alf Peterson. Smith opened a garage at 40 West Oneida Street in 1929. Before that time, he had a Ford agency on North Main Street. Eline operated a popcorn stand by the Isis Theater on State Street, worked at the Foss Clothing store, and was a committee member of the board that chose the annual Fourth of July queen. Goaslind was a former postal worker.

Four

PATRIOTISM

Prestonites have responded heartily to the call of Uncle Sam to do their part in preserving democracy during the world's conflagrations. A war memorial in front of the county courthouse honors hundreds of men and women who have represented Preston in war. The sacrifices of two men, Junior Nathan Van Noy and Leonard Brostrom, in World War II, were acknowledged with the Medal of Honor.

Brostrom was a rifleman stationed in the Philippine Islands on October 28, 1944, when the enemy poured machinegun and rifle fire from pillboxes, trenches, and spider holes, which were so well camouflaged they were invisible beyond 20 yards. Private Brostrom, without orders and with no regard for his own safety, advanced, tossing grenades through the main pillbox entrance. Six enemy soldiers left a trench in a bayonet charge. Brostrom killed one and drove the others off with rifle fire. He was wounded several times in the abdomen and knocked to the ground. Although suffering intensely and rapidly weakening from loss of blood, he slowly rose to his feet and once more hurled grenades at the pillbox. Private Brostrom died while being carried from the battlefield. His unhesitating willingness to sacrifice himself in a one-man attack against overwhelming odds enabled his company to reorganize and annihilate the entire enemy position. Van Noy, whose story appears on page 52, was killed in action in New Guinea.

Back at home, Preston housed Japanese Americans in a compound on West Oneida Street as well as German prisoners of war near the sugar factory. The Germans were sent out to local farms to work the crops while they were here. Many grew to love the area and did not want to leave.

Nevertheless, it was not easy to be a German native in Preston at the time. Although the Nuffer family had been in Preston long enough to have helped to build the OSA in the 1890s, their German heritage was a concern during the war, especially when locals participated in events such as burning in effigy a "Schitty" of outhouses gathered in the city park east of the business district.

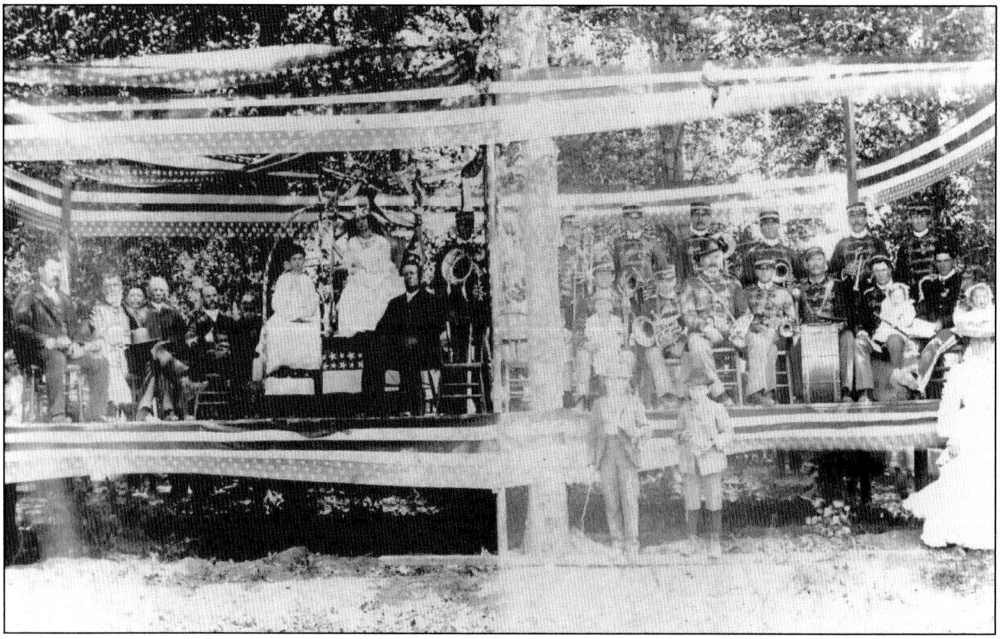

The band seen above, led by Theodore Adwin Montague, performed on July 4, 1903. Montague is on the right, wearing a large black hat. Dee and Lionel are on each side of him. On the bass drum is Phil Morgetts, and holding his son Thomas Newell (with the drumsticks) is snare drum player Thomas Carter. The baby's mother, Luda Ethel Clayton Carter, is standing at the right. Wallace Head played the bass horn, and George Moody is one of the boys in the front. Below, James Bosworth is driving this float in front of Preston Milling Company, established in 1904. Bosworth died in 1923, so this photograph was taken between 1904 and 1923. Preston's early settlers took their grain to the Muddy and High Creek mills to be exchanged for flour, then to mills in Franklin and Weston, until this facility was built.

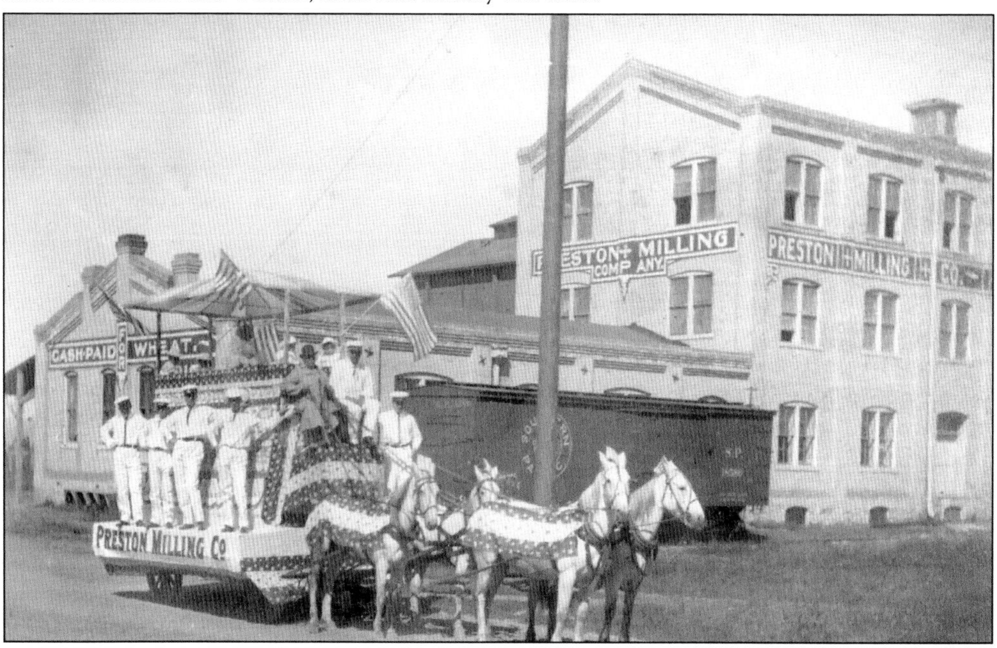

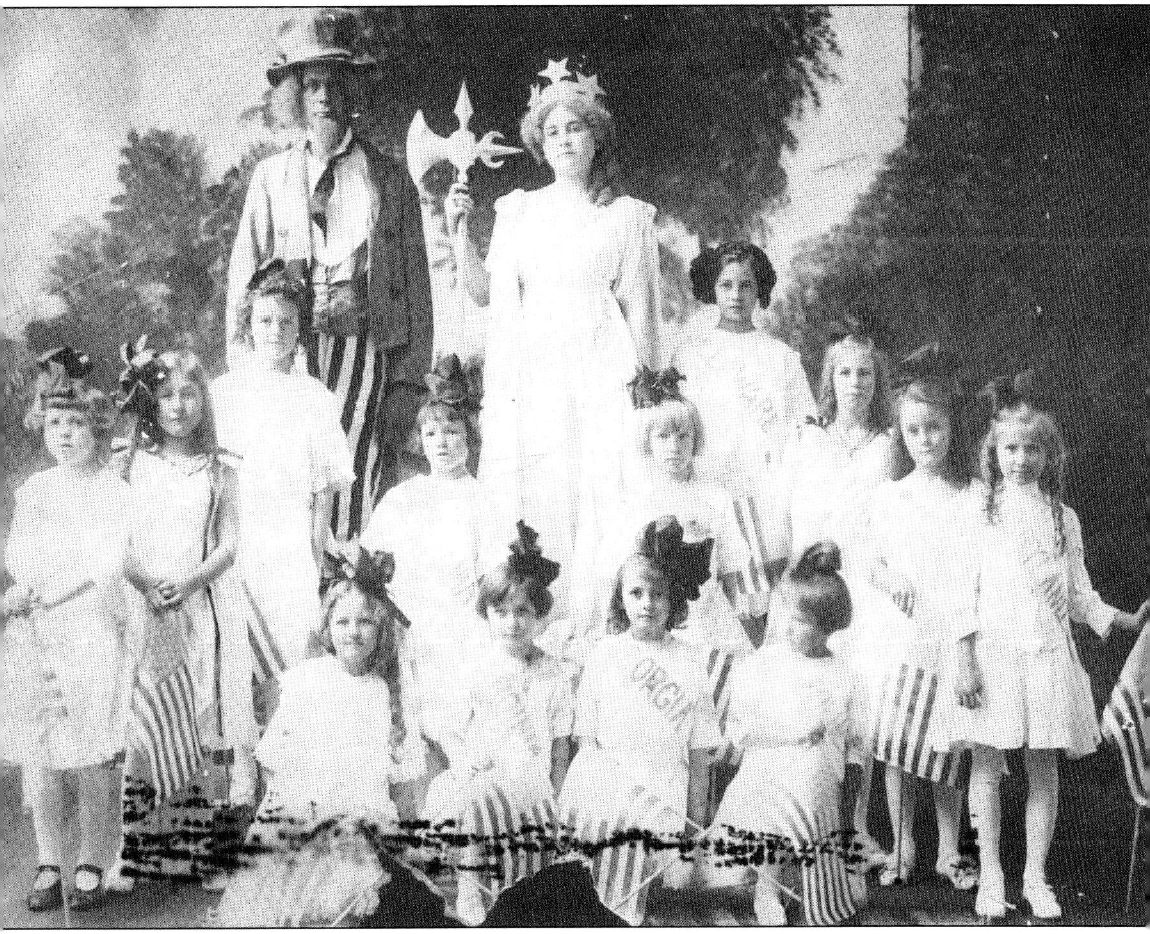

Around 1912, Preston chose Libby Hale as the "Liberty Goddess" for Fourth of July celebrations. On the left is Raidia Larsen; next to her is Louise Higginbotham. The second girl on the right is Marica States, daughter of Dr. Gilbert and Ema Mae States. The second girl from the left in the first row is Florence Fail, and third from the left is Vaiola Blood. The Stateses came to Franklin as newlyweds in 1904, she a nurse, and he a doctor. His first job was to heal the Kempton Comedy Company—all sick with food poisoning. Next, he stitched up the head of a man hit with a two-by-four by a neighbor. The Stateses moved to Preston in 1912, raised their family, and opened a hospital. Over his 20-year-career, Dr. States delivered about 3,000 babies and helped organize the Cache Valley Medical Society. He called himself a horse-and-buggy doctor until he bought the first Ford in Franklin County. He helped convince the state legislature to designate June 15 as Idaho Day and also helped to organize the first celebration.

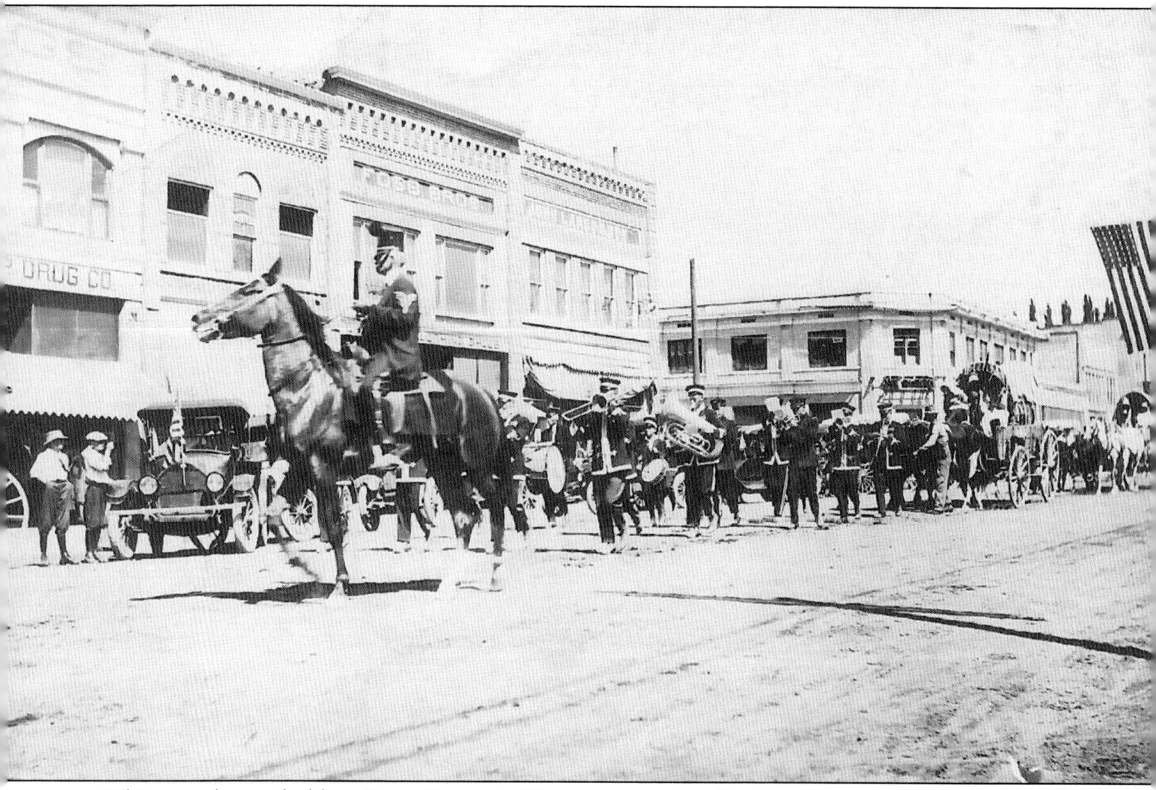

This parade was held on State Street in Preston sometime between 1916 and 1920. It was likely an Independence Day parade, judging by the large flag flown in the intersection of State Street and Oneida Street. The first three structures on the left were the original Foss buildings, built by Ezra, Cal, and Frank Foss. The first housed the Preston Co-op Drug Company, incorporated in 1899 by O.D. Merrill, Hyrum Tippets, George C. Parkinson, F.D. Geiger, William M. Daines, Dr. Allen R. Cutler, Charles D. Goaslind, and Arthur W. Hart. Ezra Foss was a pharmacist-manager there. Next was the Pioneer Meat Market, where, by 1914, wrestling matches were held upstairs. A clothing store was housed in the building emblazoned "Foss Bros." In its upper floors, Dr. Ray L. Davis opened up his dental practice. The fourth building was erected by John Larsen. Continuing north, across the street is the Greaves Block building, which housed First National Bank, Franklin County offices, and other businesses.

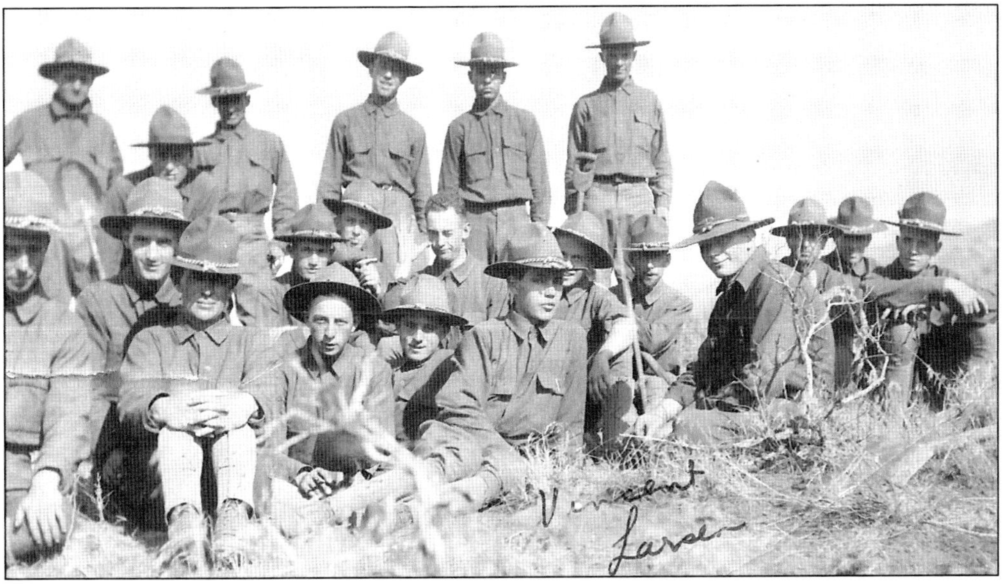

County clerk John A. Kofoed registered 21-year-old Vincent Bickmore Larsen and his father, Jacob N. Larsen (the first mayor of Preston) for World War I on June 15, 1918. At the time, Vincent was an employee at First National Bank in Preston. Preston residents sent off their solders with a parade on October 2, 1917. Below, a military parade was also held in 1943. During World War II, each community had a quota of E bonds to purchase in order to fund the war. Franklin County's quota was $275,000. Progress in meeting the quota was recorded on a meter posted on the side of First Security Bank. (Below, Jay Burrup.)

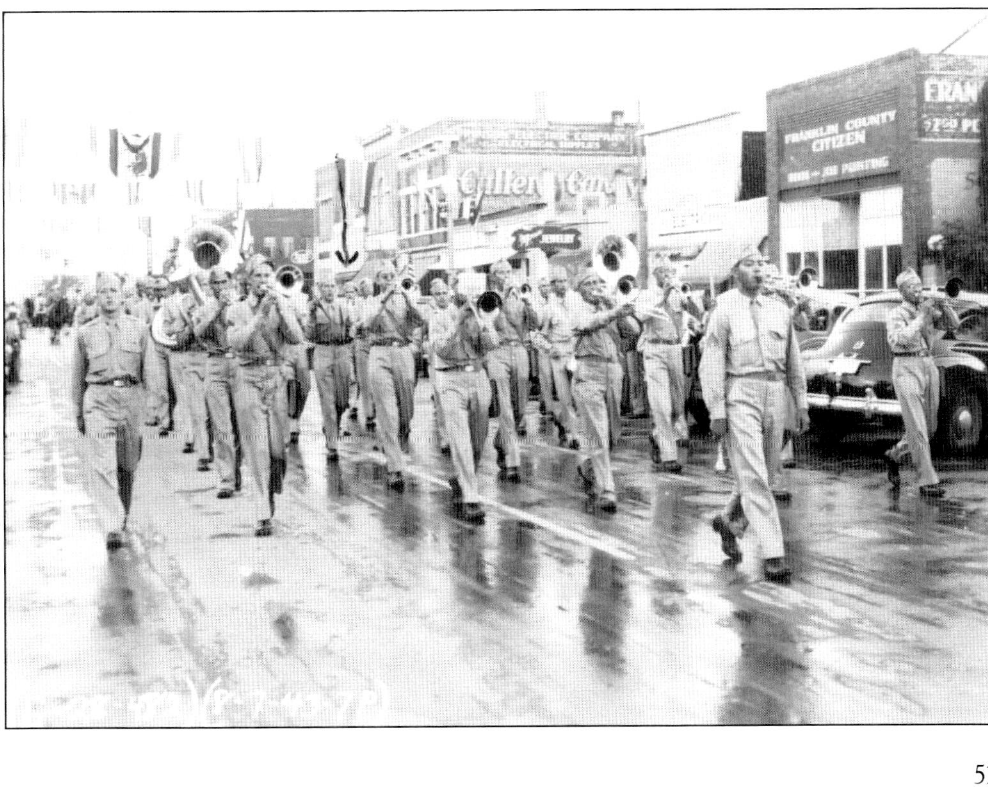

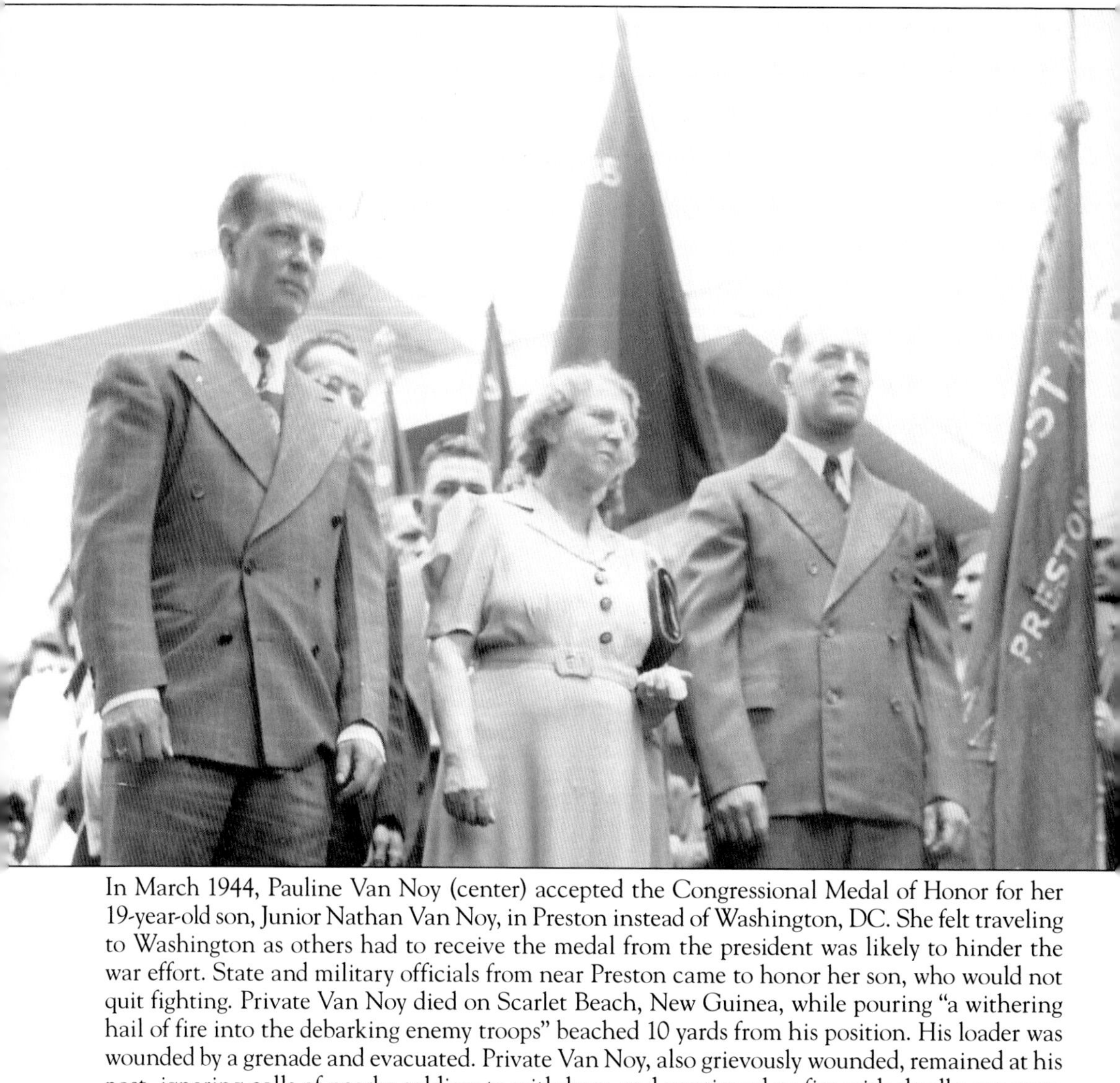

In March 1944, Pauline Van Noy (center) accepted the Congressional Medal of Honor for her 19-year-old son, Junior Nathan Van Noy, in Preston instead of Washington, DC. She felt traveling to Washington as others had to receive the medal from the president was likely to hinder the war effort. State and military officials from near Preston came to honor her son, who would not quit fighting. Private Van Noy died on Scarlet Beach, New Guinea, while pouring "a withering hail of fire into the debarking enemy troops" beached 10 yards from his position. His loader was wounded by a grenade and evacuated. Private Van Noy, also grievously wounded, remained at his post, ignoring calls of nearby soldiers to withdraw, and continued to fire with deadly accuracy. He expended every round and was found, covered with wounds, dead beside his gun. He killed at least half of the 39 enemies who landed. His heroic tenacity saved the lives of his comrades, allowing them to annihilate the attackers. (Kathy Griffin.)

Five

Business District

Business in Preston did not spring up in an orderly manner. Rather, it sprang up where it happened, as it was needed. People were quick to identify money-making enterprises, whether housed in a building, such as the first store opened up by William Chapman and James Bosworth on South State Street, or on the go, like the young men who capitalized on the heat of a summer day in 1932.

That year, the monument to the Battle of Bear River/Bear River Massacre, built by the Daughters of the Utah Pioneers, was dedicated. Charlie Eline, Denzil Petterborg, and Lamor Cole provided ice cream and soda pop to the throngs who attended. "The day was hot and 10,000 people couldn't find a drink of water. Needless to say, we did o.k.," stated Petterborg. Cole noted that cars were lined up the highway as far as the airport for that celebration. "When we ran out we had to turn people away. There was no way to get through to town for more. Although we were out of pop we did have a lot of ice left. We got cans of water from the neighbors and mixed it with the ice. People gladly used paper cups or bottles over and over and paid a nickel for the ice water."

Between 1911 and 1913, Preston boasted two electric companies, the High Creek and Idaho-Utah. From 1903 to 1912, two telephone companies, Bell and Independent, offered services to Preston residents.

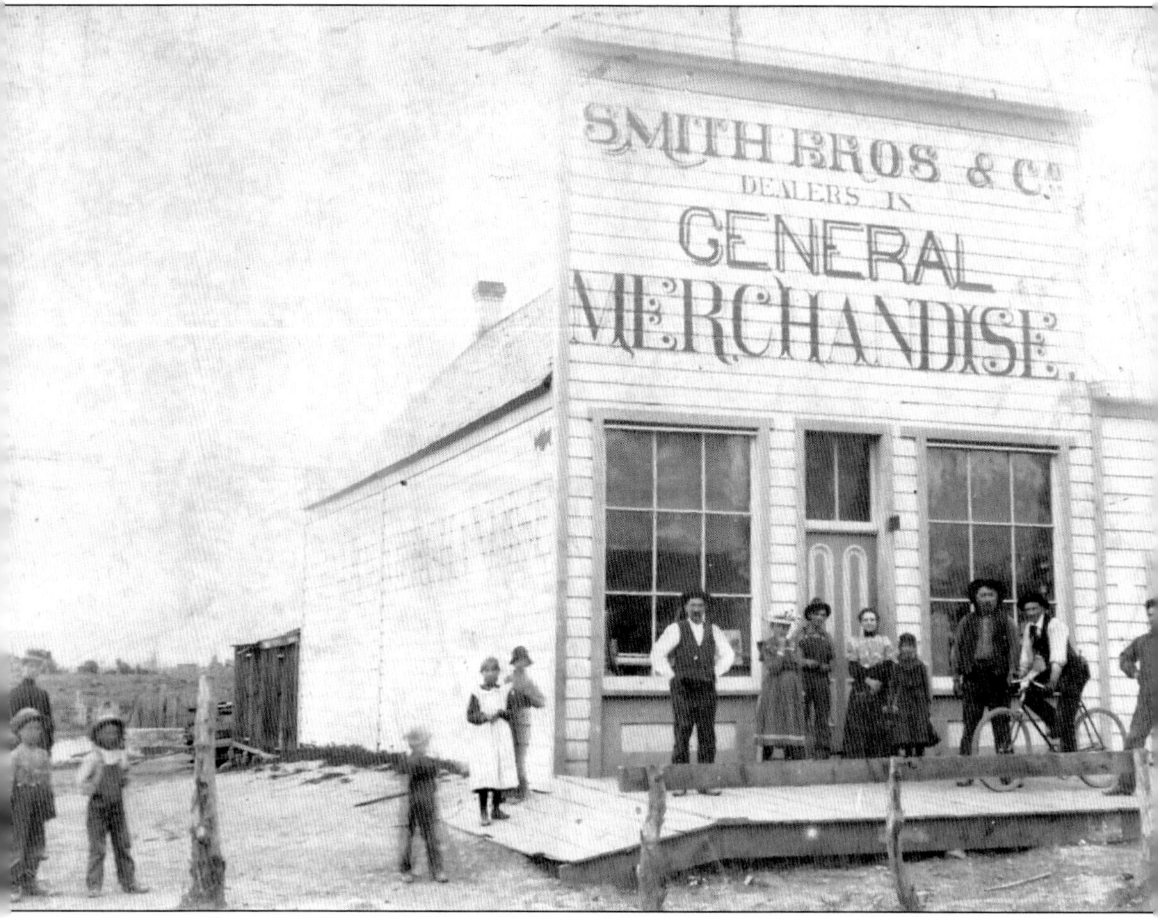

Tom Smith, one of the first homesteaders in Linrose, is wearing a white shirt in the center of this photograph taken about 1899. This store stood on the northwest corner of State and First South Streets. Smith ran the business with his brother J.G., who was on a mission to England at the time. A shoemaker, J.G. brought his business to Preston after working in Brigham City and Smithfield. He later built the yellow brick building to the north of this lot (82 South State Street), which houses Patino Store and Ross Distributing today. The man on the bike is Thomas Carter. The children are thought to be Smith's. J.G. Smith rented this building to William Tanner to sell Hamilton and Ellington pianos, Edison phonographs, and furniture after he built his brick store in 1907. After Hamilton constructed his own store at about 9 South State Street, J.C. Penney occupied this space for his Golden Rule store—his fourth store, and the first in Idaho. Chauncey and Dolly Williams once opened a candy store in the building as well.

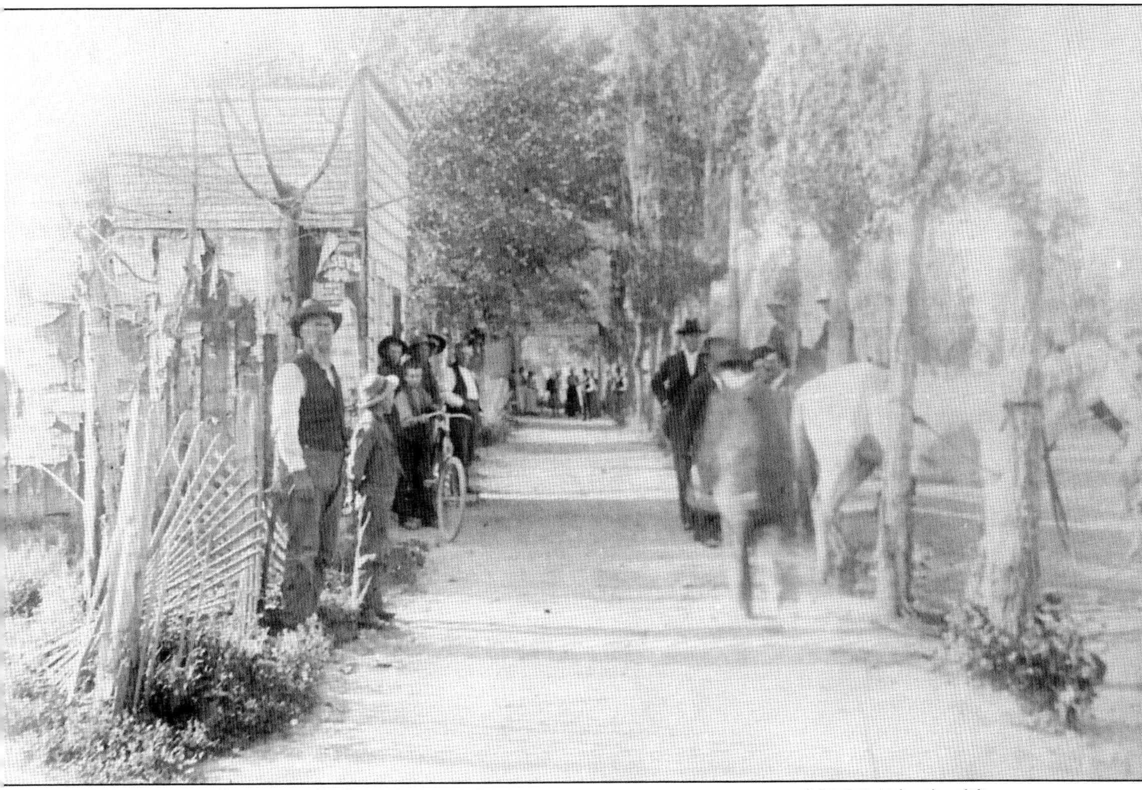

This view is looking north from Preston's main corner sometime around 1900. The building on the left is Harry Smith's barbershop. Smith could not read or write. The man in front and to the left is Nathan Taylor Packer, who operated Packer's Ferry on the Bear River between Battle Creek and Bridgeport during the 1860s. Packer and his wife, Mary Elvira, were some of the first settlers of Riverdale, where they raised their family of 15 children. He made a living as a freighter, carrying supplies from Cache Valley to the surrounding western states. He was also a Utah Indian War veteran, having served as a minuteman in Cache Valley in the 1860s. He was 12 years old when he first stood watch on Lookout Mountain (Mount Smart, or Little Mountain) in Franklin. At the end of the walkway is a group of people assembled in front of the Bosworth Hotel, opened by James Bosworth in 1892. Bosworth sold the building to Charles Hobbs in 1902.

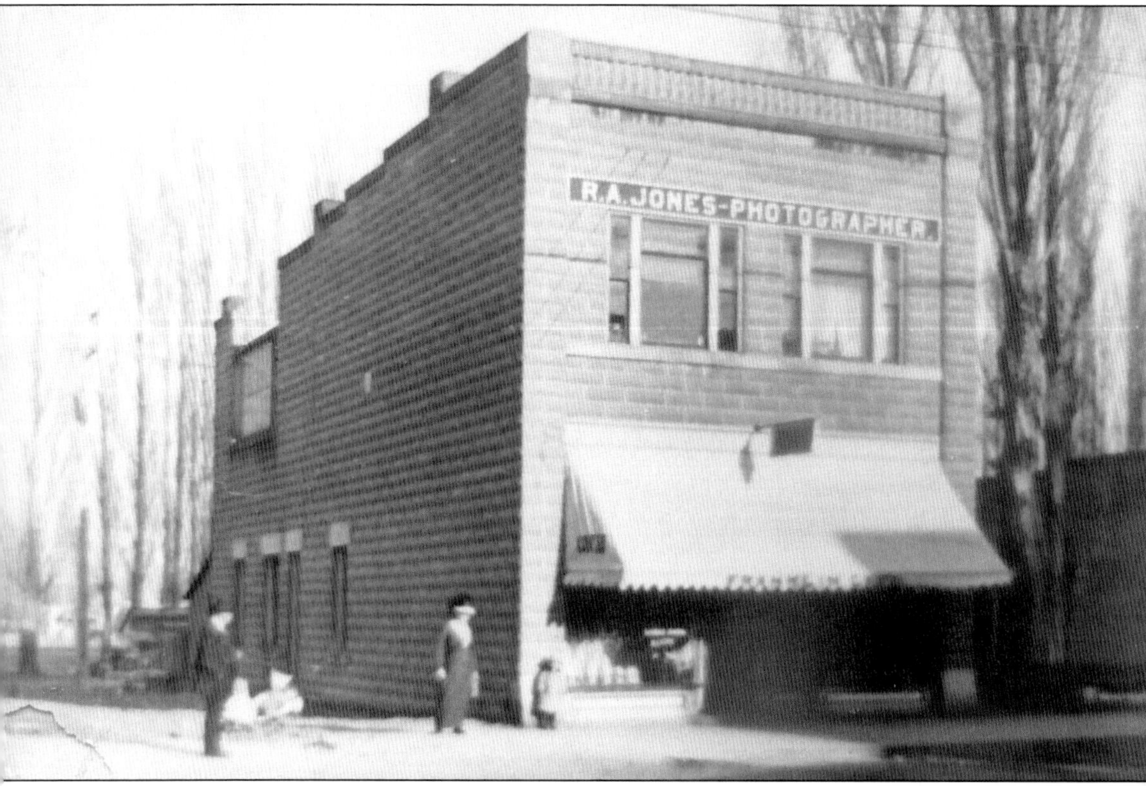

The R.A. Jones building at 43 South Main Street was on the east side of State Street. Newell Hart wrote, "Clues indicate that the building was constructed between 1910 and 1912." At first, R.A. Jones used the main floor for his photography business; he later rented the space to a Japanese family for a café, which they likely purchased from Louis M. Edison, who sold the Franklin Cafe just before his marriage in 1913. An advertisement in the October 28, 1914, edition of the newspaper noted, "Joe Stenger has been busy decorating the Jones Photo Studio preparatory for the Japs to move the Franklin Café there. This, when done, will make a swell café and one which will accommodate everybody." The photograph is attributed to Edward Viehweg, an apprentice to R.A. Jones. The words "Franklin Café" indicate that this was after the designation of the Preston area as part of the new Franklin County formed from the older and larger Oneida County on January 30, 1913.

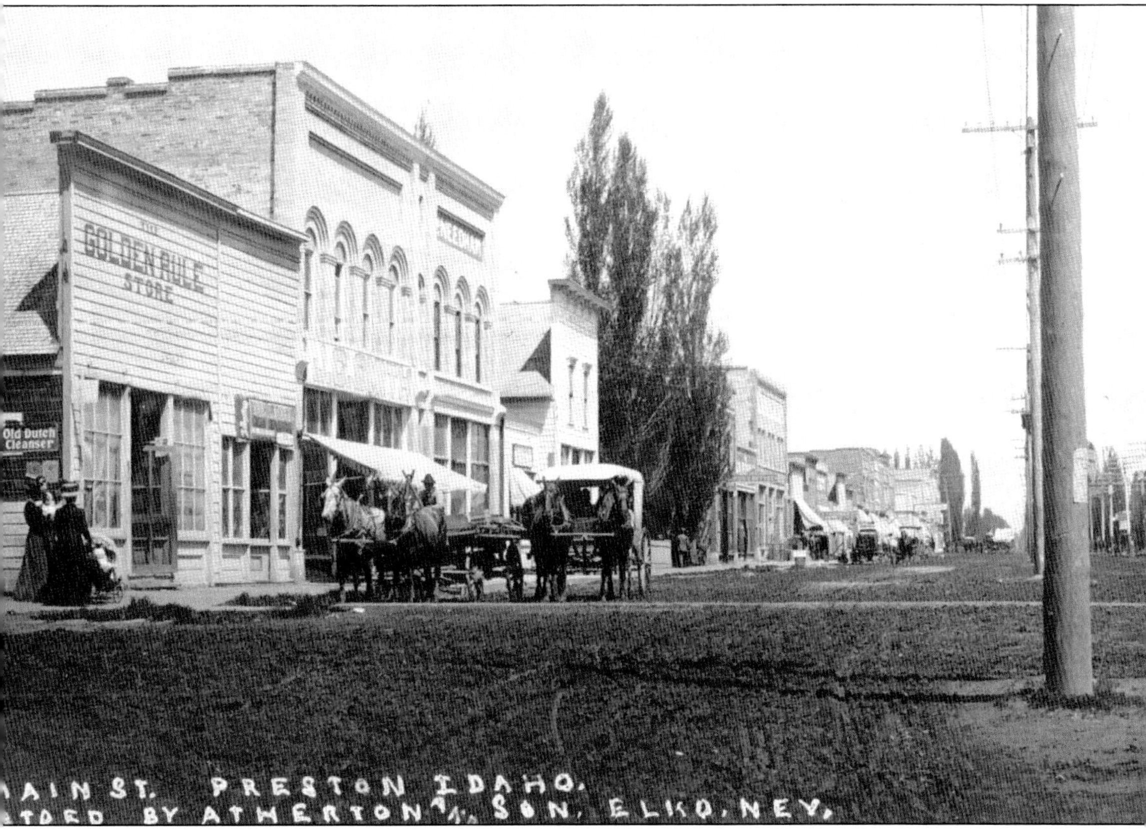

This photograph was probably taken about 1910, when N.G. Peterson came to Preston and occupied a narrow space between the Golden Rule (left) and the J.G. Smith Mercantile. James Cash Penney had moved his new concept—a department store that practiced the Golden Rule—from Wyoming into Preston in 1908, the first J.C. Penney store in Idaho. Over the next year, the Preston store generated enough profits for Penney and manager Edward Neighbors to open a Malad store. They moved the Preston store north on State Street in 1939, and it operated there until 1975. The building to the right is the J.G. Smith and Needham building, which still stands at 82 South State Street. The Needham was a newly furnished hotel upstairs and a ladies' clothing store on the ground level in 1906. Hotel rates were $2 per day. By 1911, Madsmine "Minnie" Struve had moved her millinery shop here and raised her family with her husband, William, upstairs. The poles belong to the High Creek Electric Light & Power Company, which operated in Preston from 1907 to 1913. (Jay Burrup.)

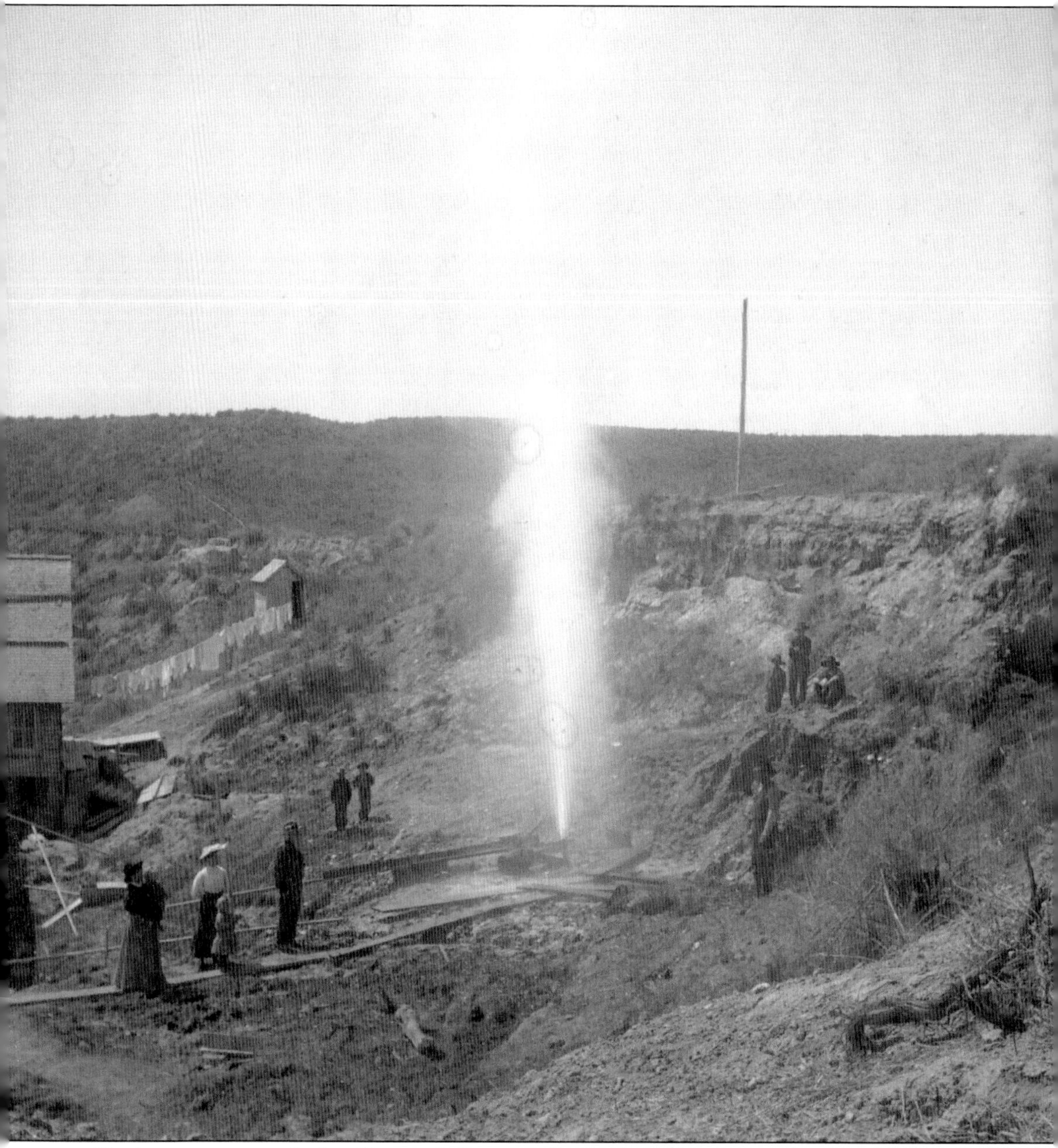

Real estate partners Arthur Hart and Clarence Chadwick built a man-made geyser and a resort at a hot spring on a bend in the Bear River west of Preston in about 1904. The building in the left foreground housed a pool and dressing rooms. Carl Viehweg was employed by Hart and Chadwick to run a crew that cut ice from the river to store in the resort's icehouse during the winter of 1905. He and his family lived in the home in the back. An advertisement in the local paper in 1906 noted that the resort was leased to Sanders and Sanders and that "the best mineral baths in the world are at the Hot Springs. Cures rheumatism and all skin diseases." The home was converted into a hotel and dance hall/saloon, and the stagecoach made regular runs between it and the livery stable in Preston. By 1911, the building was dismantled by Hart and Chadwick, and the rest of the resort slid into the river.

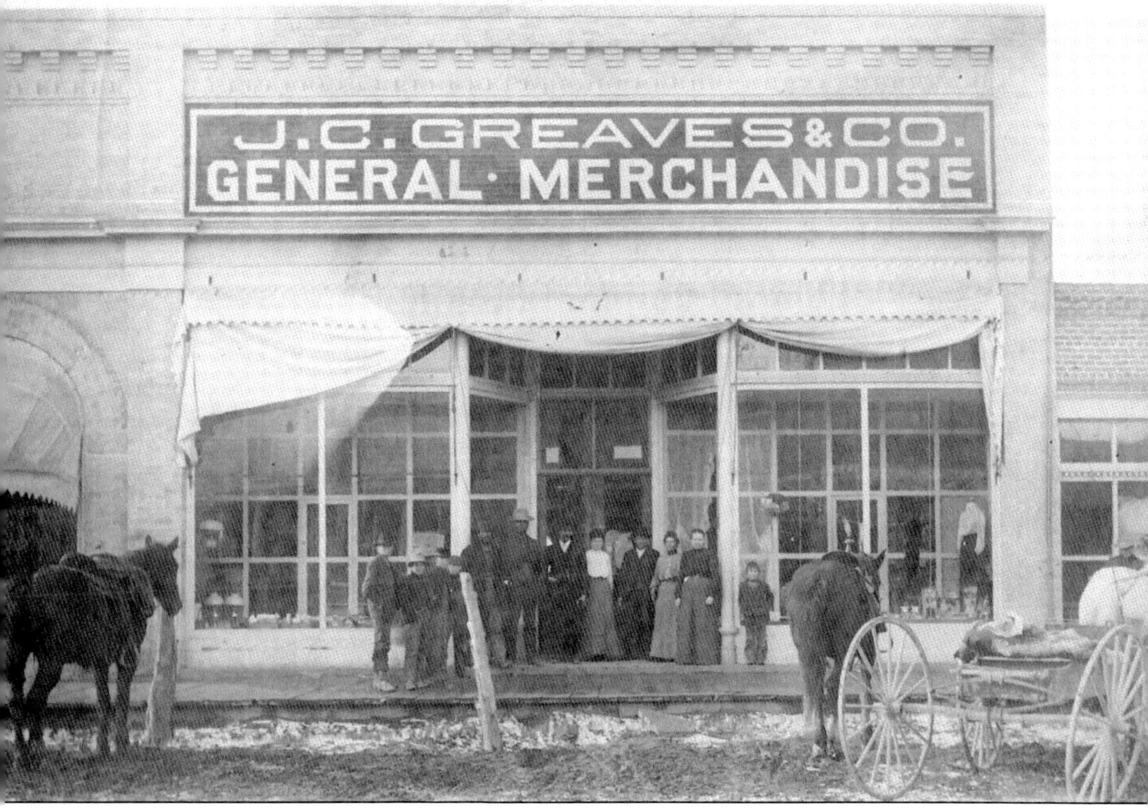

Constructed in 1904 by John C. Greaves, this building housed both a bank and a general store. It is the third store Greaves built in Preston, and it sat on the northwest corner of the intersection of Oneida and State Streets, facing east. Taken on March 11, 1908, this photograph includes Greaves's wife, Althea Card Greaves, standing on the right. The other woman might be Della Maughan, who married Clarence Chadwick and worked many years in the store. Greaves was the business manager for the *Republican* newspaper, along with Nat Davis, in the fall of 1890. In 1897, he had erected a store on North State Street. Greaves also owned a mill in the canyon east of town with Martin Johnson. Greaves, Johnson, and T.W.R. Nelson (a silent partner) opened the Bank of Preston, the first bank in town, on February 8, 1904. Greaves was also one of Preston's first postmasters, operating the post office out of his store. William B. Gibbons succeeded Greaves as postmaster on March 18, 1894. This building was flanked on the west by a barbershop.

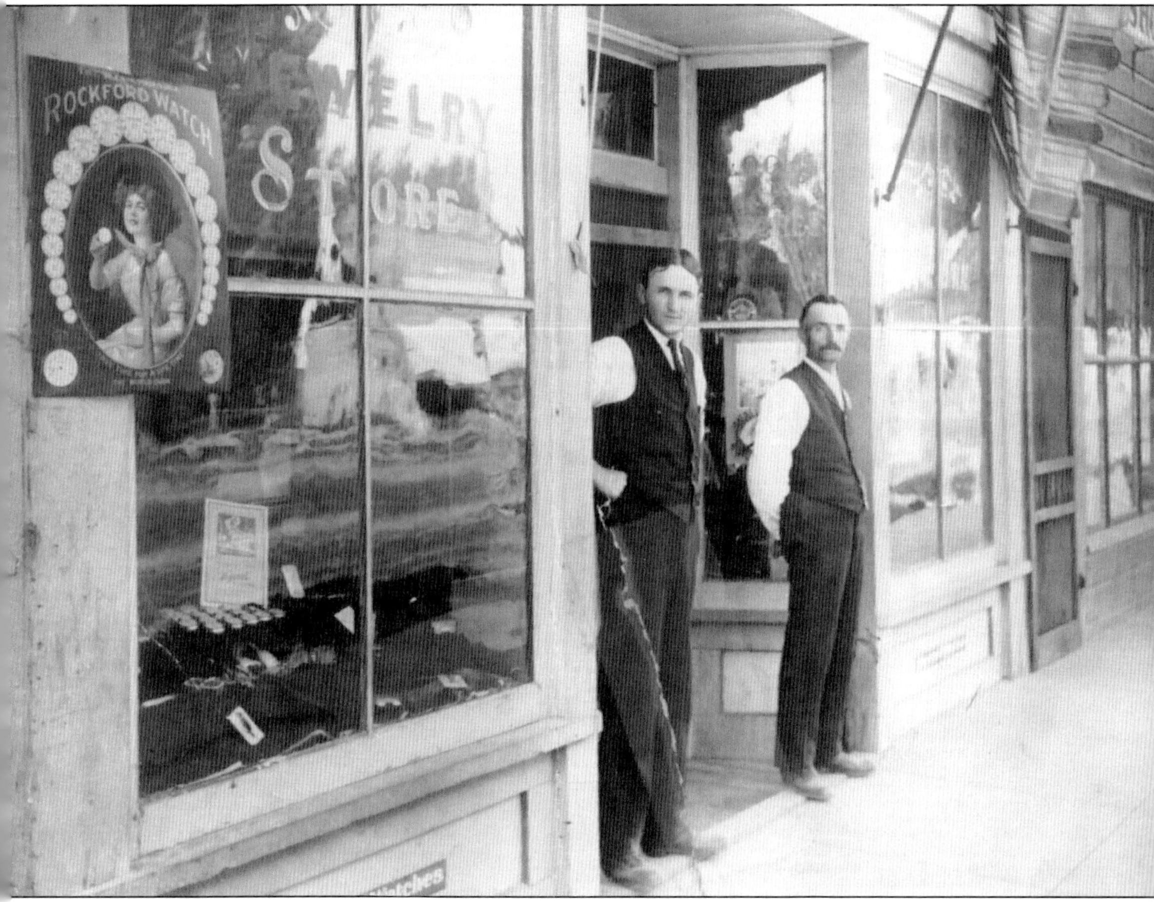

Luthy's Jewelry Store was located at 30 South Main Street. It was operated by Swiss immigrant and businessman William Luthy and his family. Pictured are William (right) and his son Joe, who later opened up Luthy's Dress Shop at about 21 North State Street. The dress shop remained open for over 50 years. Joe was involved in public affairs, running for mayor in 1935 but losing to T.R. "Dick" Bowden over controversy surrounding city finances and indebtedness stemming from when Preston's streets were first paved in the 1920s. Additionally, Joe was on the committee that organized the first rodeo in Preston in 1921.

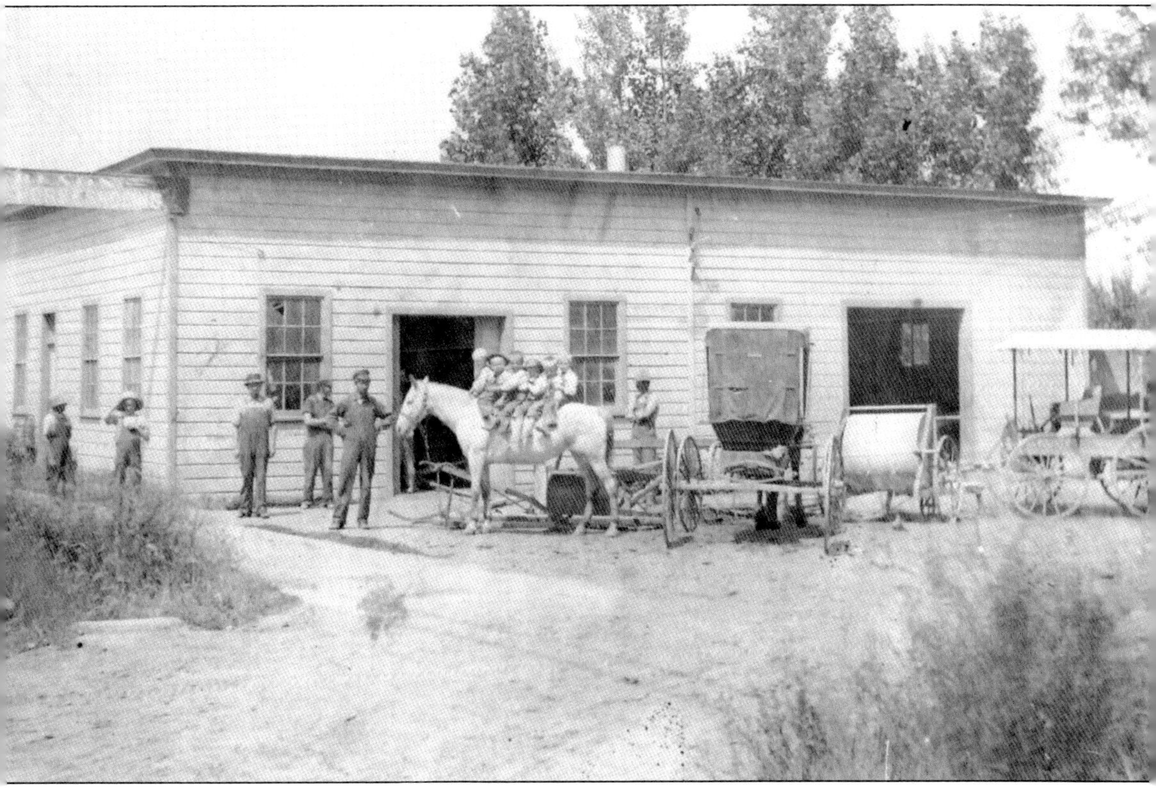

Niels Christian Carlson operated this blacksmith shop on First North Street where the Federal Land Bank building, which now houses the law offices of Jay McKenzie, is located. This picture was taken in about 1911 or 1912 and features Mads Anderson by the horse's nose. Carlson and his wife, Marie, married in 1896, then immigrated to the United States. The 1910 US census lists him as a blacksmith in Preston. The local newspaper ran an advertisement noting that on December 27, 1913, the N.C. Carlson Blacksmith Shop would sell an REO 35 power automobile No. 861 for the sum of $155 for repairing and caring for the automobile. On May 23, 1916, the *Logan Republican* reported that N.C. Carlson, "president of the Scandinavians of Oneida Stake, was a visitor from Preston" at a Scandinavian conference held in Logan. Mads Anderson, also from Denmark, operated a blacksmith shop in Mink Creek, where his shop was a town hangout for the men.

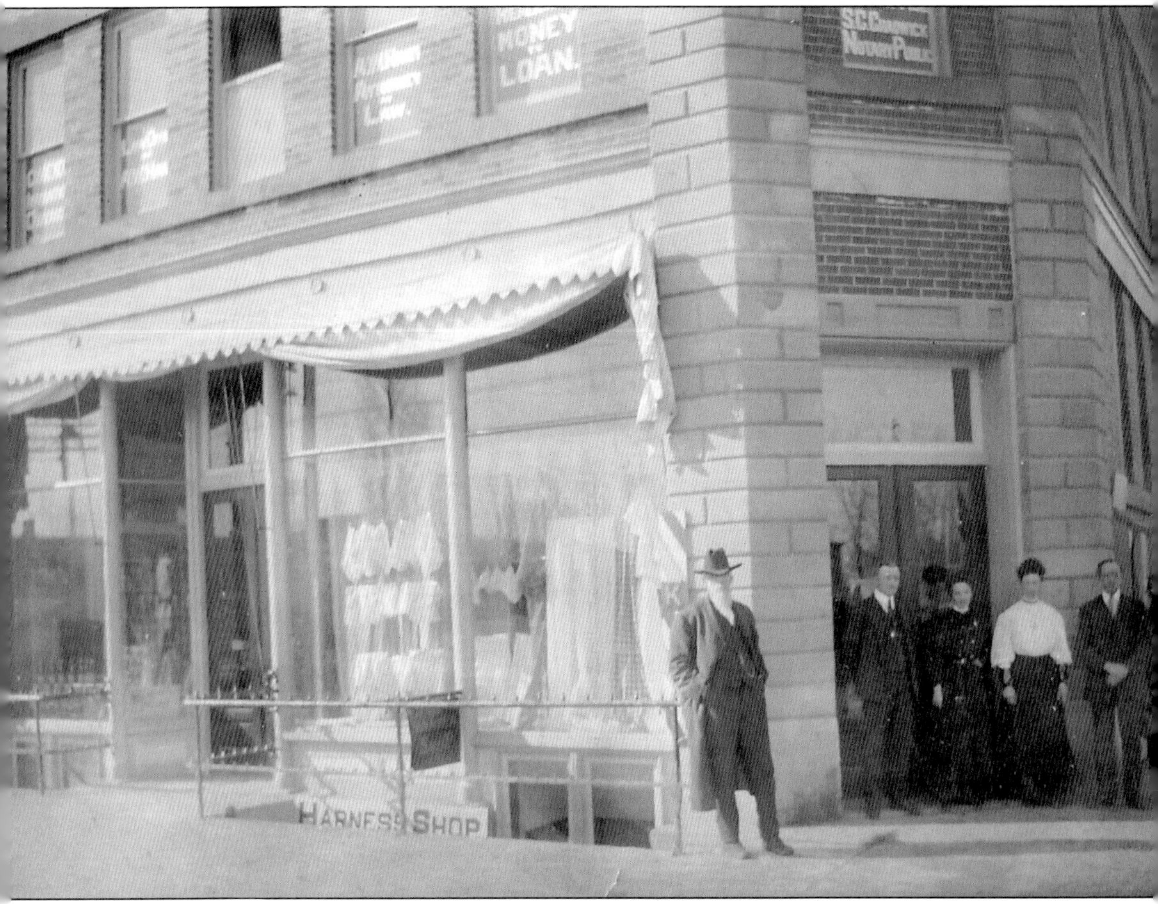

This harness shop was in the basement of the John Larsen and Sons building, which was constructed of red brick in 1903 on the southwest corner of Oneida and State Streets. It replaced a wooden building Larson had erected earlier on the site. This corner building housed many tenants, including attorney Arthur W. Hart, S.C. Chadwick, Ezra F. Wooley, P.M. Condie, P.J. Evans, A.J. Jensen, and state engineer H.B. Sternberg. The harness shop, like many other basement stores in town, was abandoned because of the high water table in Preston. Larsen was the chairman of Preston's first village board, then mayor when the city was incorporated in 1913. The building was purchased by J. C. Penney Company in 1927, which added onto the rear and operated it until 1940. At that point, the building was converted into the American Food Store. In 1966, it was purchased by James Tasso of Star Realty. Apartment units filled the upper floors.

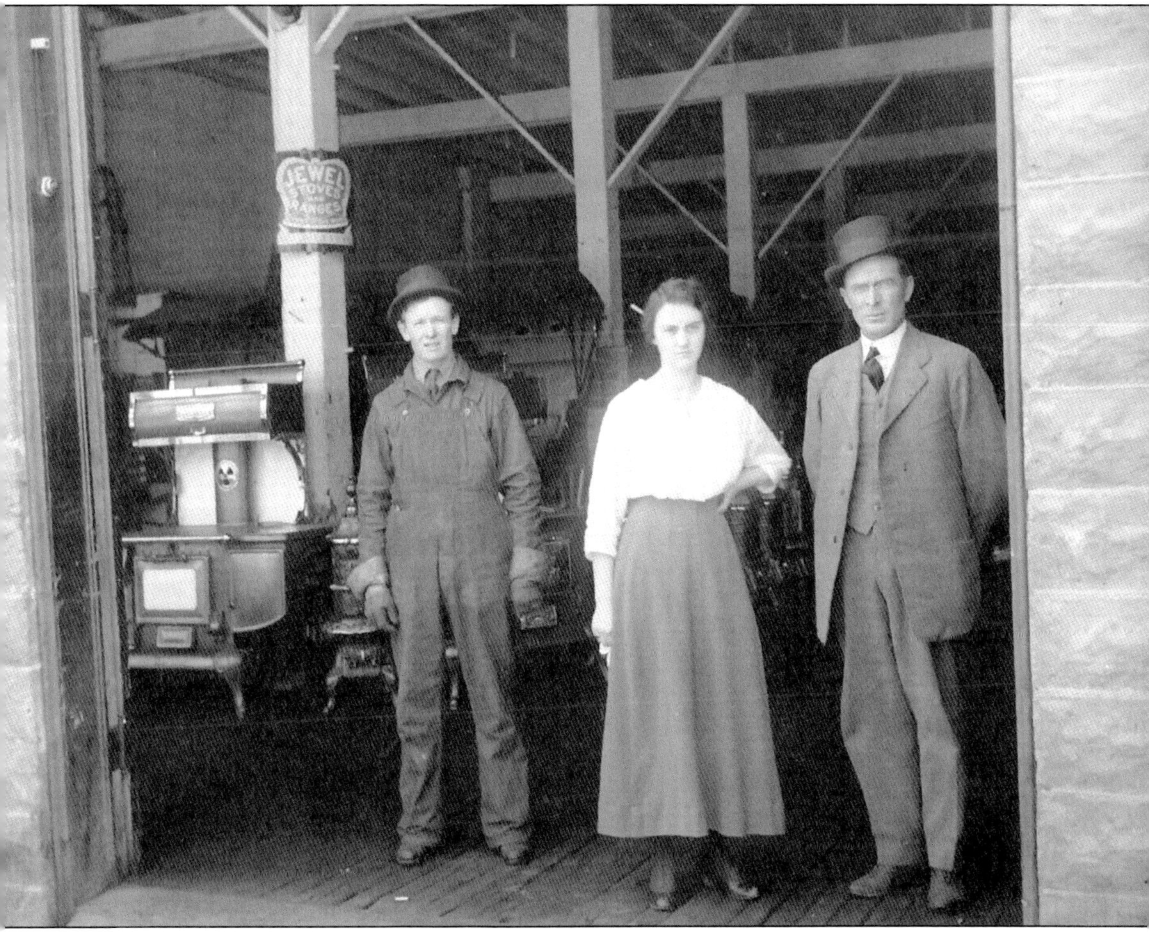

Samuel Wilkinson (left) poses with an unidentified stenographer and George L. Fail (see page 117). Wilkinson, an assistant manager of the Utah Implement Company, was transferred from Salt Lake to Preston in 1912. He purchased the business, located at 47 North State Street, in 1924, changing its name to Wilkinson-Stanger Implement Company. When he was appointed an International Harvester dealer in 1927, he moved his family to Ogden, where he owned and operated Wilkinson Farm Service. Four of Wilkinson's children were born in Preston: Donald, Sterling, Keith, and Lorraine Burdett. Information on Wilkinson was gathered from articles in the *Ogden Standard Examiner*. The woman may be Marion Cutler from Preston, who was a stenographer while serving a mission for the Church of Jesus Christ of Latter-day Saints in California in 1922. Her parents lived in Preston at least during 1903, when she would have been eight years old. Her uncle was a well-known local doctor, Allen Riley Cutler. Marion married Bernard Mac Candless in 1929.

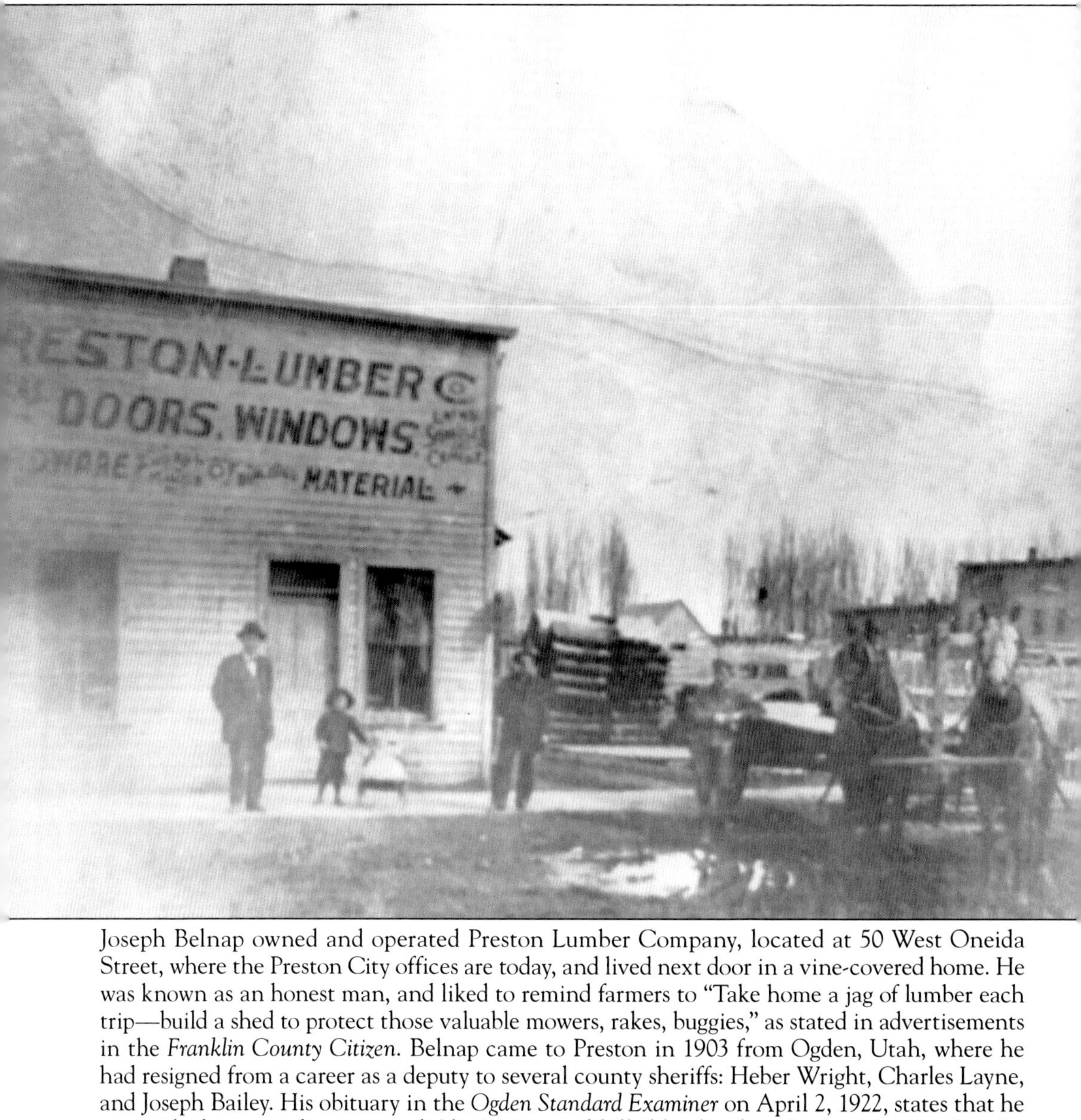

Joseph Belnap owned and operated Preston Lumber Company, located at 50 West Oneida Street, where the Preston City offices are today, and lived next door in a vine-covered home. He was known as an honest man, and liked to remind farmers to "Take home a jag of lumber each trip—build a shed to protect those valuable mowers, rakes, buggies," as stated in advertisements in the *Franklin County Citizen*. Belnap came to Preston in 1903 from Ogden, Utah, where he had resigned from a career as a deputy to several county sheriffs: Heber Wright, Charles Layne, and Joseph Bailey. His obituary in the *Ogden Standard Examiner* on April 2, 1922, states that he was with the posse that captured Abe Majors and killed his brother, Archie Majors, after the two held up a man in Brigham City, Utah. During the arrest, Ogden police chief Capt. William Brown was killed near the Utah Hot Springs. Belnap was married to Minerva P. Howard, and they had several children, a number of whom stayed in Preston: Amos Belnap, Emory Belnap, Blanche Cutler, Ida Tippets, and R. Stanton Belnap.

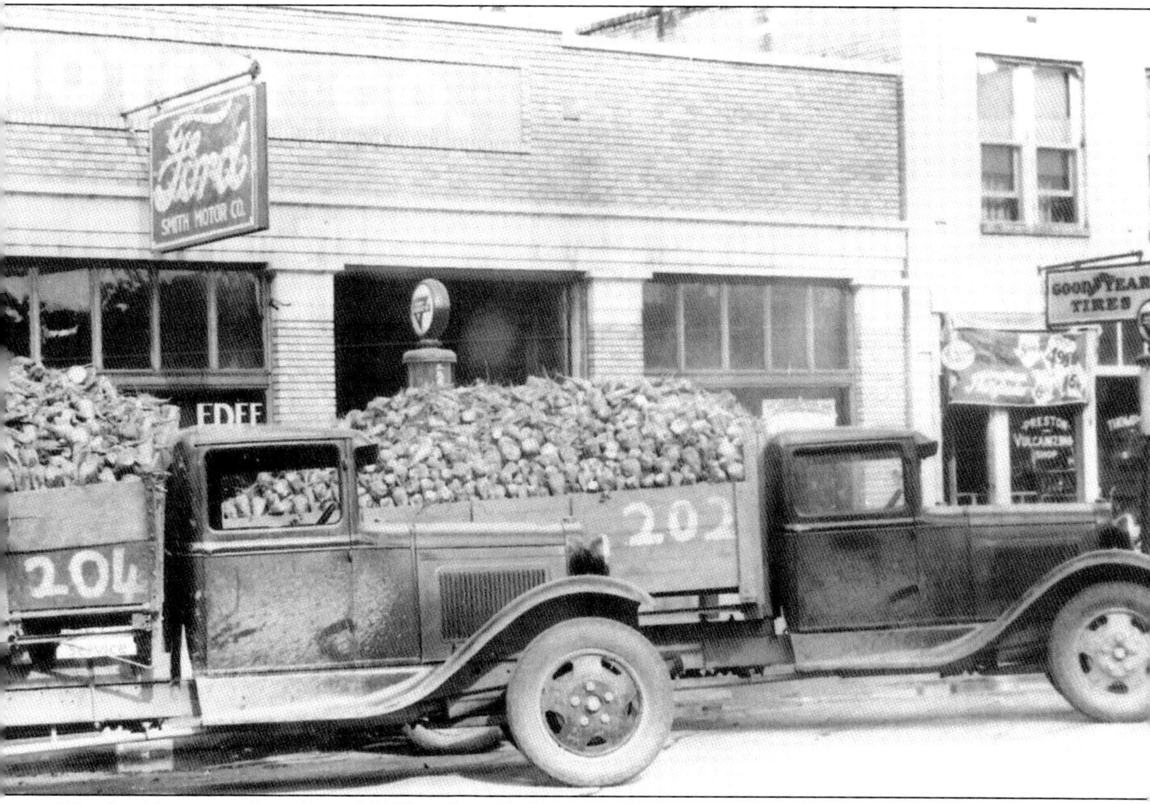

This building stood at about 40 West Oneida Street and was constructed sometime in the 1920s. Wilf Smith, who also served as the chairman of the county planning board in 1935, took the building over in 1929, moving in his Ford Agency from North Main Street. According to the *Hometown Sketchbook*, operating the business in the 1930s was difficult. Earl Nelson said 30 cars were repossessed in 1931, taken to Salt Lake and sold for whatever they would bring, but the company still went broke, and some employees never collected their wages. Gas was pumped from 6:00 a.m. to 11:00 p.m. by station attendants, who would often sleep inside until customers rang a bell for service. Self-service pumps were never installed here. Eventually, the Preston Lumber Company and Joseph Belnap's home at 70 West Oneida Street were removed to make way for a used car lot run by G.W. "Bill" McCune, who opened up McCune Motor there in 1935. The trucks pictured here are full of sugar beets grown on farms in Franklin County.

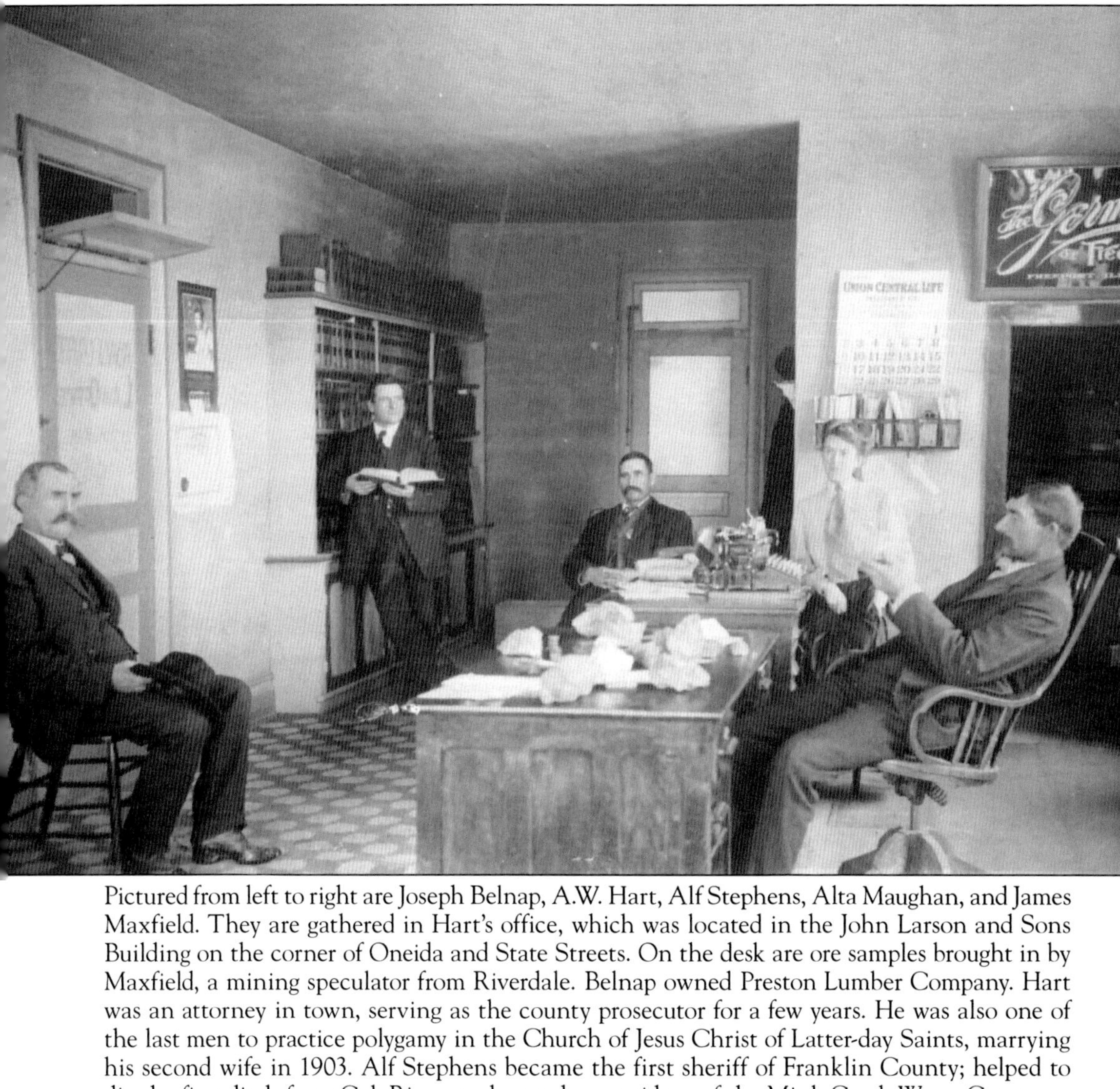

Pictured from left to right are Joseph Belnap, A.W. Hart, Alf Stephens, Alta Maughan, and James Maxfield. They are gathered in Hart's office, which was located in the John Larson and Sons Building on the corner of Oneida and State Streets. On the desk are ore samples brought in by Maxfield, a mining speculator from Riverdale. Belnap owned Preston Lumber Company. Hart was an attorney in town, serving as the county prosecutor for a few years. He was also one of the last men to practice polygamy in the Church of Jesus Christ of Latter-day Saints, marrying his second wife in 1903. Alf Stephens became the first sheriff of Franklin County; helped to dig the first ditch from Cub River; and served as president of the Mink Creek Water Company, city commissioner, deputy game warden, fire chief in Preston, and the first sexton of the Preston Cemetery. Alta Maughan worked for Hart between 1904 and 1905, so this photograph was taken during that time. She married T.C. Palmer and became the mother of eight children.

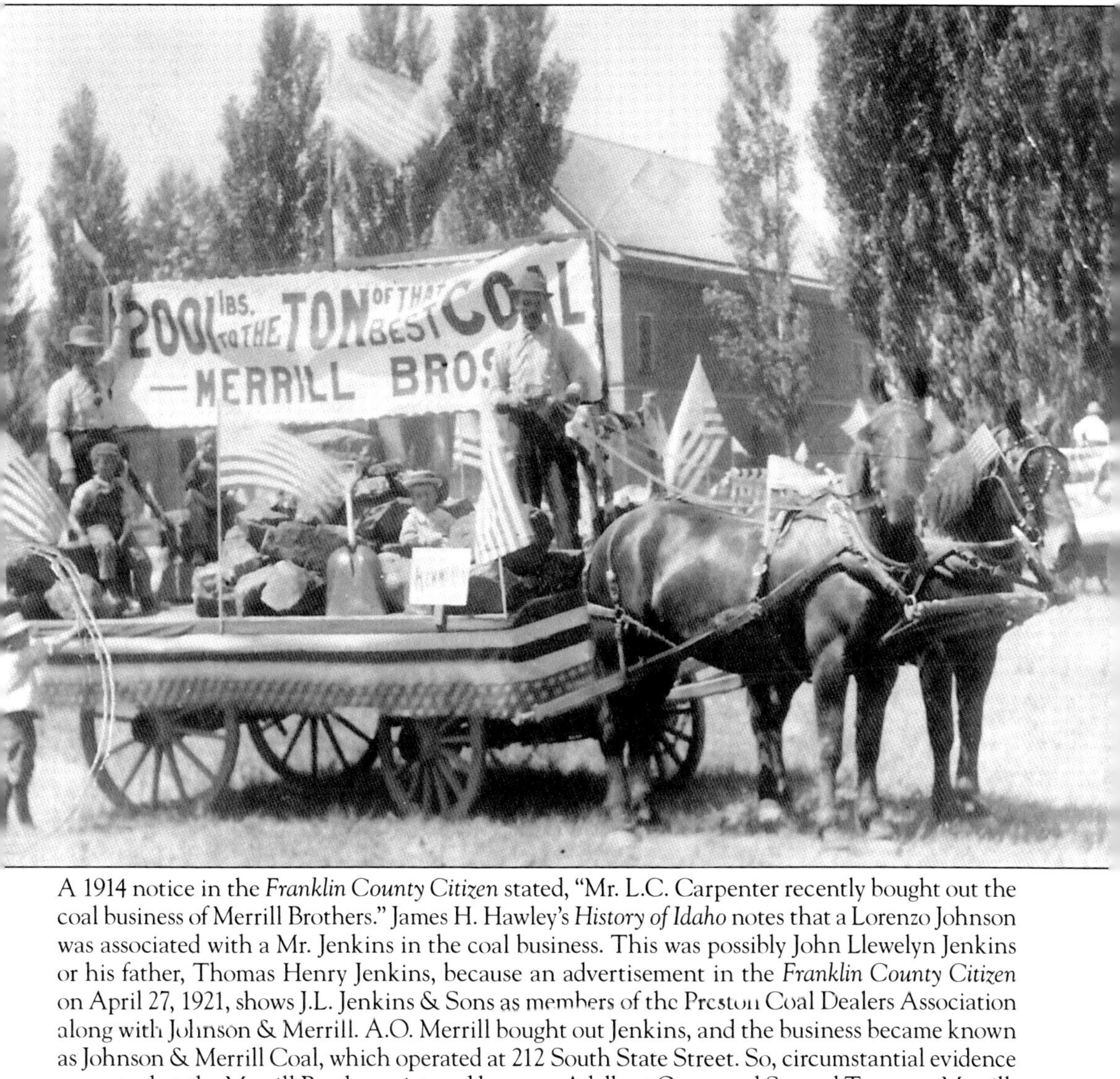

A 1914 notice in the *Franklin County Citizen* stated, "Mr. L.C. Carpenter recently bought out the coal business of Merrill Brothers." James H. Hawley's *History of Idaho* notes that a Lorenzo Johnson was associated with a Mr. Jenkins in the coal business. This was possibly John Llewelyn Jenkins or his father, Thomas Henry Jenkins, because an advertisement in the *Franklin County Citizen* on April 27, 1921, shows J.L. Jenkins & Sons as members of the Preston Coal Dealers Association along with Johnson & Merrill. A.O. Merrill bought out Jenkins, and the business became known as Johnson & Merrill Coal, which operated at 212 South State Street. So, circumstantial evidence suggests that the Merrill Brothers pictured here are Adelbert Owen and Samuel Teancum Merrill, sons of Samuel Adam Merrill and Lenora Triphena Nobel, and that the photograph predates 1914. The brothers were two years apart in age, born in 1869 and 1871. *The Trail Blazer* states that they were pioneer garage men in Preston.

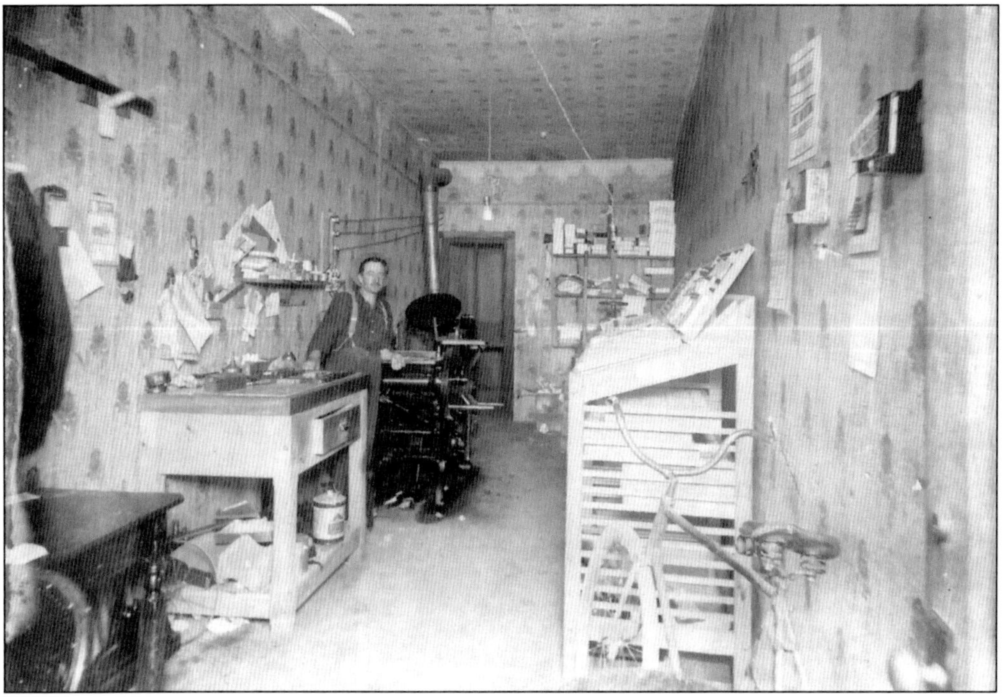

The Thomas Carter Print Shop, pictured around 1912, was located on South Main (State) Street next to the Struve Hat Shop. In 1913, Carter and A.D. Erickson, a local attorney, began publishing the *Southeastern Advocate*. Carter and Sheeley Chatterton started the *Cache Valley Clarion* in 1937. Both newspapers eventually merged with the *Franklin County Citizen*, the forerunner of the *Preston Citizen*.

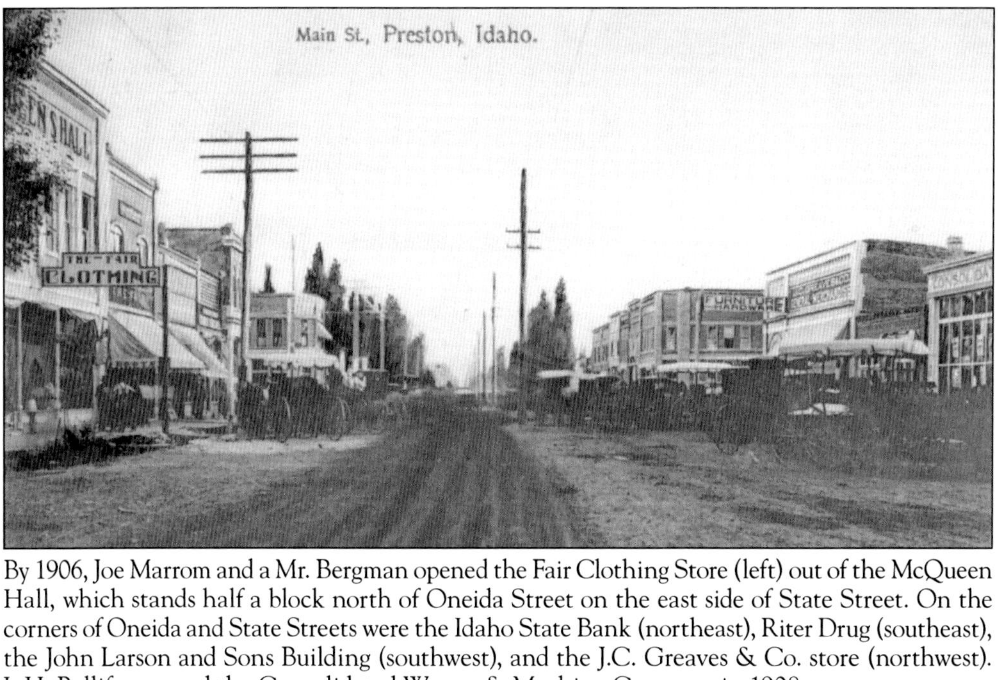

By 1906, Joe Marrom and a Mr. Bergman opened the Fair Clothing Store (left) out of the McQueen Hall, which stands half a block north of Oneida Street on the east side of State Street. On the corners of Oneida and State Streets were the Idaho State Bank (northeast), Riter Drug (southeast), the John Larson and Sons Building (southwest), and the J.C. Greaves & Co. store (northwest). L.H. Ballif managed the Consolidated Wagon & Machine Company in 1908.

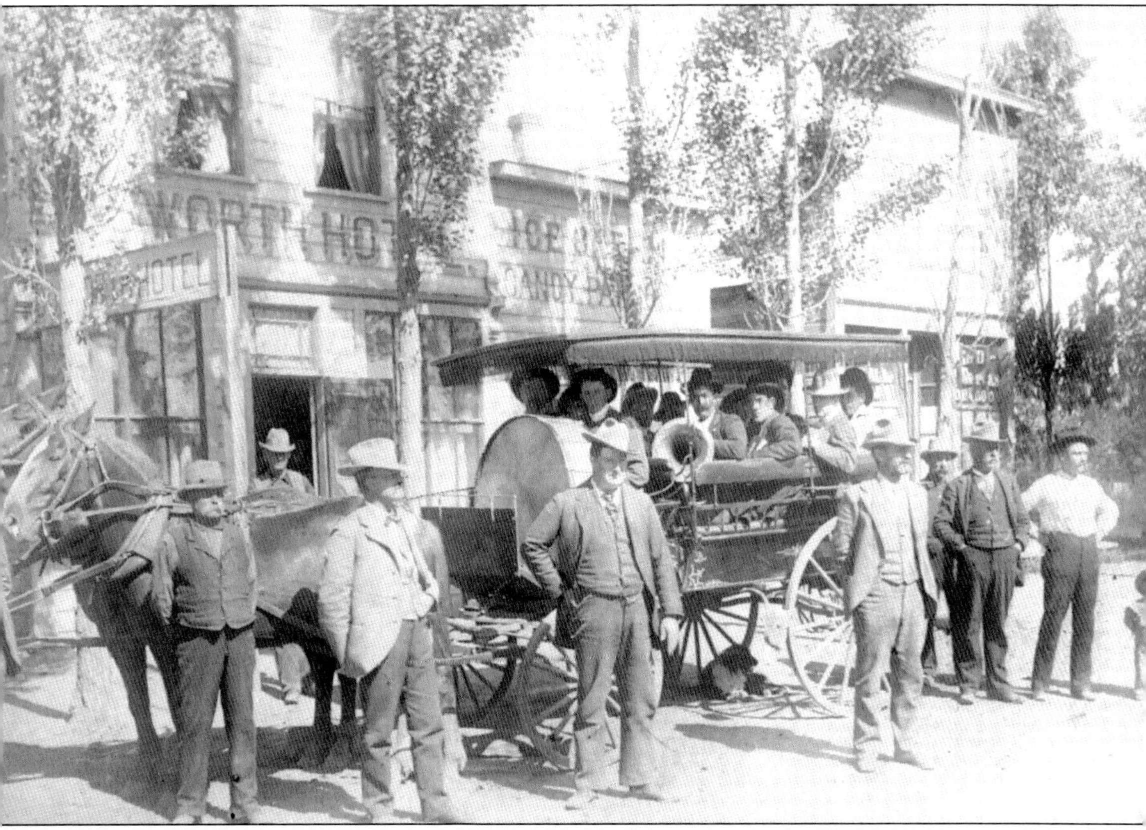

James Bosworth moved to Preston in 1881 and built the town's first hotel in 1892. It was sold to Charles Hobbs in 1902, and he remodeled it into the Wilford Hotel. Bosworth and William Chapman were also the proprietors of Preston's second store, located on the corner of State Street and Fourth South Street. They sold out to William C. Parkinson in 1884. Bosworth played the bass drum, the violin, the Jew's harp, the bones, the flute, and the banjo. A cheerful man, he would often invite the whole town out to his farm on the northwest part of Preston, then act the part of the caller for the folk dances and quadrilles. At one time, Bosworth carried water for the workmen while the railroad was laid at Promontory Point; he was present when the Golden Spike was driven, uniting the East and West Coasts by railroad. He also shaped tools for the railroad as a blacksmith at Battle Creek. He and his wife, Frances Camilla Chapman, are buried in the Preston Cemetery. Also pictured are Heber Johnson's Candy Kitchen and Harold Gee's Preston Saloon.

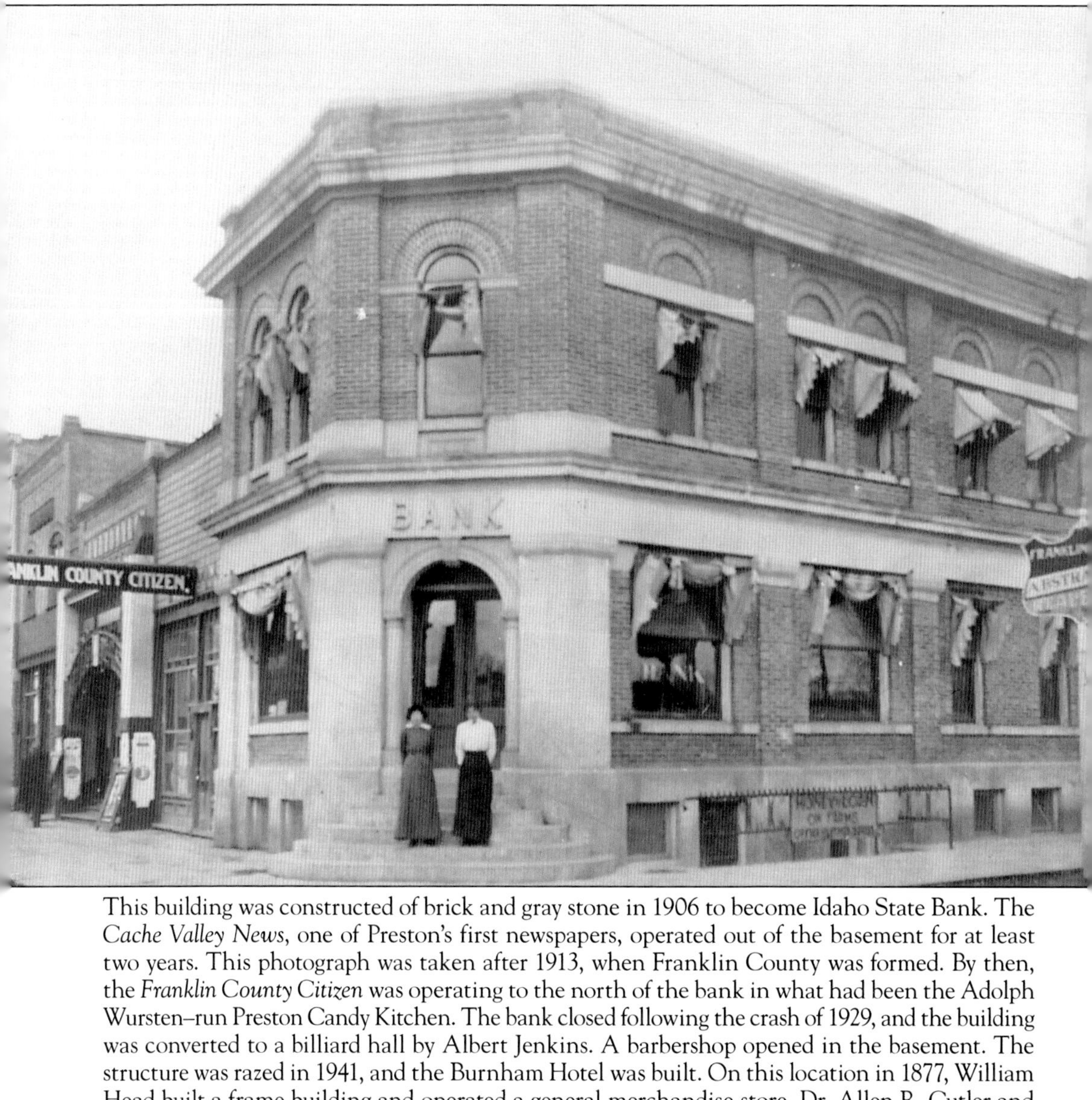

This building was constructed of brick and gray stone in 1906 to become Idaho State Bank. The *Cache Valley News*, one of Preston's first newspapers, operated out of the basement for at least two years. This photograph was taken after 1913, when Franklin County was formed. By then, the *Franklin County Citizen* was operating to the north of the bank in what had been the Adolph Wursten–run Preston Candy Kitchen. The bank closed following the crash of 1929, and the building was converted to a billiard hall by Albert Jenkins. A barbershop opened in the basement. The structure was razed in 1941, and the Burnham Hotel was built. On this location in 1877, William Head built a frame building and operated a general merchandise store. Dr. Allen R. Cutler and village clerk William M. Daines were the owners of the store when it was moved east on Oneida Street to make room for the new brick bank. In those days, buildings were moved, not torn down, noted Hart. Many village council meetings were held in the frame store.

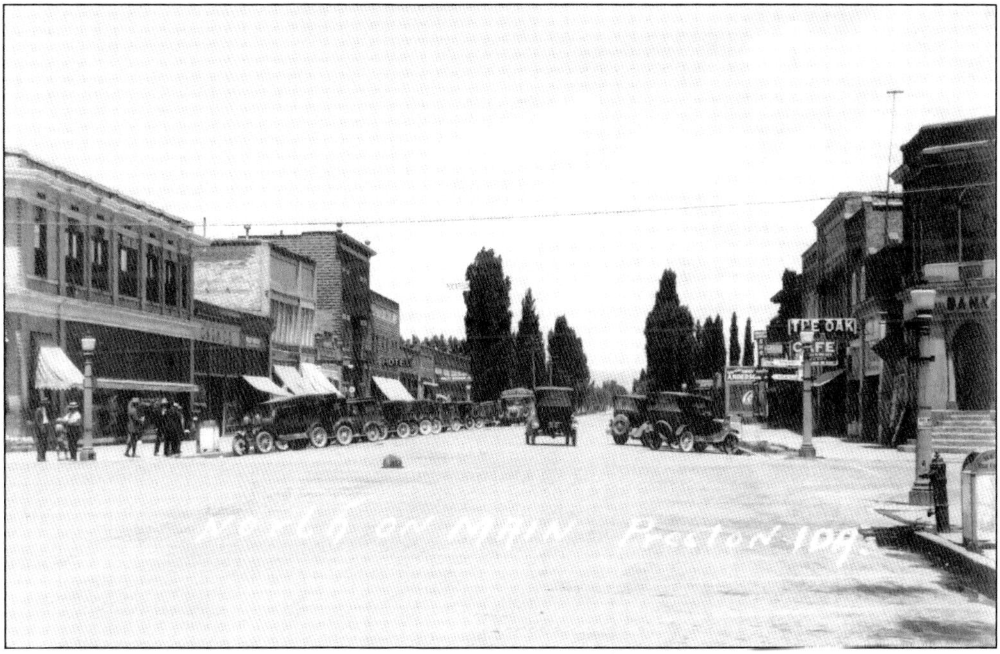

Businesses visible in this north-facing view of State Street from its Oneida intersection are, from left to right, First National Bank, Consolidated Wagon & Machine Company, Piggly Wiggly (1920s–1937), Joe Luthy's Dress Shop (1920s–1971), Wilford Hotel, and the Maxfield building. On the east (right) side of the street were Anderson Lumber, Endicott Johnson's Shoe Shop, the Wood Hotel, the Oak Café, and Idaho State Bank. (Jay Burrup.)

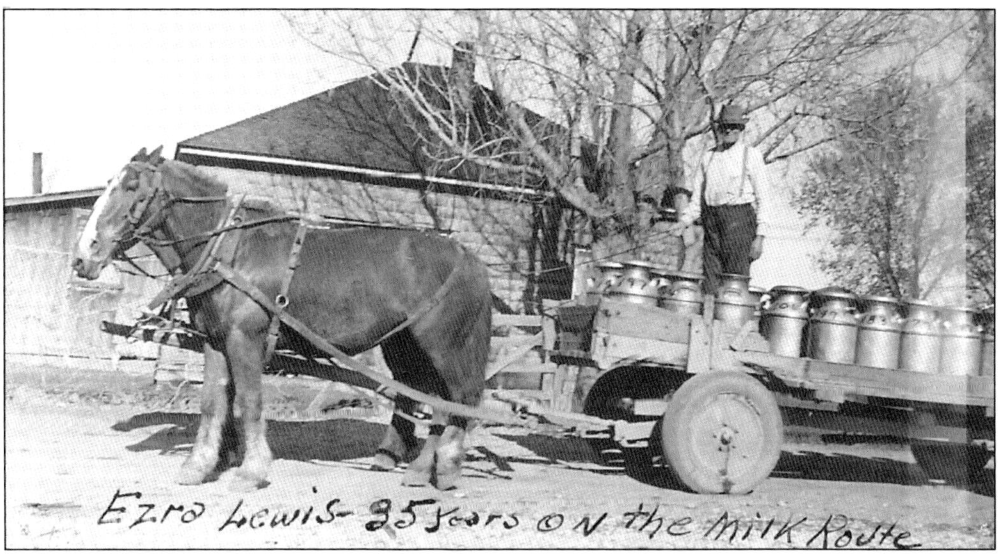

Ezra Lewis picked up milk cans daily in the Preston and Fairview areas for 25 years until 1941. He is pictured in front of his home with his horses, Jim and Puss. Puss was a buggy horse for his daughters to take to the Jefferson School until they came out one day to find her dragging the post down the street. Disgusted, Lewis put her with Jim to learn some horse sense.

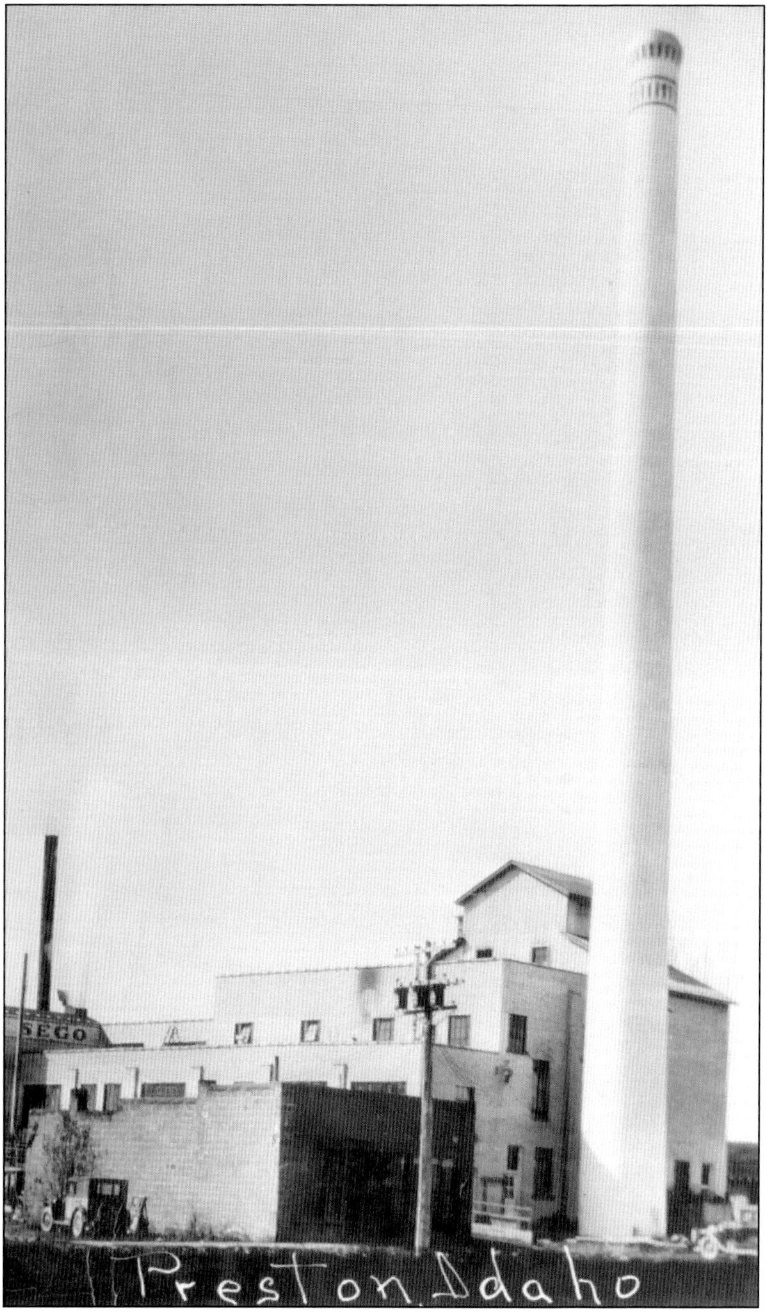

Located on First South Street between State and First West Streets, the Sego Milk Plant was built in 1928. Originally a receiving and pasteurizing station, it was soon converted to produce butter and powdered milk. By 1956, it was processing some 25 million pounds of milk and making up to 5,000 pounds of butter each day. The plant also processed milk to be shipped to Richmond, and employed up to 30 people. Before its construction, milk was taken to a condensing plant in Franklin, until it closed in 1922. Between then and the opening of this plant, people like Ezra Lewis would load milk onto the Utah Idaho Central electric train to be taken to Richmond, Utah, for processing. (Jay Burrup.)

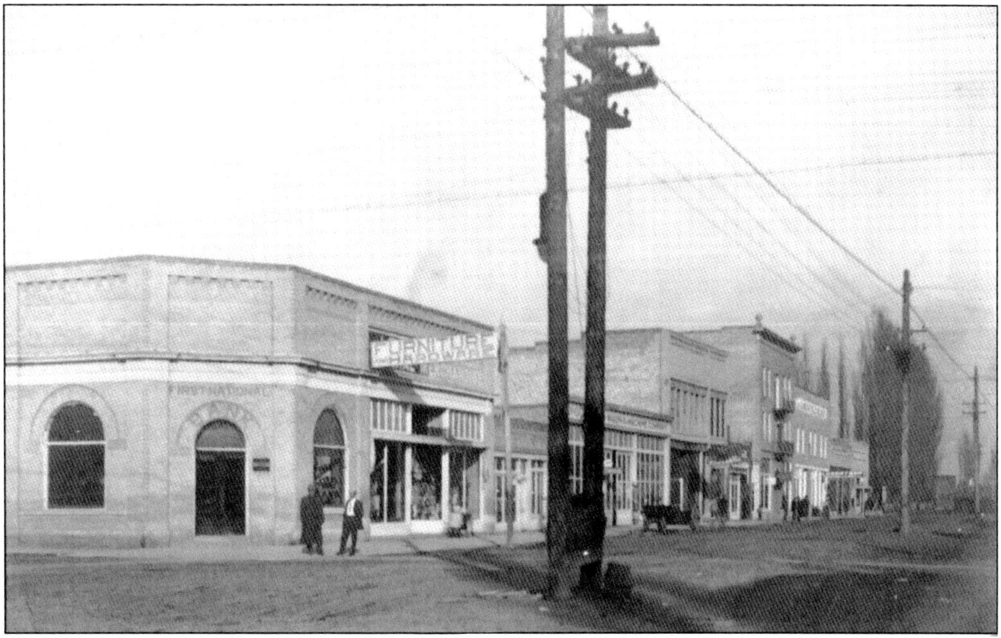

Above, this yellow brick building was constructed on the northeast corner of State and Oneida Streets in 1903 by J.C. Greaves to house his general store and the Bank of Preston. Greaves remained bank president in 1931 when the bank merged with First National Bank. Teller Alta Maughan remembered the bank had no paper money or pennies, dealing only in gold and silver pieces. Below, the building was extended on both its western and northern sides and windows squared in 1914. A second story added for office space was utilized by both businessmen and the newly formed Franklin County. In 1940, it was remodeled again to make space for the Elks Lodge, and the Golden Rule moved into the general store. The state liquor dispensary was in the west side. The Greaves Block was demolished in 1970. (Both, Jay Burrup.)

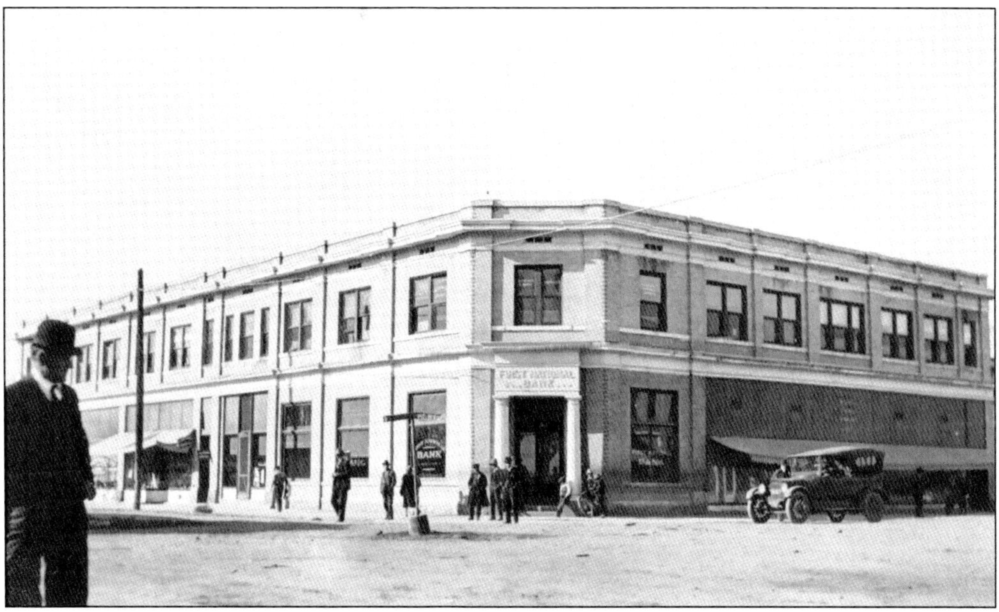

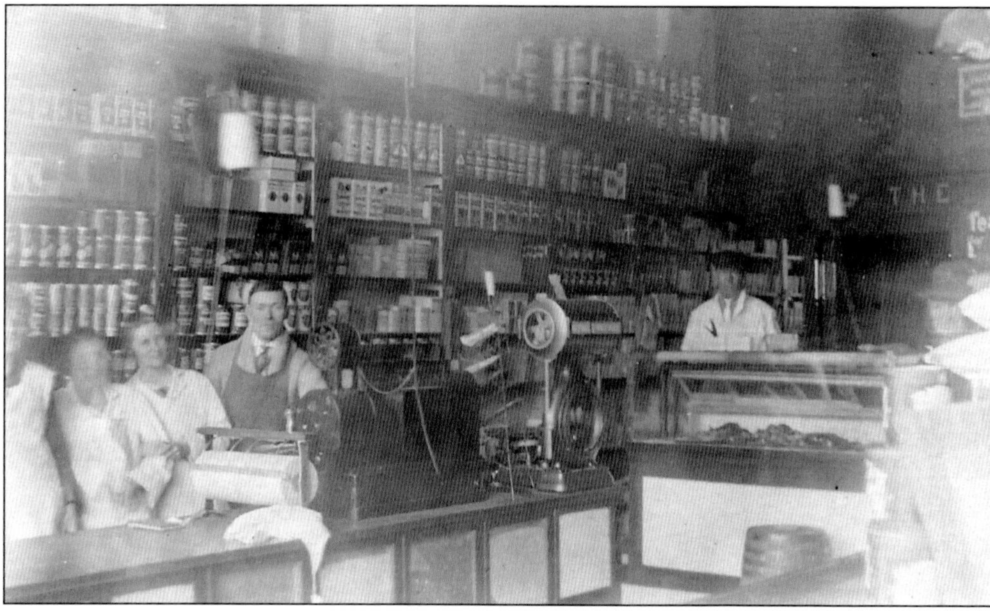

The Clayton store was opened in 1917 by brothers Thomas "Tom" and Melvin "Happy" Clayton, sister Lula, and her husband, George S. Winn. It was on the east side of Tom's home by the railroad tracks on First South Street. In the basement, George cooked, ground, and seasoned meat and put it in long tin pans to set up for cold cuts such as veal loaf, corned beef, headcheese, and wieners. Carcasses hung in an icebox in the back of the store. Produce—including pickles, candy, cookies, mincemeat, and dry beans—was sold from barrels, and shoes, boots, and some sewing items were also available. Below, the Clayton Co. store is pictured on State Street in its new location by Foss Dry Goods in the early 1920s. From left to right are Happy, Addie Clayton, Marcella Cole, unidentified, a Mr. Anderson, and James Bosworth (under the sign on the window).

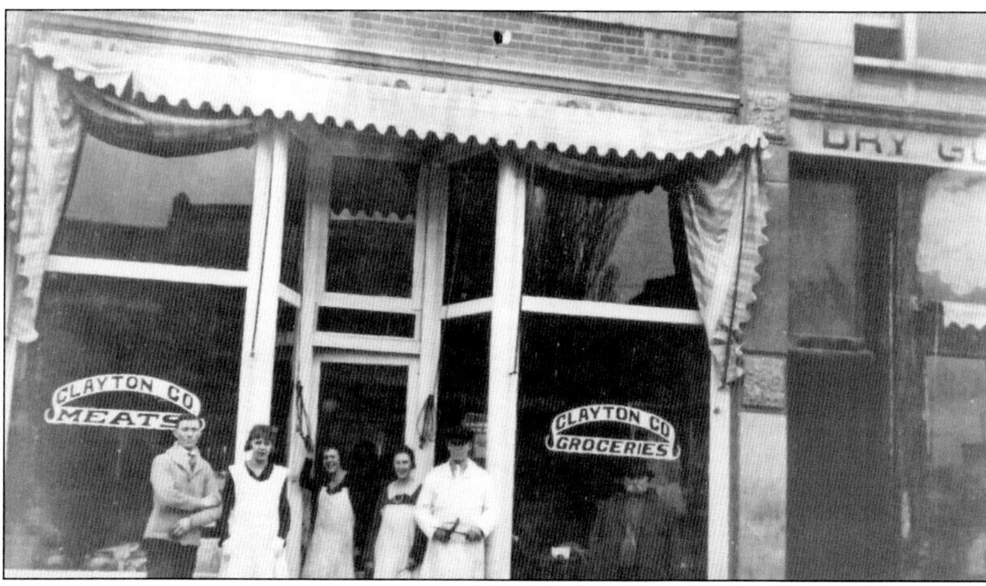

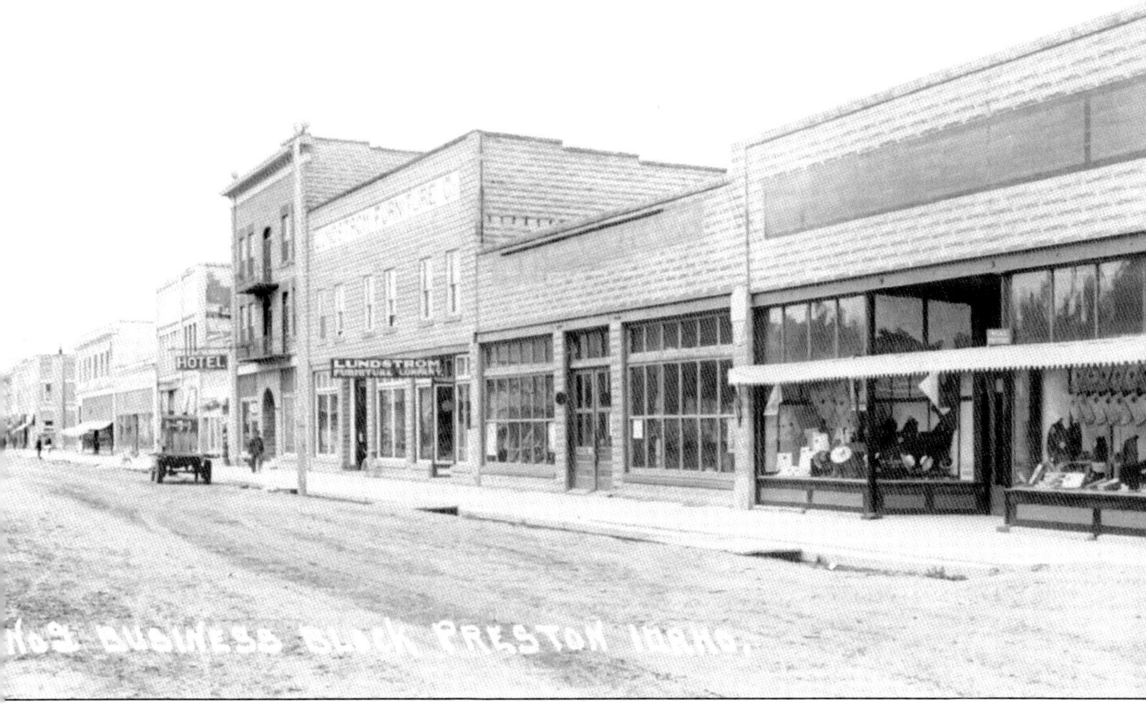

Andrew G. Lundstrom opened a branch of his Logan-based furniture store in Preston in 1908. His partners were John Spande, W.W. Maughan, John A. Carlson, J.N. Larson, and Lehi Olson. The store was managed by Lundstrom's nephew Carl Carlson, who later bought it and renamed it the C.H. Carlson Furniture Company of Preston. Following Carl's death in 1935, his brother Alvin left a position with the Utah Mortgage & Loan Company to assume the role of manager of the furniture company. Alvin died in 1958. As horses and buggies declined, the Consolidated Wagon & Machine Company (next store to the right) portioned off a space for Piggly Wiggly from the mid-1920s to 1937. At one time, the building was used as a movie house. Kids would roll barrels in to stand on so they could see over the adults. The store on the right is Luthy's Dress Shop (see page 60). (Jay Burrup.)

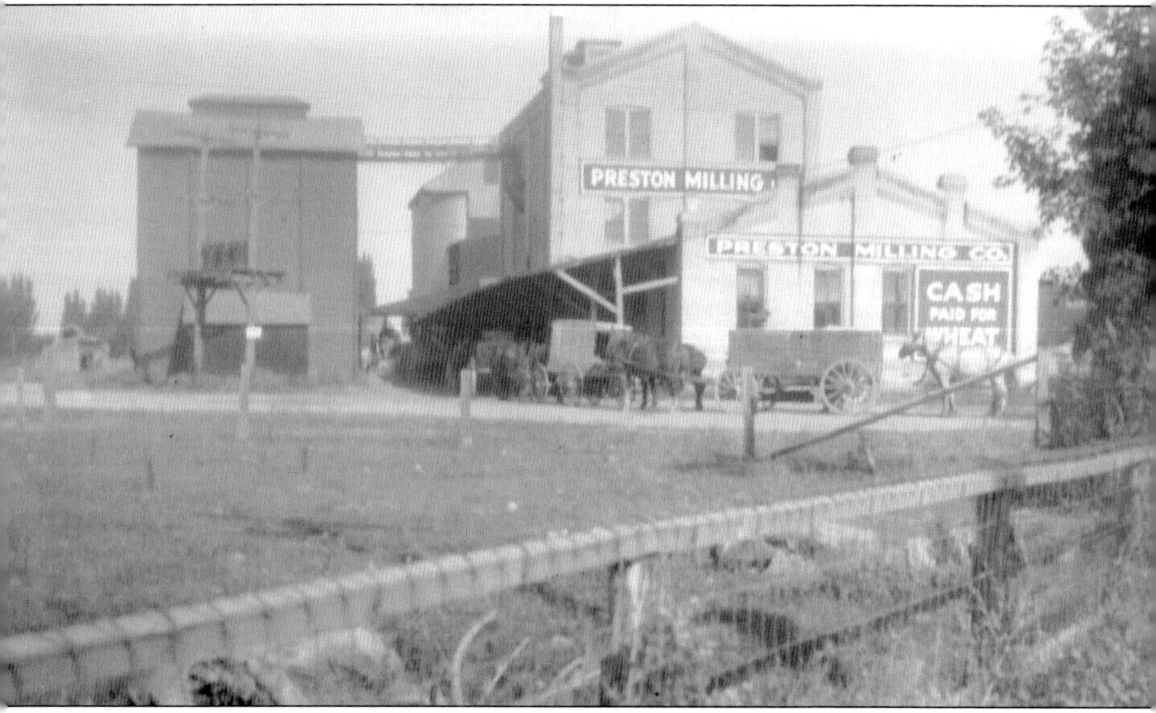

Located where Valley Wide Home & Ranch operates today at 264 South State Street, this mill was built in 1904 by the Peery family of Ogden, Utah. They hired Frank Manning to construct the foundation from rock blasted from a quarry in Battle Creek by Edison Fuell. The mill operated on steam power until 1907, when electricity came to Preston. During peak usage hours, the electricity was insufficient, and the machinery slowed down. Lester Higginbotham, a relative of the Peerys, managed the mill until Joshua Rallison took it over in about 1913. According to Cley Rallison, Joshua's family moved to Preston in 1912. His father and Charley Hobbs went into the coal business, which did not last long, so Joshua went to the mill. About this time, the Peery brothers divided up their holdings, and Harold J. Peery took over the milling industry. Joshua went to work for Peery and purchased stock in the company, which he held until the mill was sold in the 1930s.

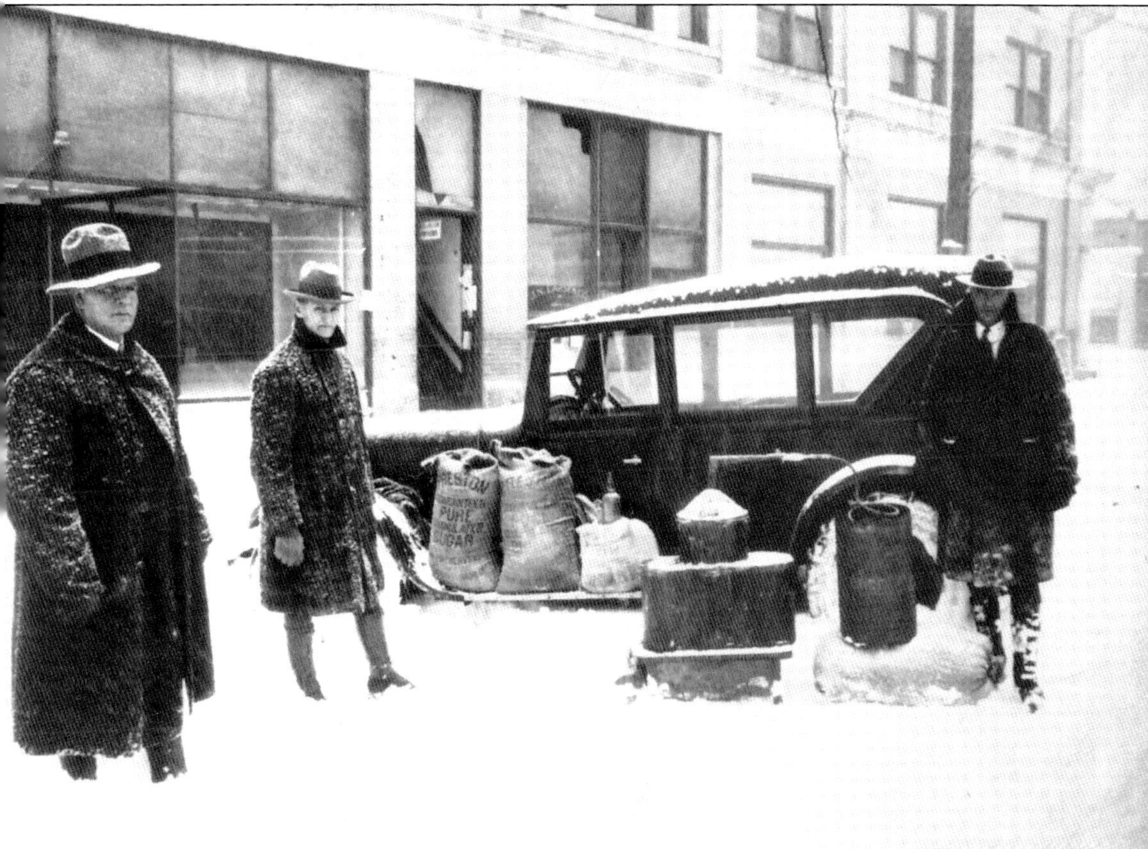

From left to right, Dave Davis (Preston police chief and head village marshal as early as 1908), W.D. "Bill" Head (Franklin County sheriff from 1923 to 1939), and an unidentified man stand in front of the Greaves Block building with moonshine contraband—bags of grain, an adapted boiler, and a carbide can with delivery tube—in the mid-1920s. Head recalled, "I can't remember the bootlegger's name. He didn't live around here. He had this still near Weston and did his bootlegging around Logan. This still was hid away in an old mine up in Black Canyon west of Weston. I chased this guy around through the snow and the quakin' aspens. The snow was knee deep up there." The open stairway behind them leads to the sheriff's office and other county offices. The truck is a 1928 or 1929 Chevrolet and has chains on the wheels.

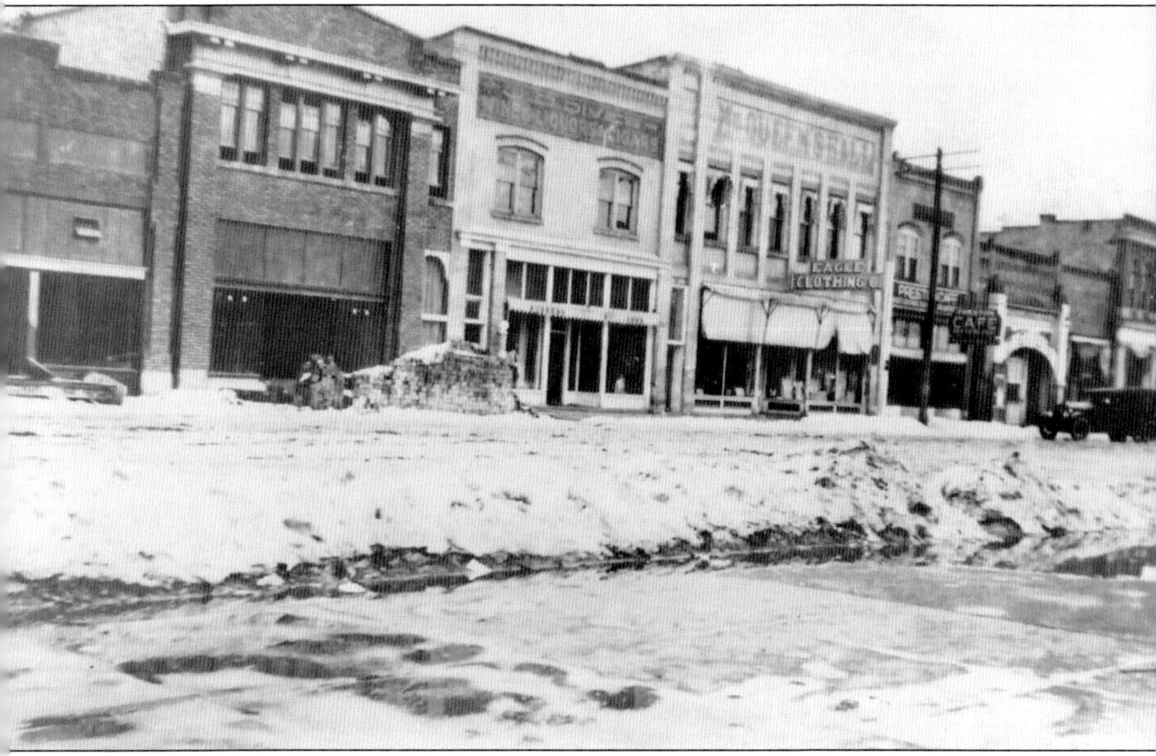

State Street northeast of Oneida Street had many saloons, cafés, and billiard halls prior to 1909, when Prohibition drove the beer business underground. McQueen's Hall (16 North State Street) was built by John Naisbitt McQueen around 1905 and housed a clothing store when this photograph was taken in the 1920s. A furniture store followed, then Preston Electric until 1958, when Idaho Appliance & Sport opened. The second floor was used for traveling shows, boxing matches, basketball practice, roller-skating, wrestling, and moving pictures. The second building from the left was erected by Chris Gundesen in 1920. It has housed City Motors, Jimmy Hoggan's appliance store, Ern Britenbaker's bike shop, Clyde Checketts' Maytag, and attorneys J.D. Williams and Lowell Castleton. The Dives Saloon, constructed in 1904, became a café/hotel, then an automotive supply store, Harry's Place (a pool hall), and Jensen T.V. Next is the oldest building on the block. A saloon prior to 1909, it later housed several cafes. On the edge is the Zeus Theater, built in 1911–1912. The next was the home of the *Franklin County Citizen*. On the end is Idaho State Bank.

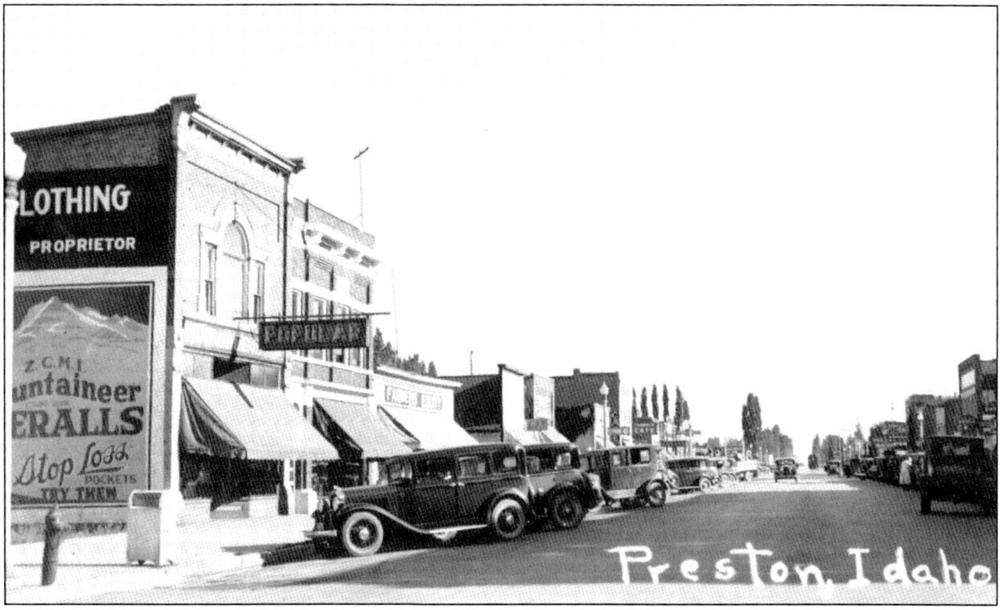

The Popular Clothing Store stood on the east side of South State Street around 1929, just south of Riter Drug and an empty lot on the southeast corner of the State and Oneida Streets. Other stores, from left to right, are Farmers Equity (a frame building said to have been a livery stable built as early as 1903, it housed the Preston Produce Company in 1912 and was used to sell Maxwell automobiles in 1915), several cafés, Bell Telephone, Petterborg-Nash garage and Chevrolet dealership, and the new Persiana dance hall. A train car heads south at the end of the street, and on the west side, the Griggs' first café is visible at about 40 South State Street. The view below, taken several years later, shows a section farther south on State Street. Russ Cranney purchased the Petterborg-Nash dealership in 1949. (Jay Burrup.)

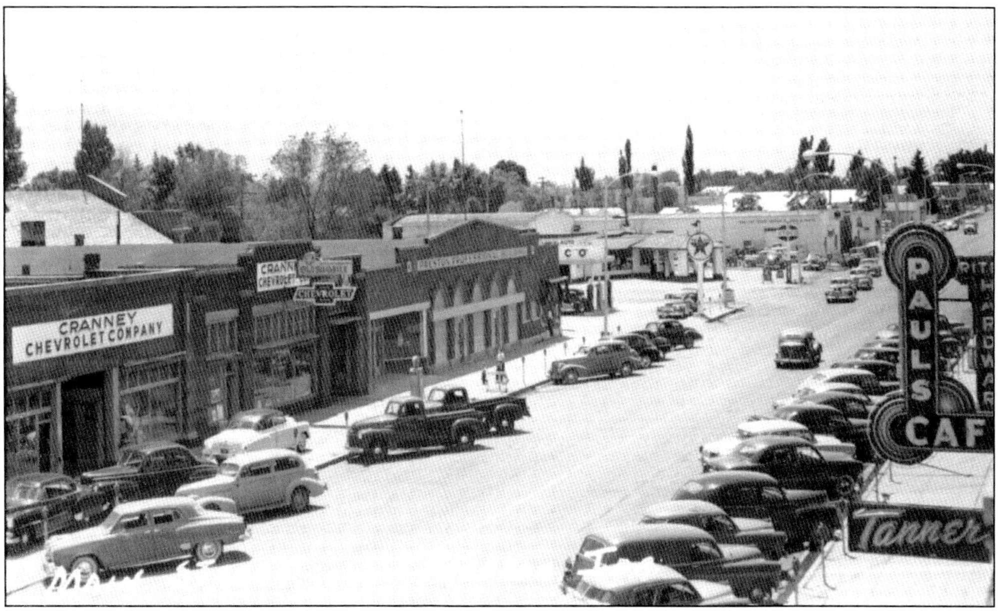

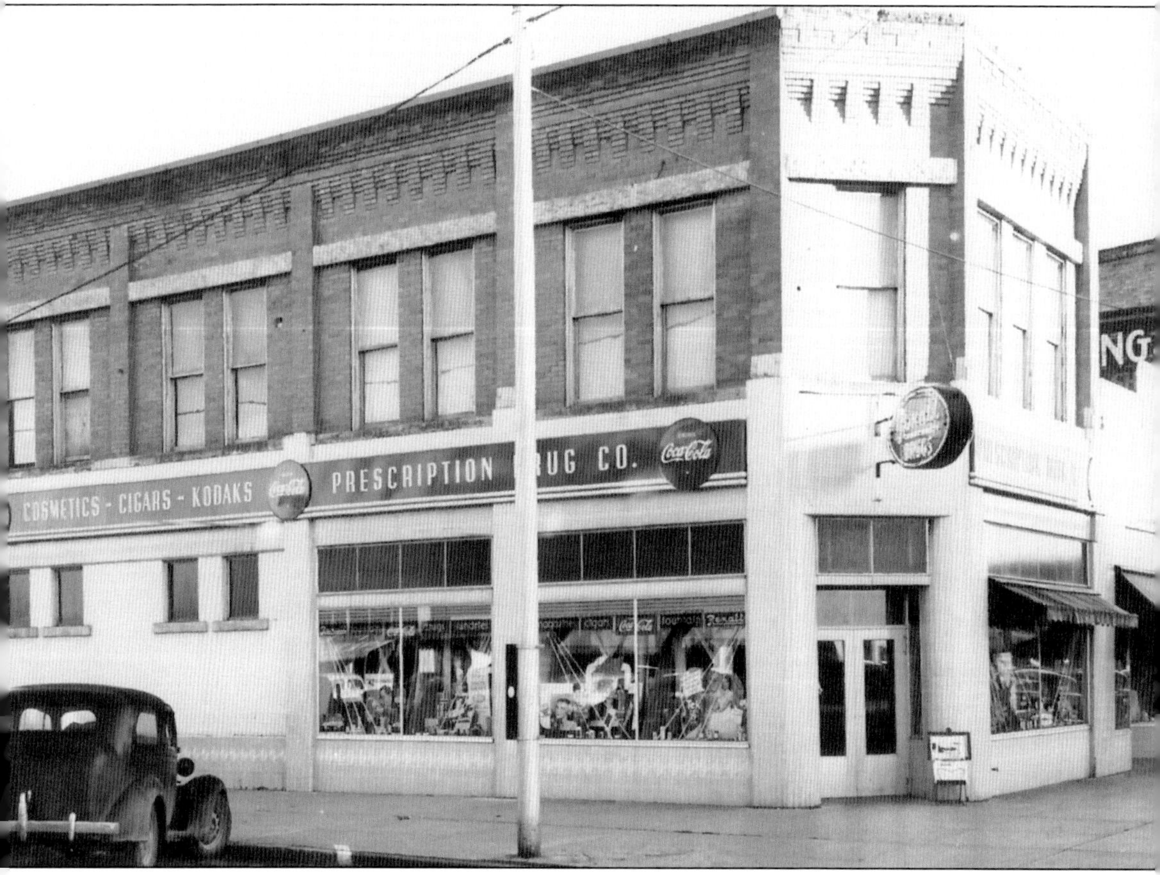

Prescription Drug, pictured here around 1945, stood on the southeast corner of State and Oneida Streets. It succeeded Riter Drug, which was the original occupant of the redbrick building when it was constructed in about 1900. The building housed the Bell Telephone switchboard upstairs and was the town's nerve center, according to the Hometown Sketchbook, with the phone number "1." Prescription Drug bought Riter's by 1930, then Mel Burrup purchased it in 1945. From then until the building was razed in 1970, the store housed several businesses. In 1940, C.A. Lundahl, a businessman from Logan, Utah, who owned the main building, built two smaller stores on its sides. Sid Biggs rented the one on the east side for a barbershop, then a gun and sporting store. Harley and Mabel Greaves rented the one on the south side for their style shop.

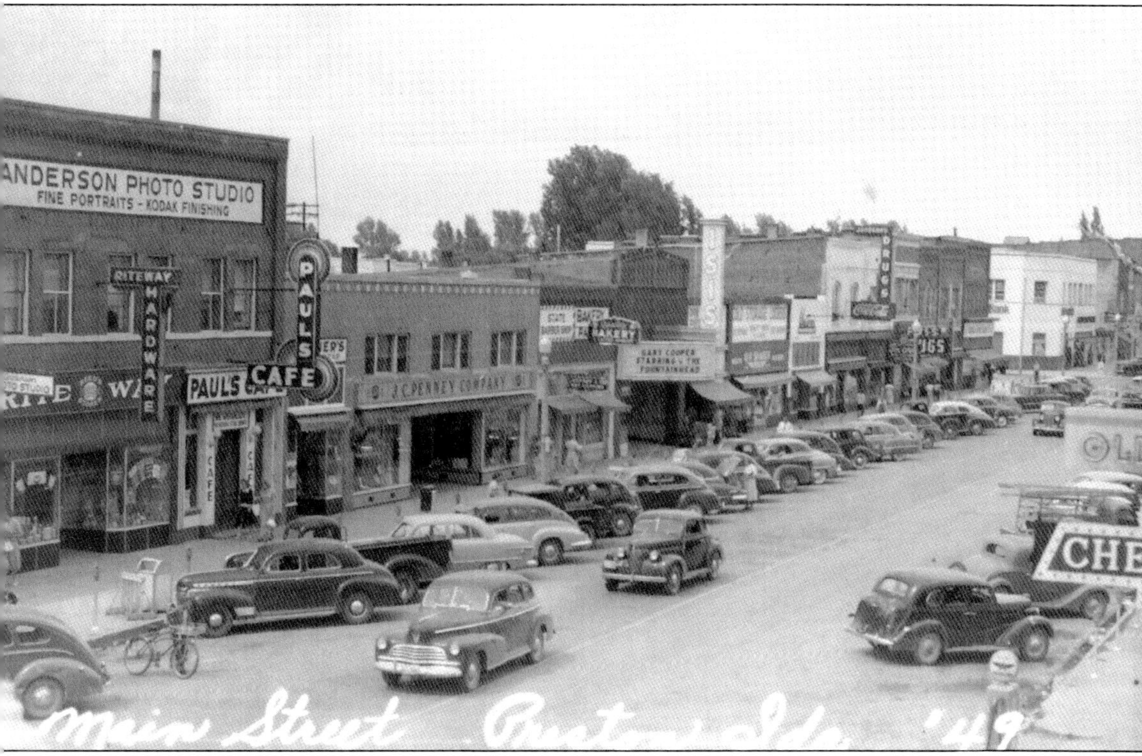

This view of the west side of State Street on the block just south of Oneida Street shows the businesses that operated there in 1949. They are, from left to right, Anderson Photo, J. C. Penney Company (Kings today), State Barber Shop, Quality Bakery, the Isis Theater (at that time featuring Gary Cooper in *The Fountainhead*), Don Greaves Food Market, O.P. Skaggs Cold Storage Lockers, Johnson's Drug, Western Auto Supply, the Owl, Foss Drugs and Fountain Shop, Harold's Barber Shop, Goodyear Shoe Repair, and the John Larsen and Sons Building, which housed the American Food Store. South of Anderson Photo on this block, but not pictured, were Paul's Café, Idaho Billiards, and the Grand Theater. (Jay Burrup.)

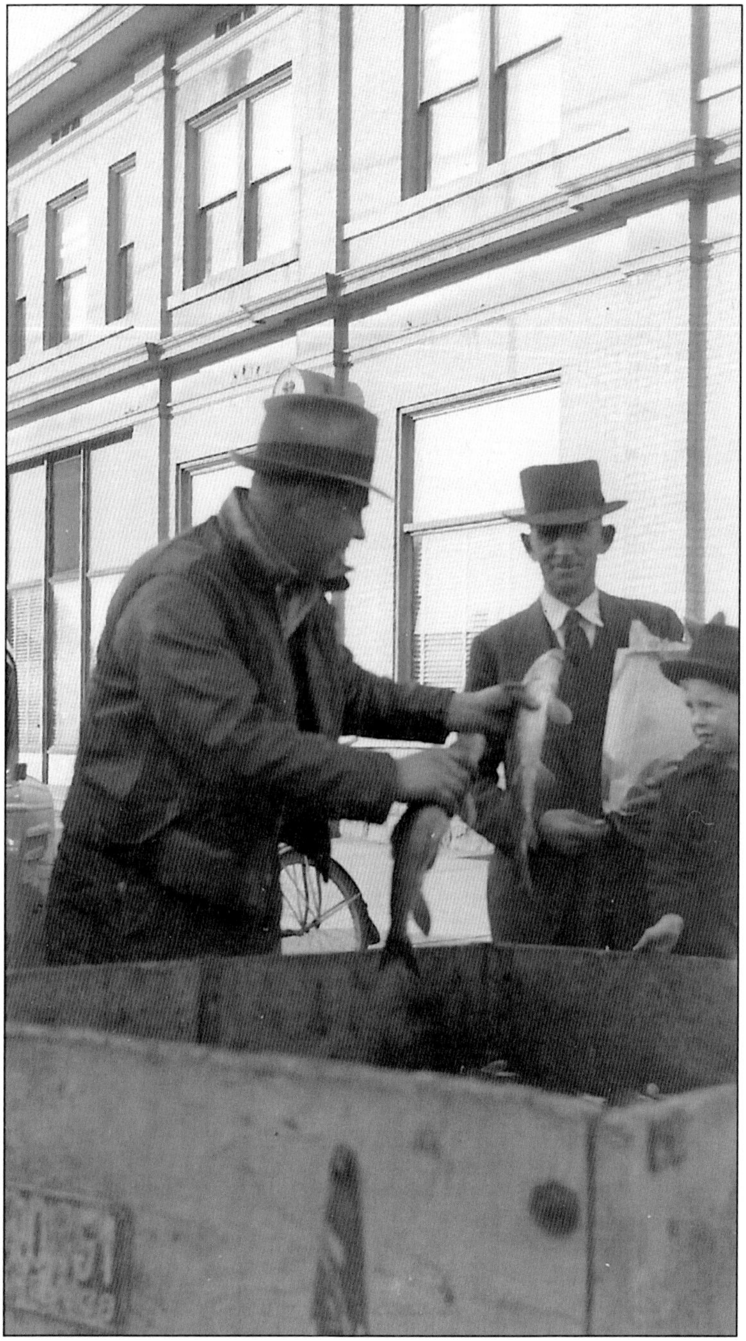

In this late 1930s photograph, Orville Talbot sells Alvin Brower a fish in Preston. According to Talbot's nephew LaVern Talbot, Orville would seine the Bear River, then sell the fish in town. The license plate on the trailer box appears to state 1938. Orville once used the seine to retrieve the body of a nephew who drowned in Twin Lakes, LaVern recalled. A son of his, Ray, grew up to become the Franklin County sheriff. His other children were Darwin, Beth, and Carma. Like most men of the time, Orville had a little farm, which included a few cows and chickens. It was located in Winder.

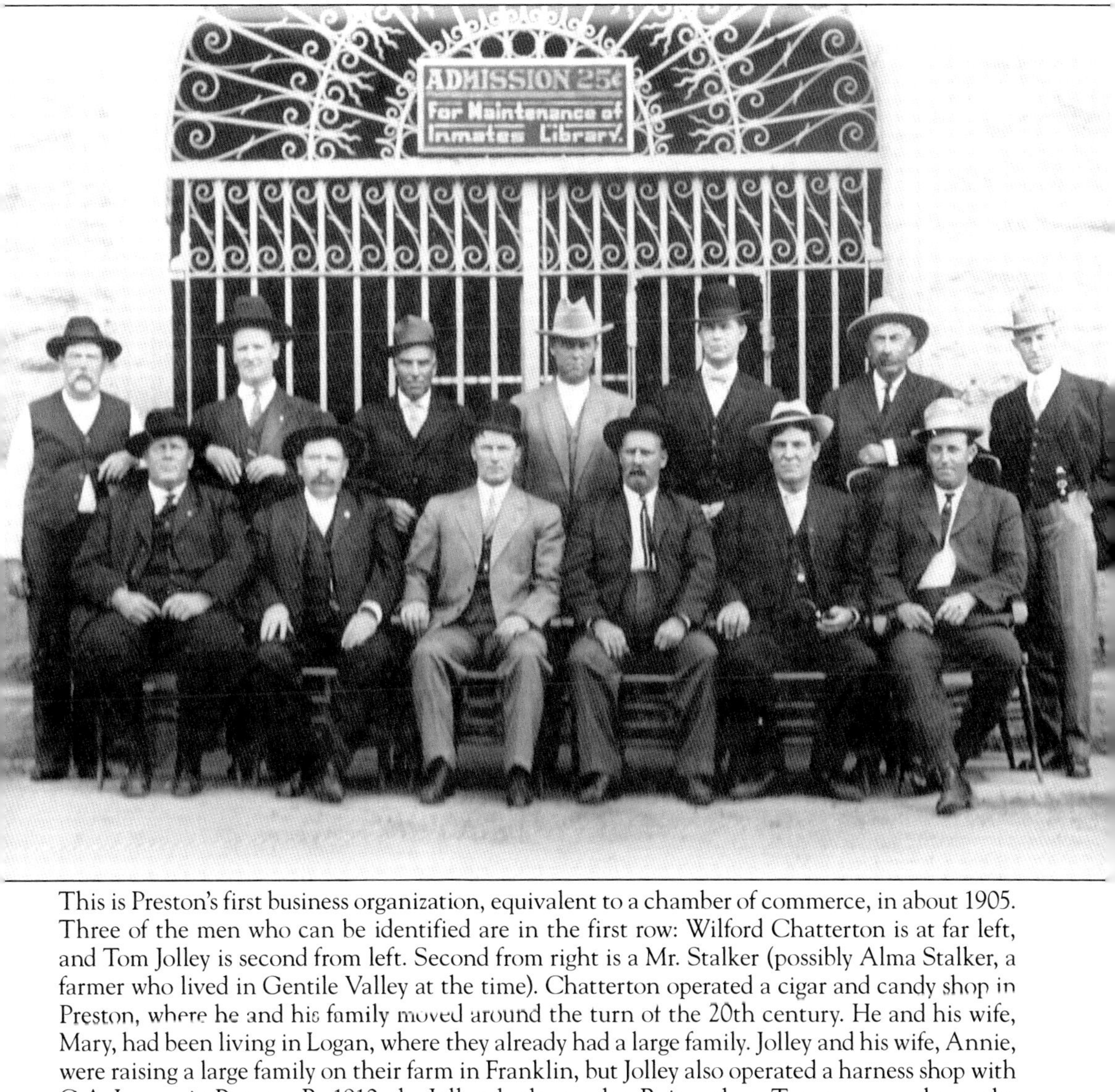

This is Preston's first business organization, equivalent to a chamber of commerce, in about 1905. Three of the men who can be identified are in the first row: Wilford Chatterton is at far left, and Tom Jolley is second from left. Second from right is a Mr. Stalker (possibly Alma Stalker, a farmer who lived in Gentile Valley at the time). Chatterton operated a cigar and candy shop in Preston, where he and his family moved around the turn of the 20th century. He and his wife, Mary, had been living in Logan, where they already had a large family. Jolley and his wife, Annie, were raising a large family on their farm in Franklin, but Jolley also operated a harness shop with C.A. Larson in Preston. By 1910, the Jolleys had moved to Boise, where Tom was a warden at the state penitentiary. He came back to Preston in 1913 to retrieve Charles Edwards, who had been sentenced by Judge Bridge on forgery charges.

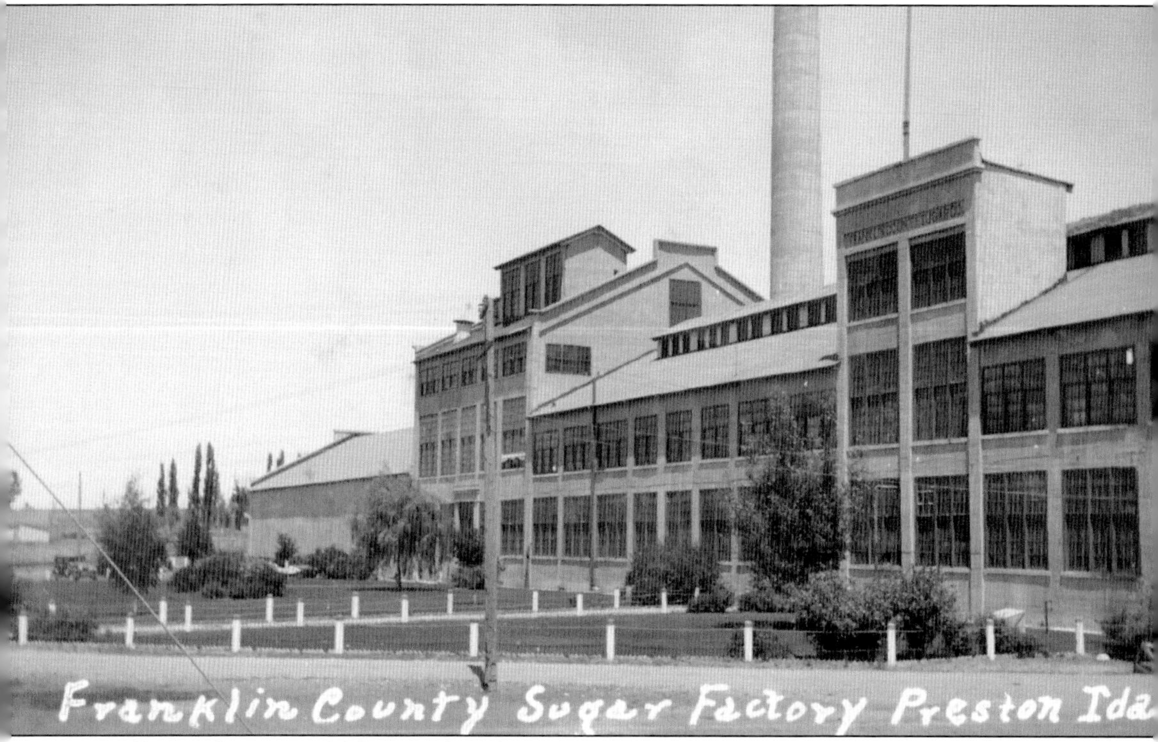

Following five years of delays attributed to supply shortages caused by World War I and speculation on other factories, the Franklin County Sugar Factory was finally built in 1922. It was the first sugar factory to be constructed with a generator and powered by electricity, said Bills Owens, Preston native and sugar factory historian. Farmers harvested 3,400 acres of sugar beets in October that first year. Usually, the factory would start slicing beets by October 10 and finish processing the harvest in December. In low-yield years, however, the process would be finished by November. A crew of 20 to 30 people worked on maintenance and packaging/shipping sugar at the factory year-round. Owens said local farmers built Twin Lakes reservoir to help raise sugar beets. Despite having a bumper crop in 1962, the factory held its last campaign that year. (Bill Owens.)

Six

TRANSPORTATION

A century ago, people were moving from horses, buggies, and trains into the age of airplanes and automobiles. Dr. States brought the first automobile to Preston on April 1, 1912 (see page 49). Local author Mark Hart recorded seeing those first Tin Lizzies:

> Down Preston's main street came a horseless carriage sputtering like a one-lunged halibut boat. Dogs by the dozens were cavorting about, barking delightedly. Horses, with nostrils extended, reared frantically from their hitching posts. Merchants and customers alike appeared on the wooden sidewalks. A patron with his face half shaved stood by a barber with a razor in his hand. It seemed the whole town was there, standing amazed and mesmerized, eyes agape, as Louie Ballif, the local implement dealer, rattled down through town in the most electrifying surprise of the year—of the century, in fact. Wearing goggles and a light tan duster, with gauntlets that hit him at the elbows, Louie sat very erect as he grasped the steering stick with both hands. As this strange vehicle rattled by, a young squirt—Ernie Porter, by name—shouted in a stentorian voice, "Hey, Louie, get a horse! Get a horse!" Everyone guffawed.

Within a couple of years, Hart wrote, the first airplane to touch down in the county arrived:

> We kids were down on the south forty hoeing [sugar] beets [as many of the youth did until the late 1970s, when sugar-processing companies consolidated and moved away from the area]. We heard a terrifying noise, a thundering noise, the likes of which we had never heard before. Like a tornado, it approached from the southwest. What made it more alarming was that we couldn't see anything coming, yet the sound became louder by the second. It hadn't occurred to us to look up. Suddenly, we discovered an airplane about 200 yards immediately above us. It had a much greater impact on us than Louie's Tin Lizzie. It was the first airplane we had ever seen in flight. Moments later it landed, as did the geese, over in Bosworth's hay field; and one could see hundreds of Prestonites racing toward the spot. It was an exhilarating experience and a great day.

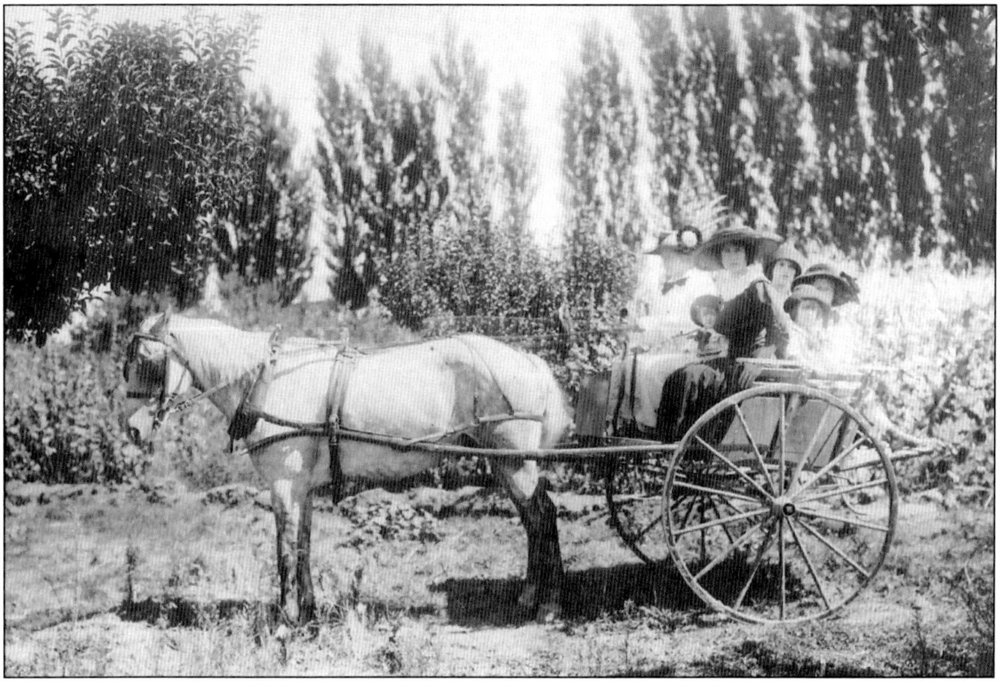

Florence Fail Mitchel wrote about this photograph, "I remember many picnics at this farm. Many young marrieds and their children would gather—great long tables were set out of doors—abundance of good food—fun and laughter—about 1912–1913. Note the poplar trees." Florence grew up in Preston when horses were the main mode of transportation. The Fail, Higginbotham, and Evans women and children spent much time together. Mitchel identified the image below as having been taken in 1912 or 1913 at the Higginbothams' farm. From left to right are Fay Evans Edison, Leah Higginbotham, and Florence's mother, Daisy Fail.

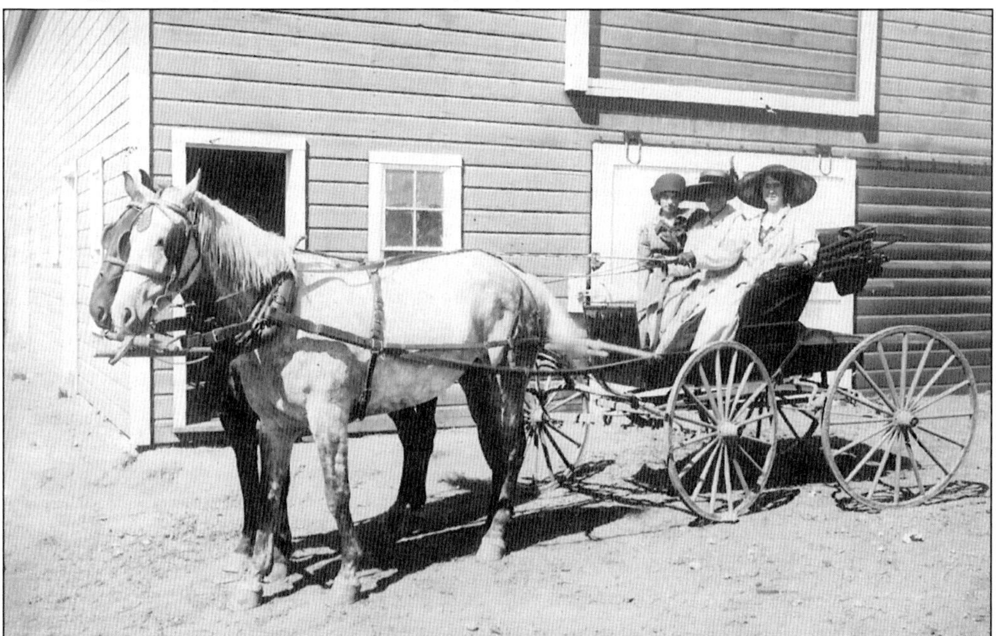

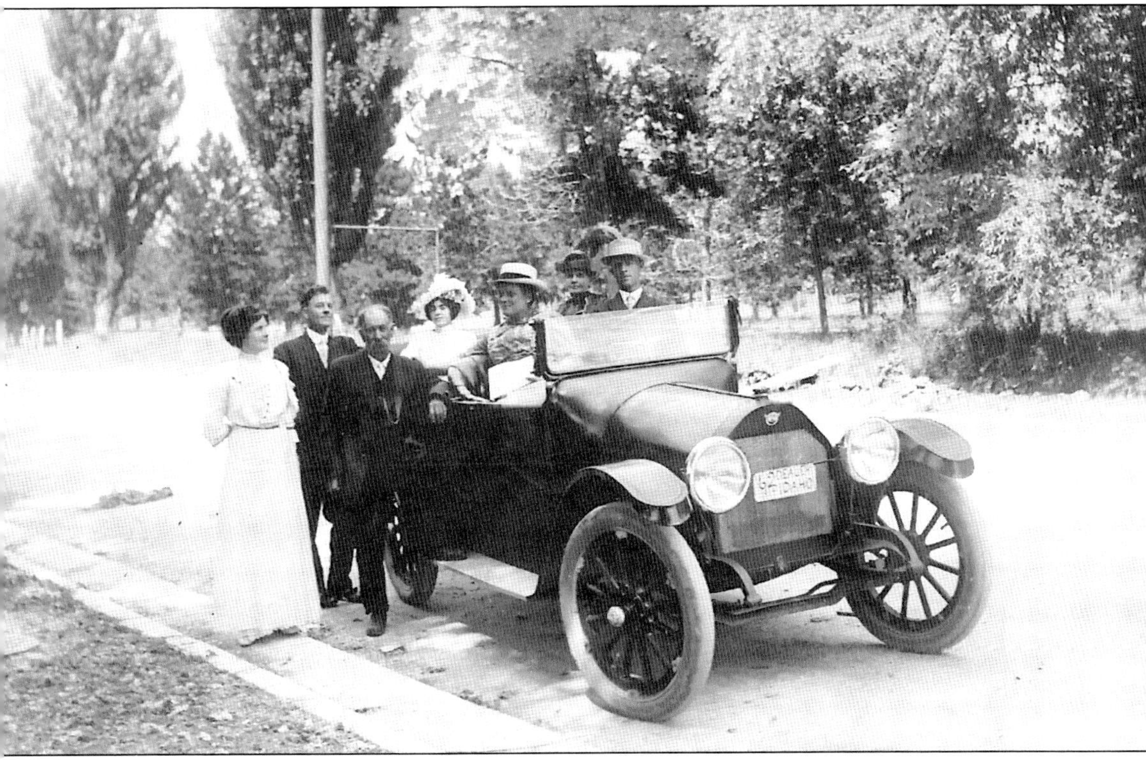

Out for a pleasure ride in an REO Speed Wagon touring car in 1914 are Birdie and Clarence Kendall (up from Salt Lake City, where he was a carpenter), John Tibbets, Dora Hansen, a Mrs. Wineburger, Mary Jane Tibbets, and Clarence Hansen. Birdie was a sister to Clarabelle, the wife of Clarence Hansen, a farmer and railroad motorman during the 1920s. (He was described as "always full of life and wit" by Jack Roe.) Hansen and Dr. J.C. Peterson proposed the construction of a new dance hall to Baltzar Peterson in order to get his financial backing. They opened the Persiana in 1928, and the hall was a raging success for many years. While watching Halley's Comet streak through the sky on May 7, 1910, Clarence and his son Levon speculated on what could happen if the comet were to hit Earth. In his later years, when buses replaced trains for public transportation, Clarence drove a bus around the Agricultural College (Utah State University) campus. (Kathy Griffin.)

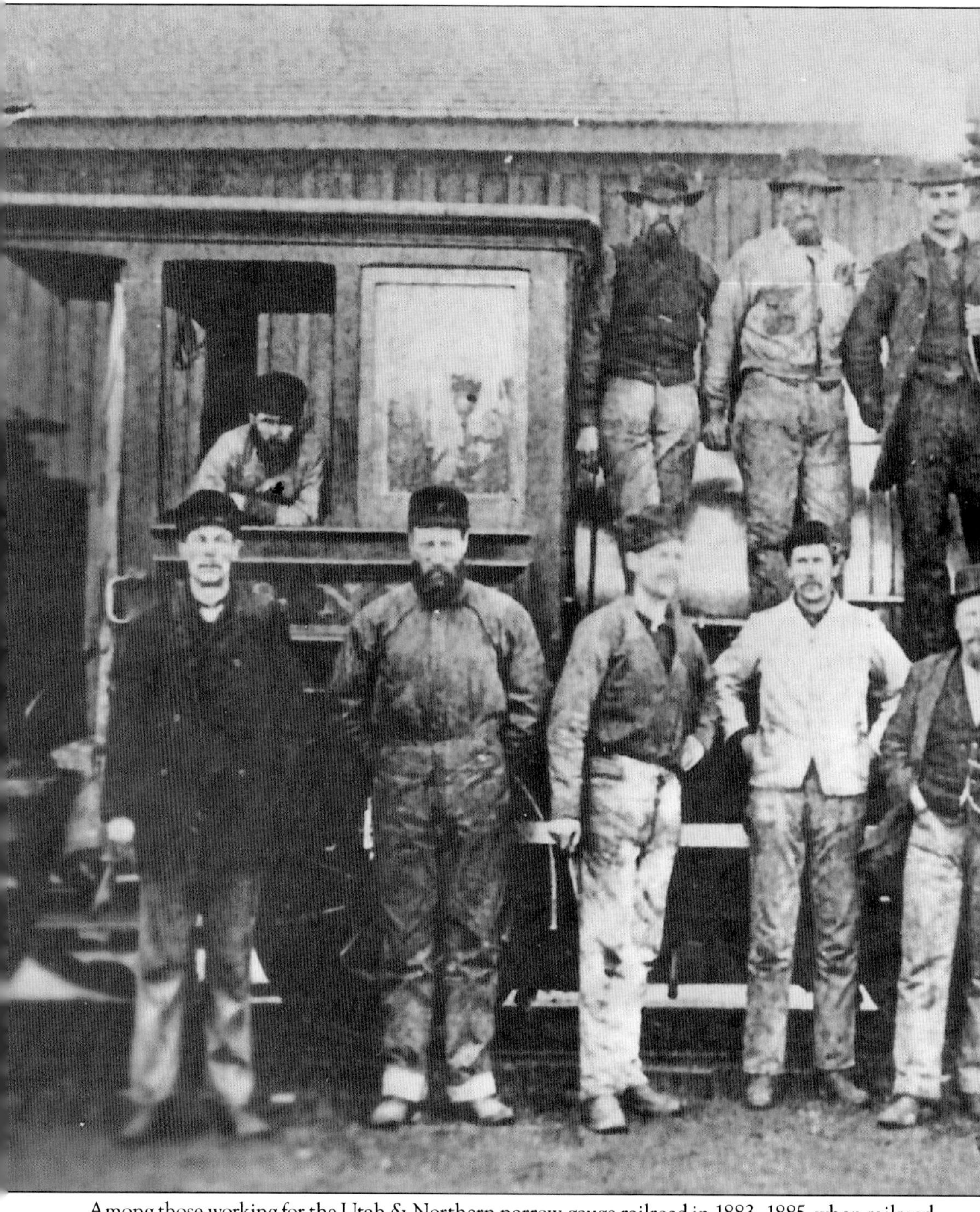

Among those working for the Utah & Northern narrow-gauge railroad in 1883–1885, when railroad historian Arthur Peterson dated this photograph, were Jack Murdock, Jens Steffensen, William Lowe Young, William Carter, George Carter, Bill King, Bill Knowles, Charles Paul, Charles Pond, Hubel Chatterton, and John Shields. Ted Murdock of Dayton told Newell Hart that his father, Jack, could be third from left in the first row. Ern Carter told him, "If my father is on here at all

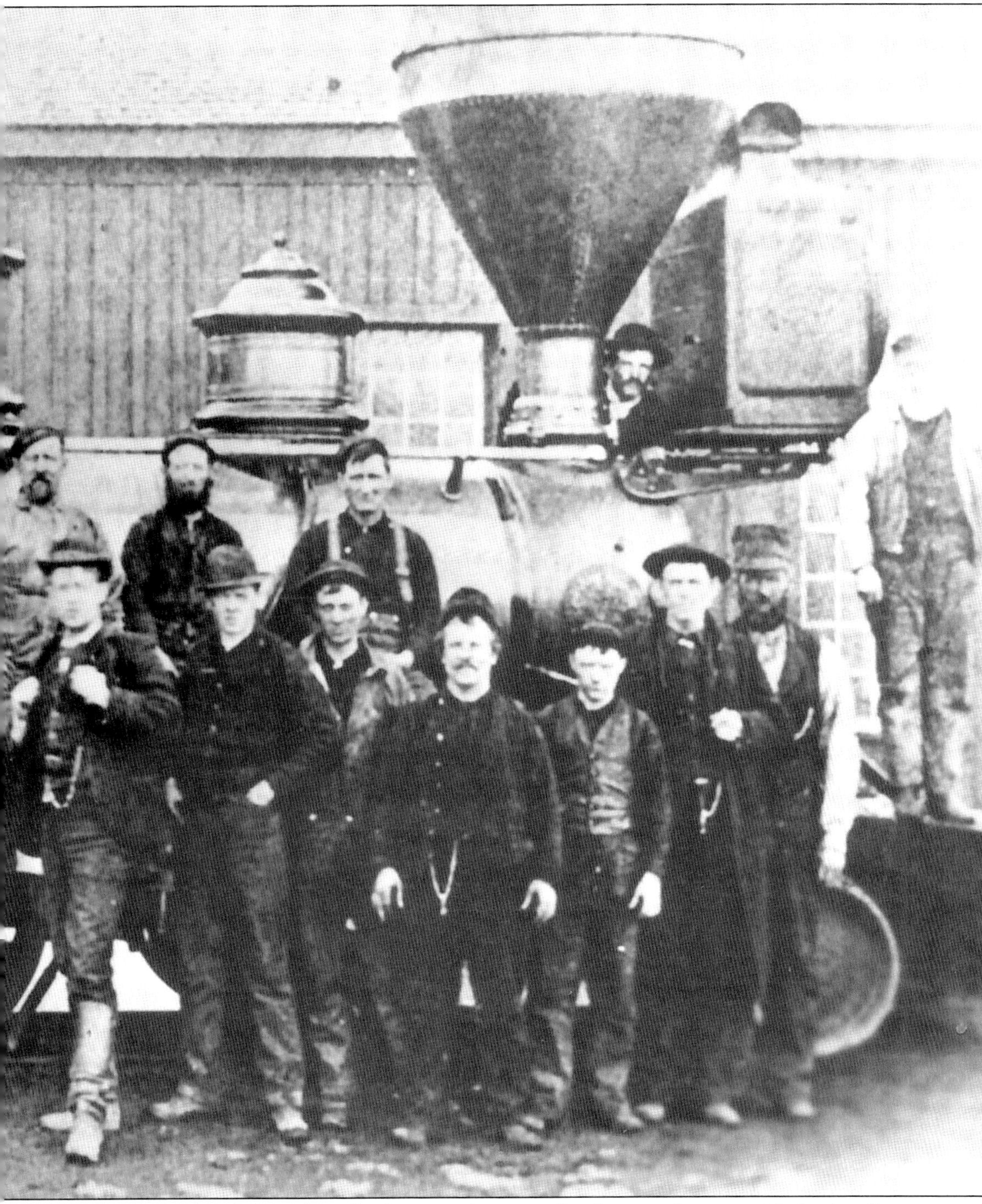

it would be the fourth from the right, he was a short man," indicating the man with the dangling watch chain. Edna S. Casperson said the white-bearded man at far right resembled her father, Jens Steffensen. This photograph was taken at an engine terminal. Battle Creek was a terminal where both crews and engines changed. Helper engines were serviced there.

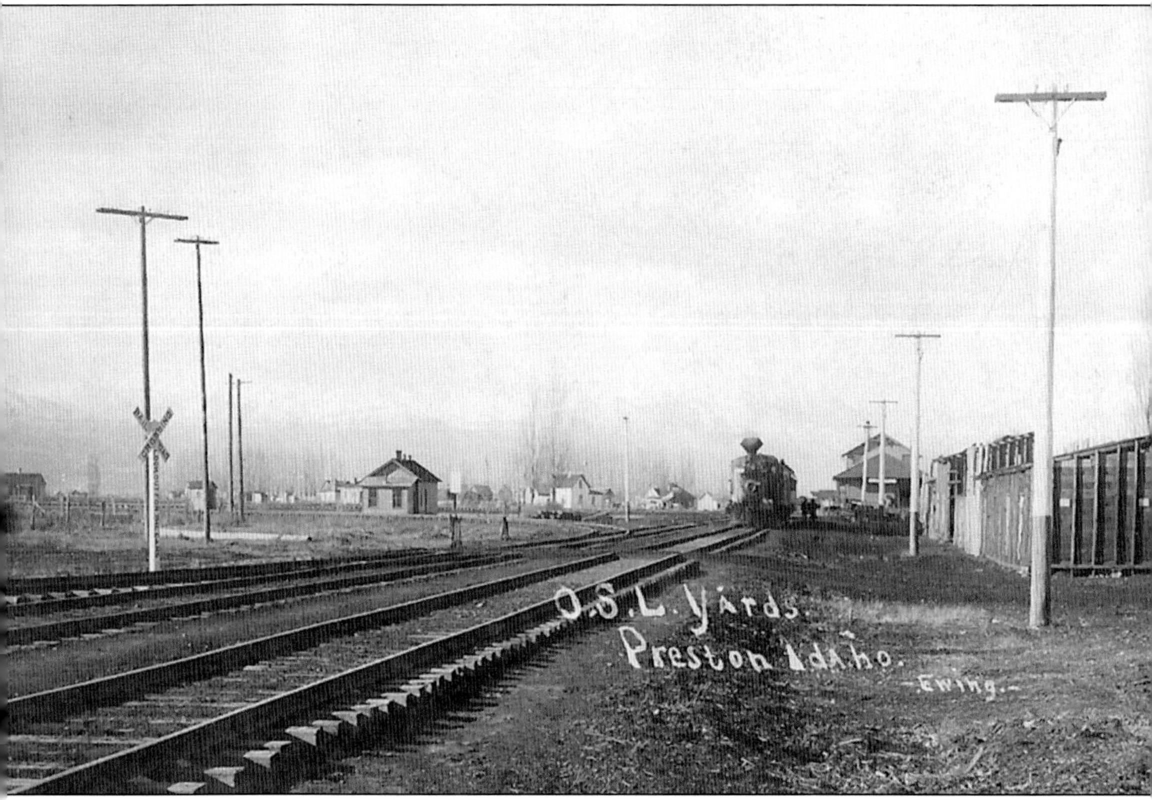

The railroad came through Preston in 1876, pushed from Franklin to Battle Creek, a location on the river bottoms north of Preston on Highway 91 near the monument erected by the Daughters of the Utah Pioneers to commemorate the Bear River Massacre. This view of the track is looking northwest from Second South Street in about 1910. "OSL" stands for Oregon Short Line, a company organized on July 27, 1889, by merging several other companies from Utah, Idaho, and Oregon. The OSL began running a daily round-trip 100-passenger car to Preston from Cache Junction in 1911. By 1914, another company, the Utah Idaho Central, arrived in Preston with a line of rails for its electrical cars. Daily service from Logan to Preston began on May 1, 1915, with stops along the way. By the 1940s, the train made four trips in and four trips out of Preston every day except Sundays and holidays.

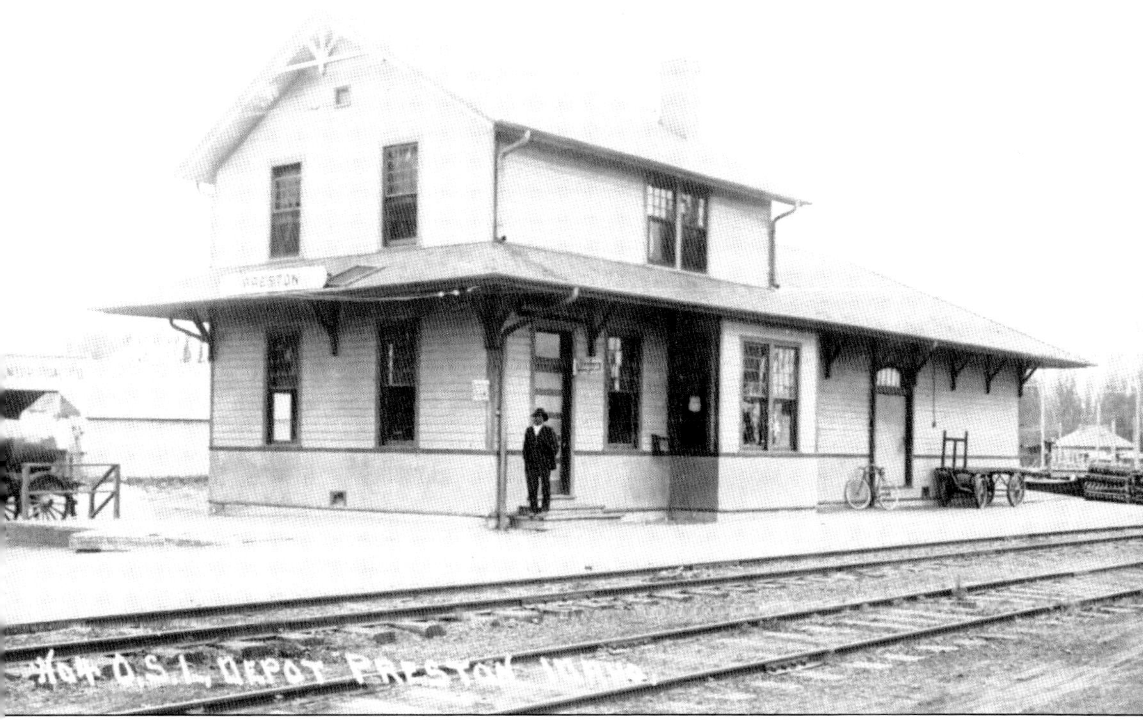

Leaving the OSL Depot in Preston at 7:00 a.m., 8:00 a.m., 2:00 p.m., and 5:15 p.m., the train stopped at eight locations before reaching Logan, and twenty-six before reaching Ogden, where passengers could catch the Bamberger Railroad into Salt Lake City and points in between—a five-hour trip. The train stopped at a variety of undesignated places. The rickety ride earned it the nickname "Galloping Goose." Keith Christensen once recalled that "the goose" was a great place for pep rallies between the competing high schools in Preston, Richmond, Hyrum, and Logan. "We'd get 200 or 300 students together and they would have a special run to the games for us. They pretty much gave us the run of the place." By the 1940s, passenger use had dropped considerably, and by the end of World War II, there were talks of shutting the Utah Idaho Central down. On February 15, 1947, the Galloping Goose made its last run to Preston. Today, just the standard line remains. (Jay Burrup.)

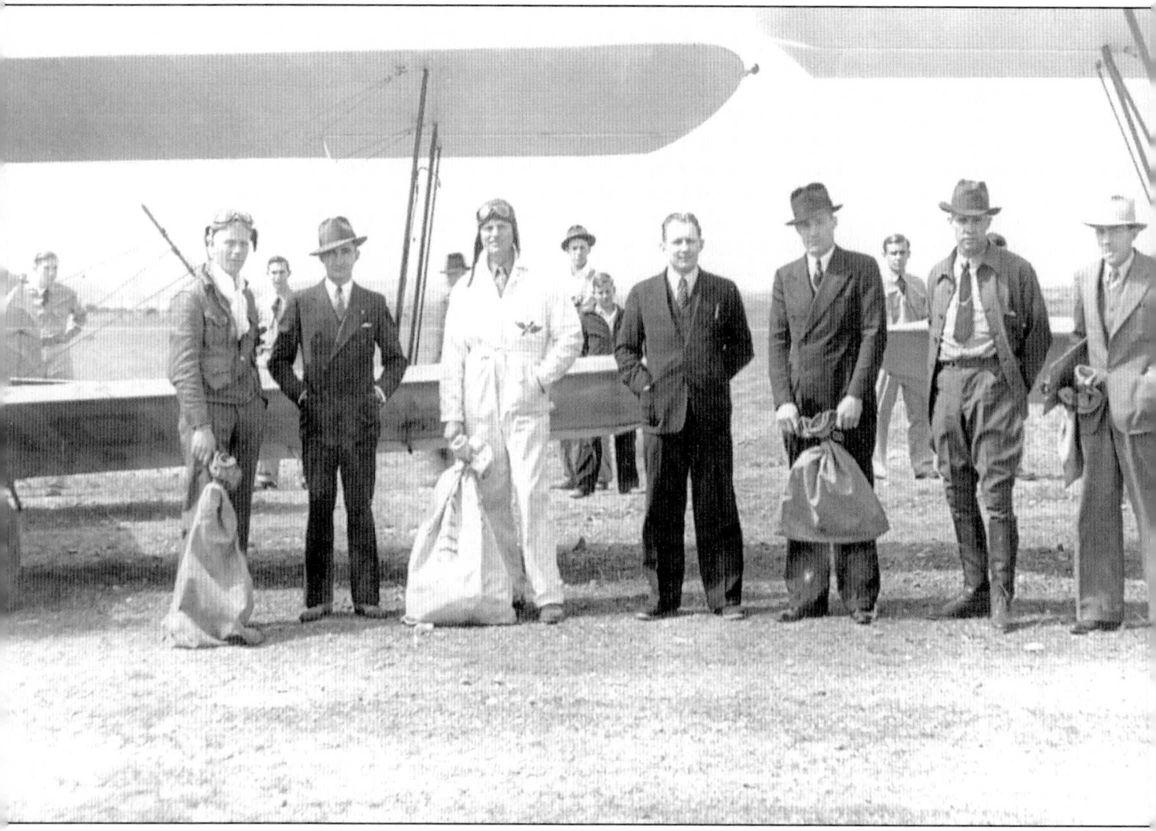

Preston was designated an airmail landing field connecting routes between Salt Lake City and Pocatello in 1934. Officials were on hand to recognize the milestone in Preston's modernization. The airport had been built the previous year under the leadership of Mayor Lorenzo Hansen by matching funds provided by the federal government's WPA project. Men used teams and wagons to cut two runways. It was the first all-direction airport in Cache Valley and could be used in any wind condition. The runways were covered with shale when it was finished. The land on which Preston's airport is built was deeded to the city on December 13, 1933, according to city clerk Jerry Larsen.

Seven

PUBLIC PLACES

Public places in a community reflect a collective commitment to stick around and make a place succeed. Preston's first public building was multipurpose, if not multi-roomed. Religious, educational, and civic meetings were held in the one-room schoolhouse built in 1877. As the population grew and businesses sprang up, those buildings served both private and public purposes. Town council meetings were held in Bill Head's general merchandise store on the northeastern corner of State and Oneida Streets for many of those early years. The post office was another gathering spot, until post men began taking the mail out to the recipients. Today, those centers have moved to private businesses such as coffee shops. It is there that news (both true and false) begins a swift journey along the grapevine to the far reaches of the community, where it can grow and morph until official statements can be made through the local newspaper and radio station.

Preston has experienced two large growth spurts. The first one was around 1914 with the town's designation as the new seat of the fledgling Franklin County. Construction abounded. Citizens collaborated to construct the Nelson Gymnasium for their high school students and garner Andrew Carnegie's support for a shiny new library. The newspaper and cafés were renamed to reflect the county's name change, and new county offices were constructed above the bank in the Greaves building.

Then, in the 1930s, Pres. Franklin D. Roosevelt's New Deal provided funds for public buildings across the country. Preston residents took advantage of the opportunity, and in 1939, built themselves a courthouse, a new high school, and the current post office. Also that year, a new tabernacle was built at the corner of 200 South Street and 200 East Street for the Franklin Stake of The Church of Jesus Christ of Latter-day Saints.

The year 1939 marked a difference in how Prestonites began building their public edifices. Before that time, people pooled their resources—cash or talent—and built what they needed as a community.

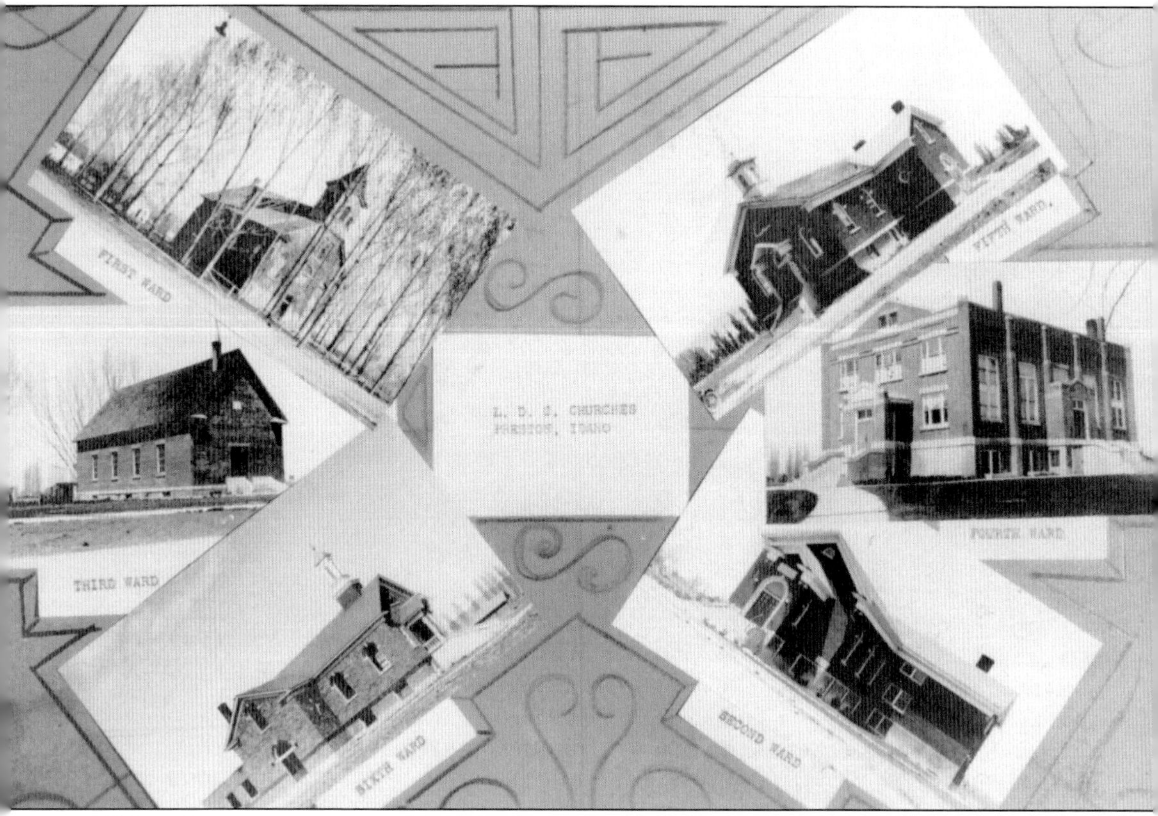

When Preston was young, church buildings were also civic centers, and many more church buildings stood in Preston than do now. Historian Newell Hart immortalized the Preston Sixth Ward building through his writings in the *Cache Valley Newsletter* and in his books, which were based on his experiences as a child growing up in the early years of Preston and attending church in that building. Pictured are some of those early buildings. Of them, only three remain: the Second Ward building, standing at First South Street and 200 West Street, was sold in 1976 and has been remodeled into a bed-and-breakfast; the Sixth Ward building, standing on West 800 South, is a private residence; and the Fifth Ward chapel standing on East Oneida Street is also a private residence. The First Ward building stood near 200 East 200 South. The Third Ward Building stood at 155 North 200 West. The Fourth Ward building stood at 200 East 200 North. The Catholic church stands on East Oneida Street, and the Presbyterian church, formerly an LDS chapel hauled from Glendale in the 1950s, stands at 206 East 200 North. (Jay Burrup.)

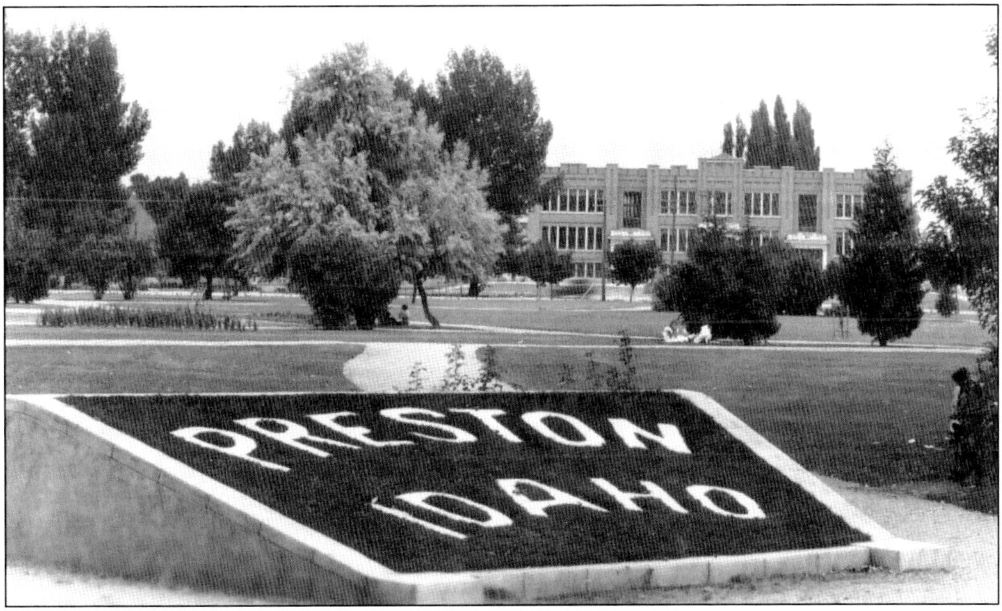

Preston laid out a beautiful park in 1920 under Mayor Joe Marrom. Bill Head, Preston's chief of police, and Will Hawkes Sr. used a two-horse grader to cut wide, circular paths into the hard-packed, weed-covered dirt lot where "a lot of baseball games had been played," remembered Head. They followed the design of a landscape artist from "the college in Logan." Shale from Dayton Canyon covered the paths. Residents helped to plant trees and shrubs, identifying the varieties with stakes. Joseph Geddes and Al Watson were groundskeepers. In 1928, Mayor Ren Hansen commissioned the beautiful Danish Gateway, a wrought-iron gate hand forged by Pete Jorgensen, Junno Kjar, and Chris Gundesen that still stands at 35 South State Street. In 1974, the city gave the park to the Church of Jesus Christ of Latter-day Saints. Today, it is known as Benson Park. Below, the Central School can be seen looking north through the park.

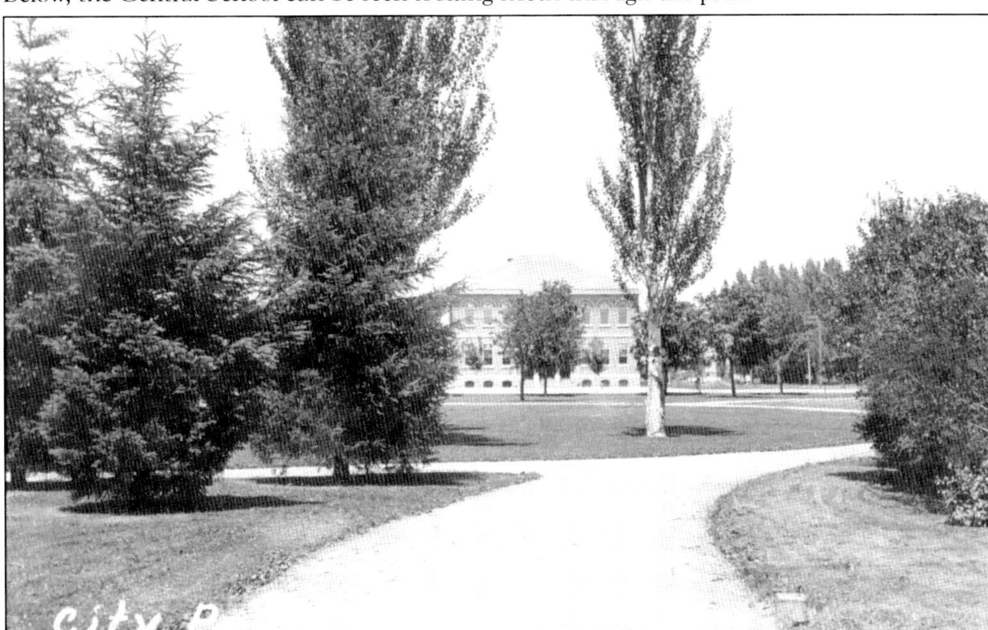

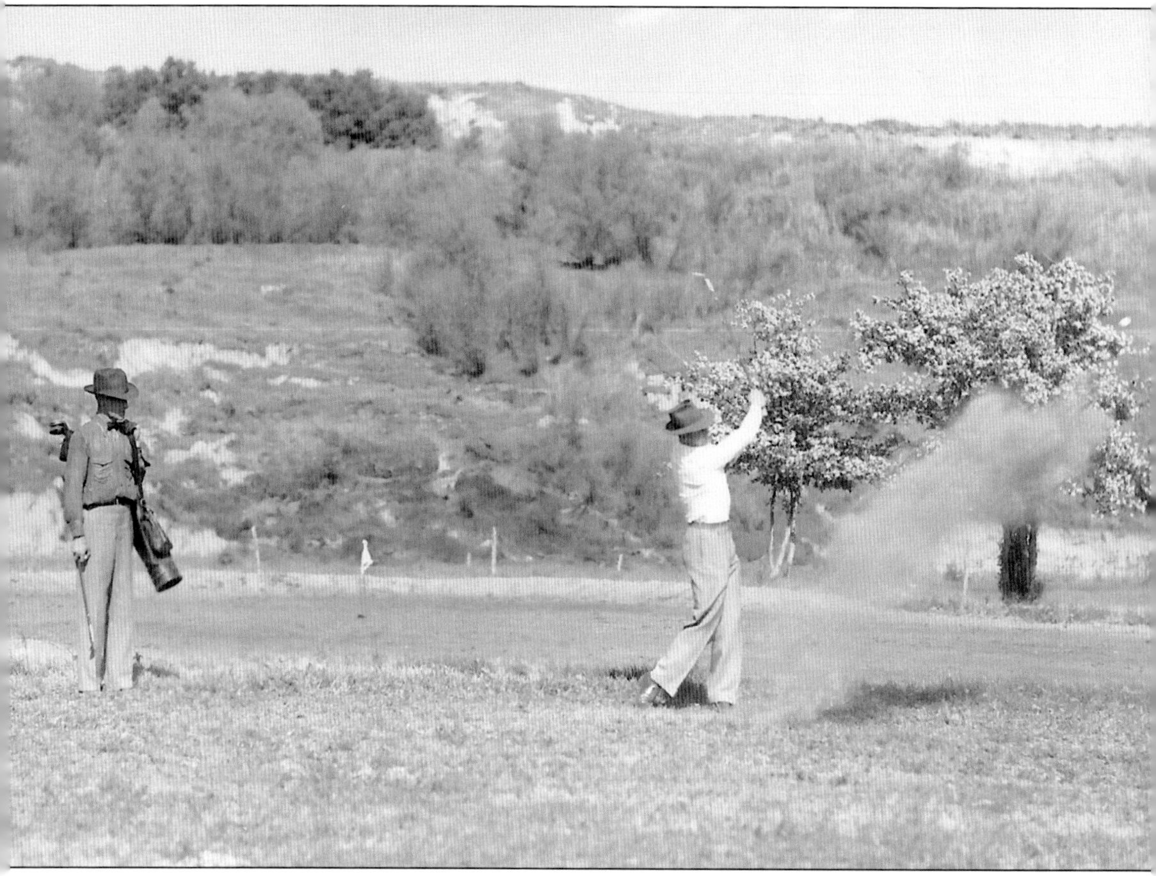

West on Oneida Street, down the bluffs and onto the banks of the Bear River, a golf course was built in 1932. Sand was packed to create the "greens" that followed the west bank of the river from the gates south until the waterway bends back west again. At that point, golfers would take a swinging bridge to the east bank of the river for additional holes. The course included a clubhouse and Pioneer Park, a place for the kids to play while parents golfed. By the 1940s, the course was in decline. World War II put the kibosh on recreational activities. Today, Dav Frew's Angus bulls graze around a rock pillar entryway, shaded by Russian olive trees and surrounded by pastures utilized by neighboring farmers. Frew, who was born the same year the course opened, remembers the fury incurred by thoughtless golfers who tromped through his father's crops to get their lost balls. "They even burned the field once to find their balls," he said. (Preston Golf and Country Club.)

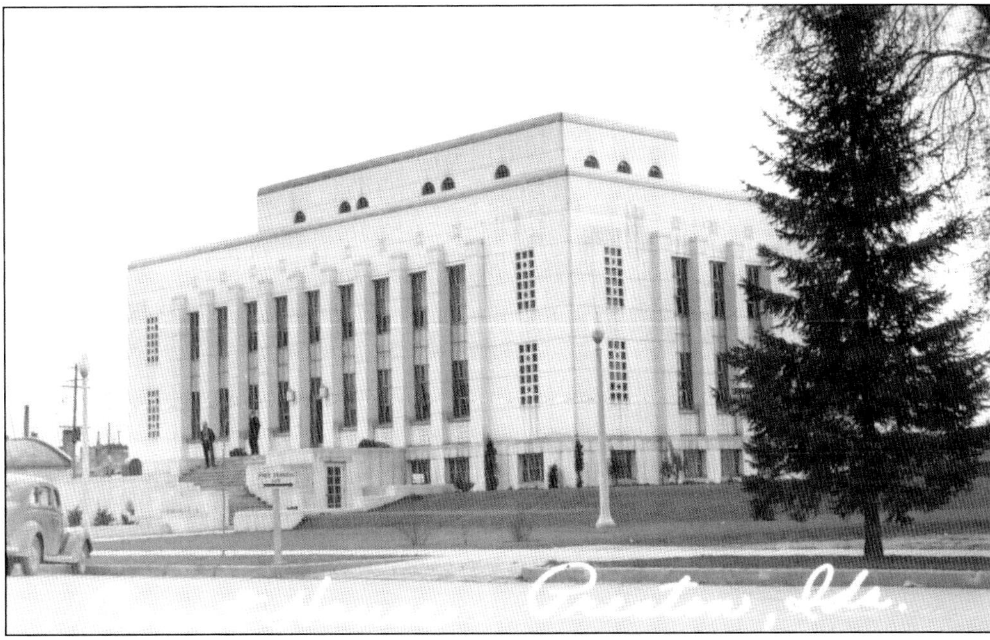

The Franklin County Courthouse (above) was built in 1939, the first structure in the county erected specifically for this use. The building was designed by Salt Lake City architect Hyrum C. Pope in the Art Deco style. It was built with $60,750 in federal WPA funds and matching county funds, costing $135,000. It includes a jail on its top floor. The building was listed in the National Register of Historic Places in 1987. Also in 1939, the county built Preston High School, the federal government built the post office, and the Church of Jesus Christ of Latter-day Saints began construction on the long-hoped-for Franklin Stake Tabernacle (below) on the corner of Second East and Second South Streets. It took a year to build, costing $91,000, and was dedicated in August 1942 by LDS president David O. McKay. Rust-colored drapes were hung on the windows, and the building was steam heated with a coal stoker and had air-conditioning. It would seat up to 1,400 people with the recreation hall open. (Both, Jay Burrup.)

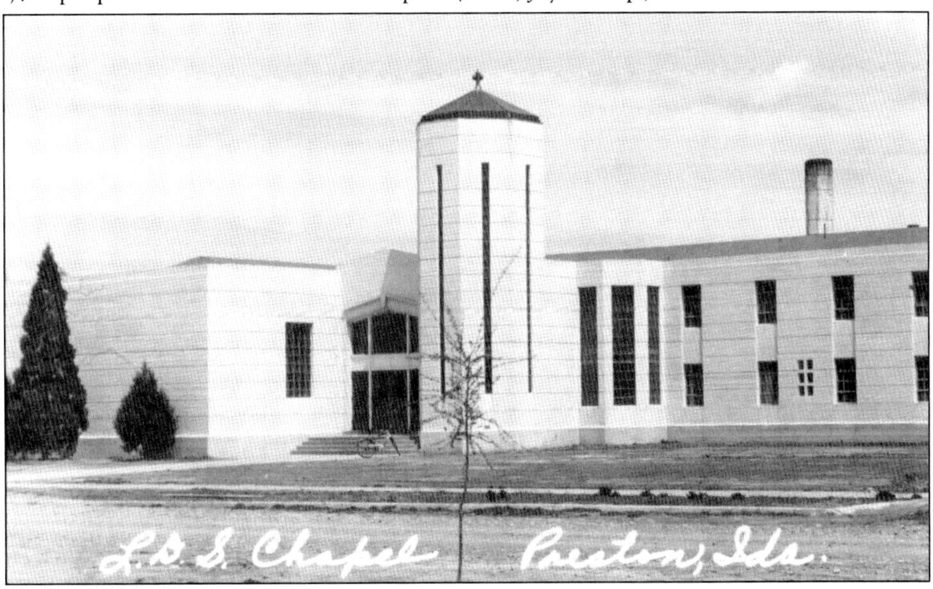

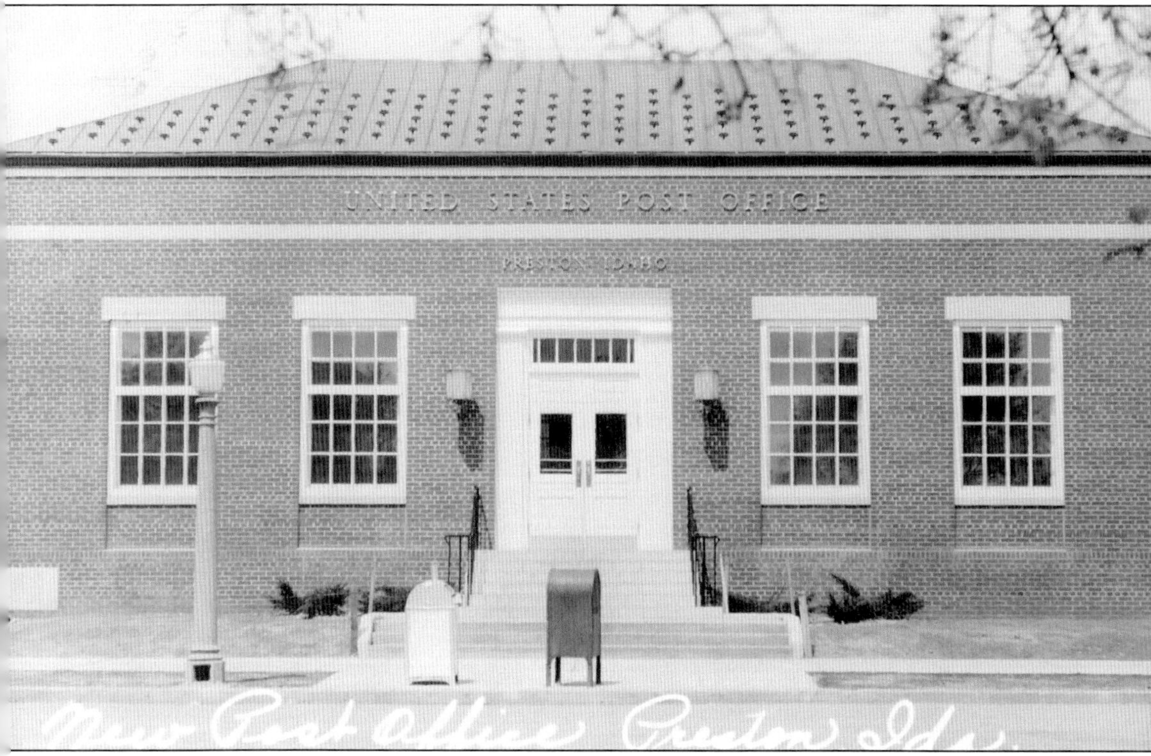

The Preston Post Office was constructed in 1939, the first time a building was constructed for the sole purpose of distributing mail in Preston. William Chapman was named Preston's first postmaster in 1881. The post office was established on August 28, 1882. For a short while, Chapman handled the mail in a section house near the rail tracks, then in his and James Bosworth's store at about 264 South State Street. Other postal locations were at about 10 North State Street and on Oneida Street in the west side of the Greaves Block. The newspaper reported that county residents were thrilled to have the new building, but "house to house delivery destroyed a somewhat cherished social custom . . . the daily gossip sessions in the post office," wrote Newell Hart. Inside, as part of a national program to distribute works of art throughout the country, Edmond J. Fitzgerald memorialized the Bear River Massacre in 1941. He painted a scene in which Col. Patrick O'Connor led the US Cavalry against a Shoshone encampment in 1863. Upwards of 450 Shoshone men, women, and children were killed, ending local conflict with Native Americans. (Jay Burrup.)

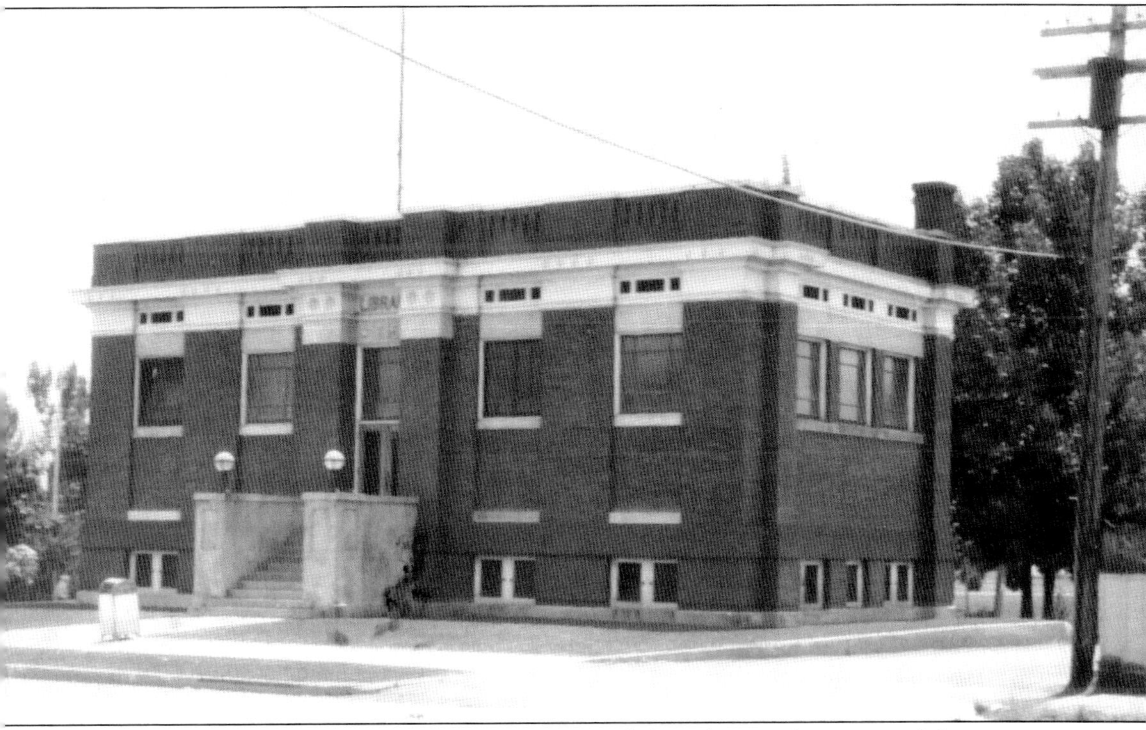

Steel magnate and philanthropist Andrew Carnegie believed it was his responsibility to give his wealth back to the people because they were responsible for making his fortune possible. Furthermore, Carnegie believed that "a man who dies rich dies in disgrace." Wanting to help people who helped themselves, in 1911, he began assisting communities in building libraries. Local leaders from the Church of Jesus Christ of Latter-day Saints made application to Carnegie, wanting the resource for area children and youth. He granted $10,000 to build the library in 1914, with the understanding that local residents would be assessed a tax each year to help maintain the facility. In the United States, 1,689 libraries were built—11 of those in Idaho. This structure was completed in 1915 and was located on East Oneida Street on the east side of the alleyway between Benson Park and US Bank. The library was torn down in 2005, and a new benefactor, David Sant, was immortalized with the construction of the Preston Larsen–Sant Library in 2002. (Jay Burrup.)

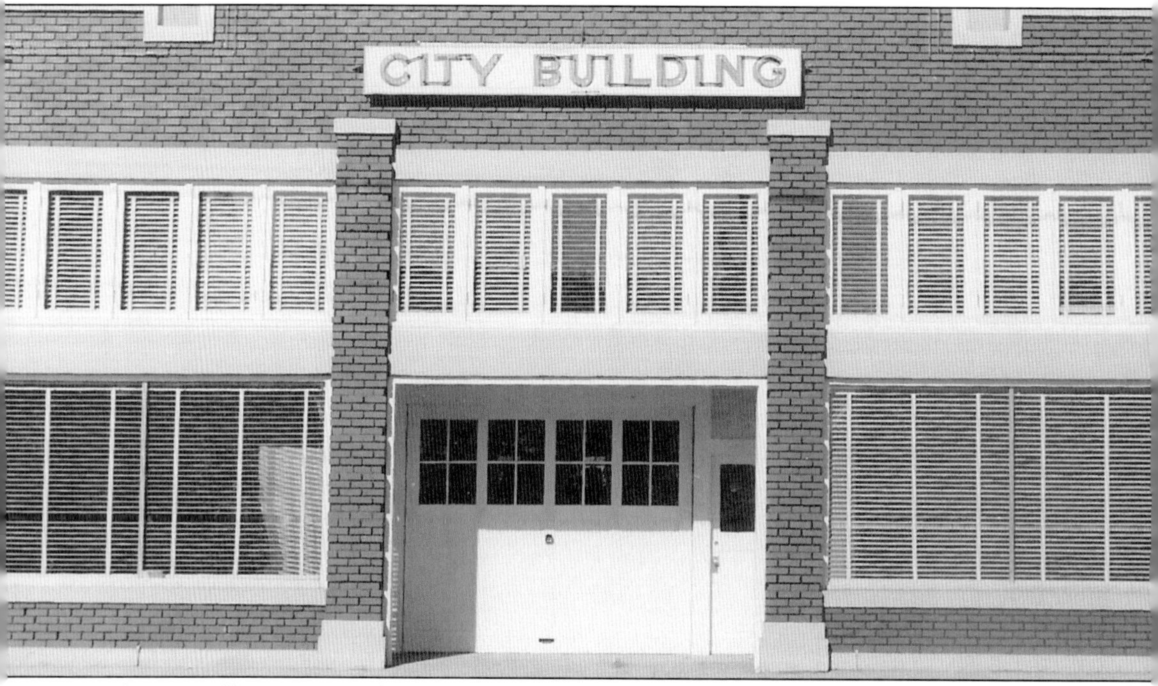

The city's offices once stood on the empty lot east of 77 West Oneida Street. Built in about 1916 by brothers James and Joseph Johnson, this building was originally a Studebaker and Paige showroom called the Guarantee Motor Company. The Johnsons sold the building in the mid-1920s, and the garage was used to sell Cleveland, Chandler, and Oakland cars by Whit Kimball and his brother. During the winter of 1931–1932, heavy snows caved in the roof. The following spring, Paul Larsen, a local musician admired by Newell Hart and his musician brothers, converted the damaged building into the Moonbeam Dance Hall. It operated just during the summer of 1932 and competed with the Persiana, "but was crowded at every dance," wrote Hart. Preston purchased the building in 1936, locating the council room upstairs; clerk and treasurer offices were located at left and right. In the 1970s, the city remodeled, added on a new council room, and converted the windows to doors for parking its fire truck, ambulance, and fire-rescue truck. The building was demolished in 2005. (Jay Burrup.)

Eight

Private Homes

Like settlers throughout the West, the first Preston residents built their homes out of whatever was available. During those first years, dugouts were many. Homes were built of logs and added onto as needed. Often, floors and roofs were dirt and canvas, respectively, until crops could be sown. They were then replaced with more durable and much cleaner alternatives as time and materials became available.

Homes were also self-sustaining enterprises for many of these early settlers. They raised gardens, crops, and animals for food and trade. They understood what it meant to "make hay while the sun shines," because if they did not, they often went without basic necessities. Store-bought items were available, but at a price and distance. Homemaking skills, such as cooking, cleaning, and sewing, were prized, for they were what put the finishing touches to the shelters created for protection from the elements. Homes were also where the memories were made for generations and generations of children. Author Mark Hart immortalized a fruit orchard near the home he grew up in that stood on the southwestern section of Preston. Tales of adventures had there by the children of the entire neighborhood come to life in his book *Apple Blossom Daze*. "Inside the grove were track-meet grounds, basketball standards, running tracks, and willow camp hideouts," he wrote.

By the 1890s, people were beginning to build substantial, spacious Victorian-style houses. They were often filled with local talent as families and friends entertained within their walls.

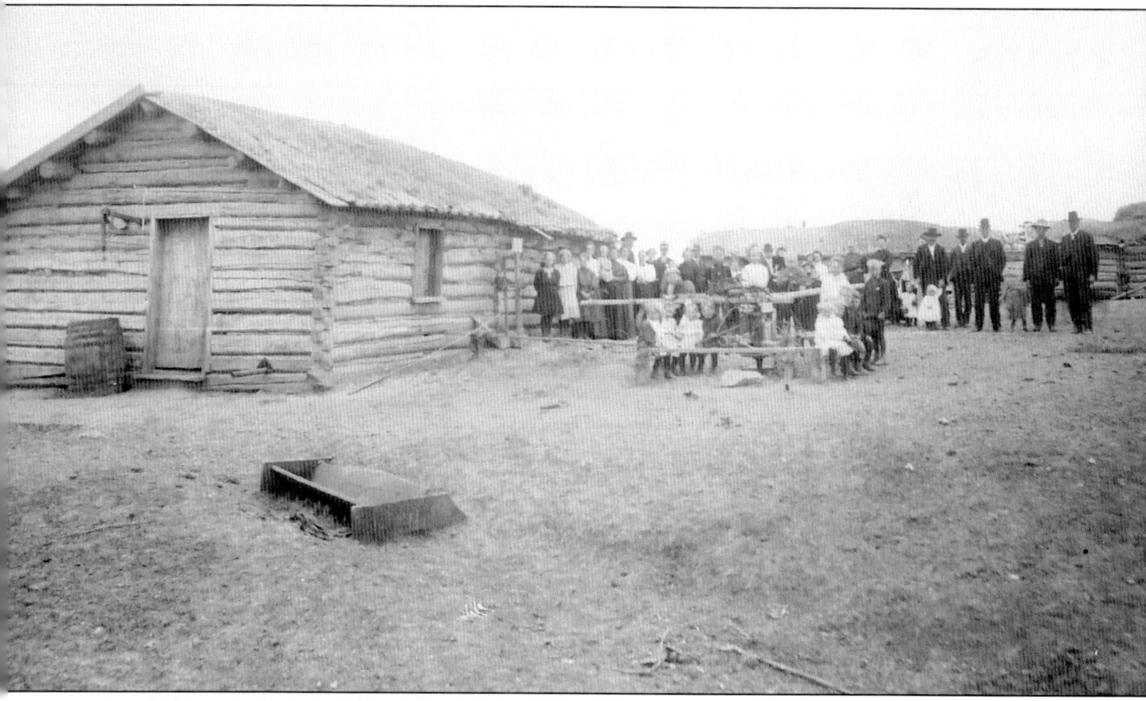

In 1868, an early winter freeze jammed the Bear River. Ties cut in the mountains east of Preston and floated down the River to Corinne, Utah, did not make it on time to be a part of the transcontinental railroad. David C. Jensen gathered some of them up, logged a few more from Worm Creek Canyon, and built this home in 1871 on the Preston flat. His family became the first permanent residents of Preston, or Worm Creek, as it was known at the time. Before then, people would move out from the Franklin Fort to farm and ranch during the summers, but return during severe weather. This picture was taken in 1884 at the funeral services of David's first wife, Serena. Pictured are Hyrum D. Jensen, Elmer Jensen, Samuel D. Jensen, George Shaffer, Christina J. Shaffer, Joseph Jensen, Junius Jensen, Sylvia L. Jensen, Sarah J. Alder, Margaret Jensen, Sarah Jensen, Julia Konstance Jensen (younger sister and sister wife of Serena), Jane Jensen, Richard Jensen, Black Charlie Peterson, Sara Peterson, Dagmar Jensen, Nora Smart, James Smart, Fredrick Jensen, and May Jensen. (Kathy Griffin.)

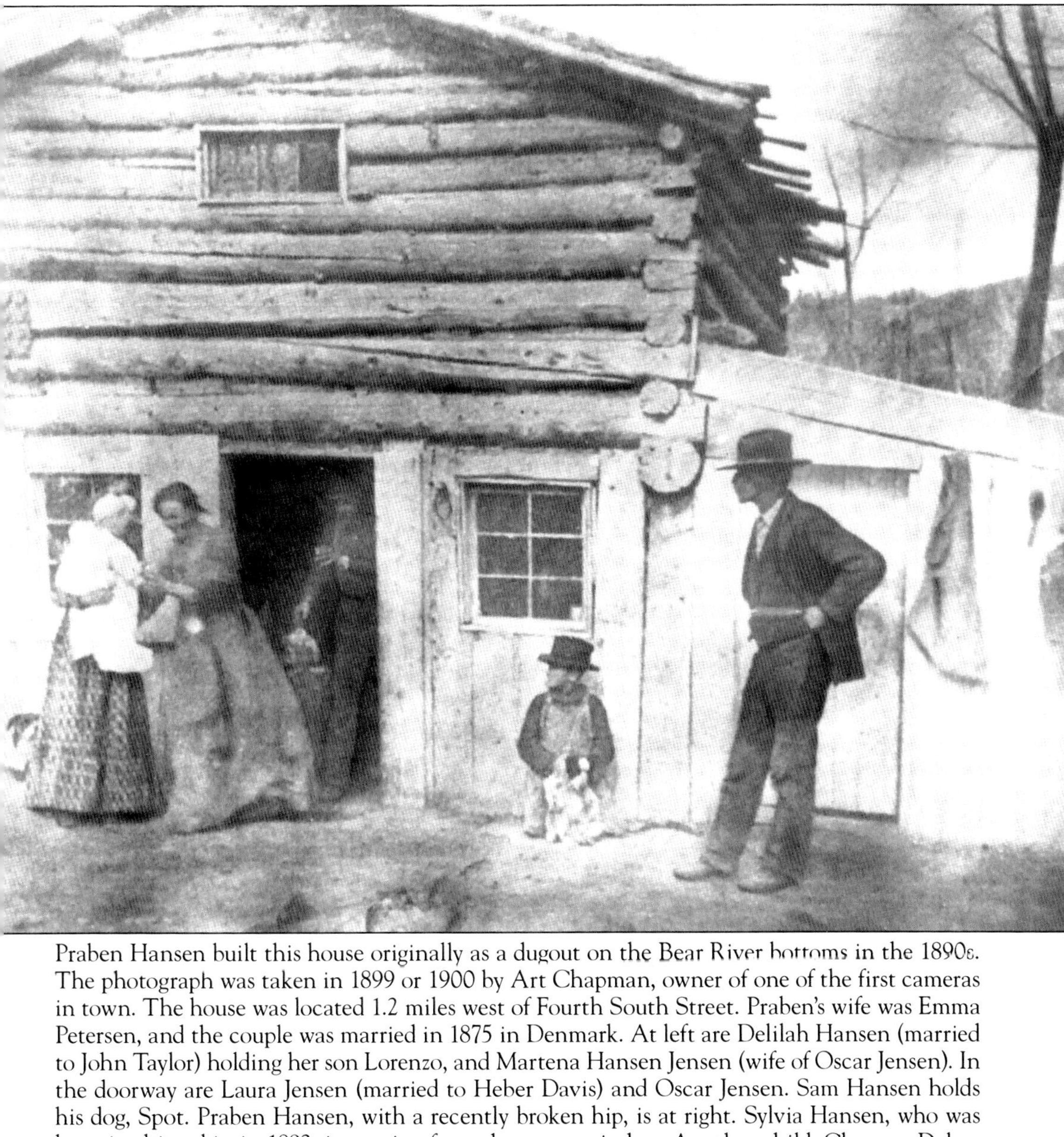

Praben Hansen built this house originally as a dugout on the Bear River bottoms in the 1890s. The photograph was taken in 1899 or 1900 by Art Chapman, owner of one of the first cameras in town. The house was located 1.2 miles west of Fourth South Street. Praben's wife was Emma Petersen, and the couple was married in 1875 in Denmark. At left are Delilah Hansen (married to John Taylor) holding her son Lorenzo, and Martena Hansen Jensen (wife of Oscar Jensen). In the doorway are Laura Jensen (married to Heber Davis) and Oscar Jensen. Sam Hansen holds his dog, Spot. Praben Hansen, with a recently broken hip, is at right. Sylvia Hansen, who was born in this cabin in 1892, is peeping from the upper window. Another child, Clarence Deloss Hansen, grew up to build the famed Persiana Dance Hall in Preston. (Kathy Griffin.)

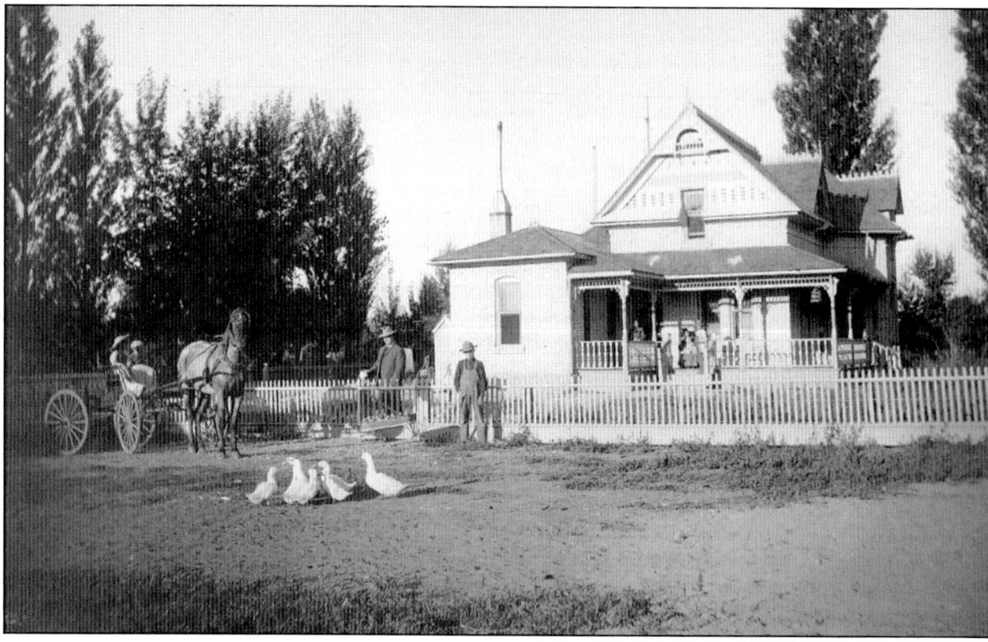

Above, Arthur W. Hart's home was built in 1904, one mile south and three quarters of a mile west of Hart's law office in the newly completed John Larson and Sons Building in downtown Preston. Hart is at the gate, leaving for work. Members of the family are on the porch, and James Osmond, a nephew from Bear Lake, stands in front of the fence. Below, the David and Elizabeth Greaves Eames farm, two miles north and one half mile west of the State Street–Oneida Street intersection, is pictured in about 1913. Aeriel Guy Eames, married to Edna Geddes Eames, is driving the buggy on the left. Lillie Eames Benson with her twins, Carmen and Harold, are in the backseat. David Eames is driving the black buggy. Elizabeth is sitting next to David, with Gladys Benson, Lillie's oldest daughter, between them.

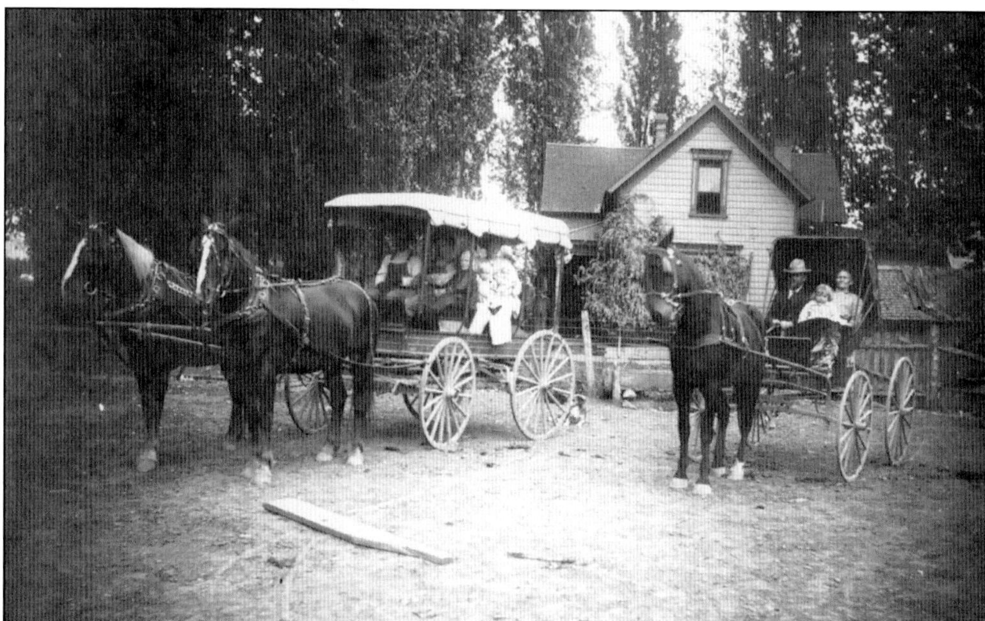

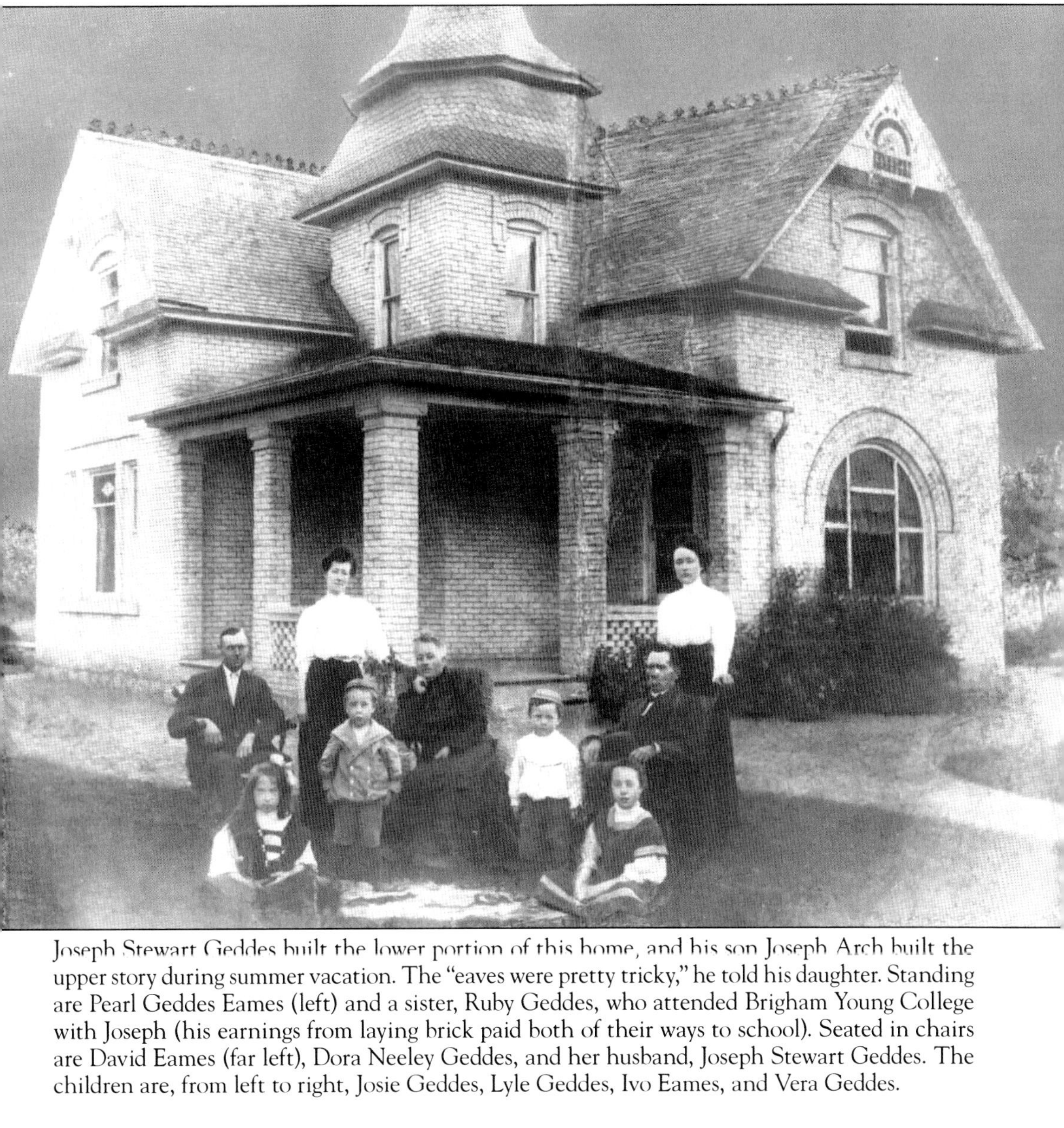

Joseph Stewart Geddes built the lower portion of this home, and his son Joseph Arch built the upper story during summer vacation. The "eaves were pretty tricky," he told his daughter. Standing are Pearl Geddes Eames (left) and a sister, Ruby Geddes, who attended Brigham Young College with Joseph (his earnings from laying brick paid both of their ways to school). Seated in chairs are David Eames (far left), Dora Neeley Geddes, and her husband, Joseph Stewart Geddes. The children are, from left to right, Josie Geddes, Lyle Geddes, Ivo Eames, and Vera Geddes.

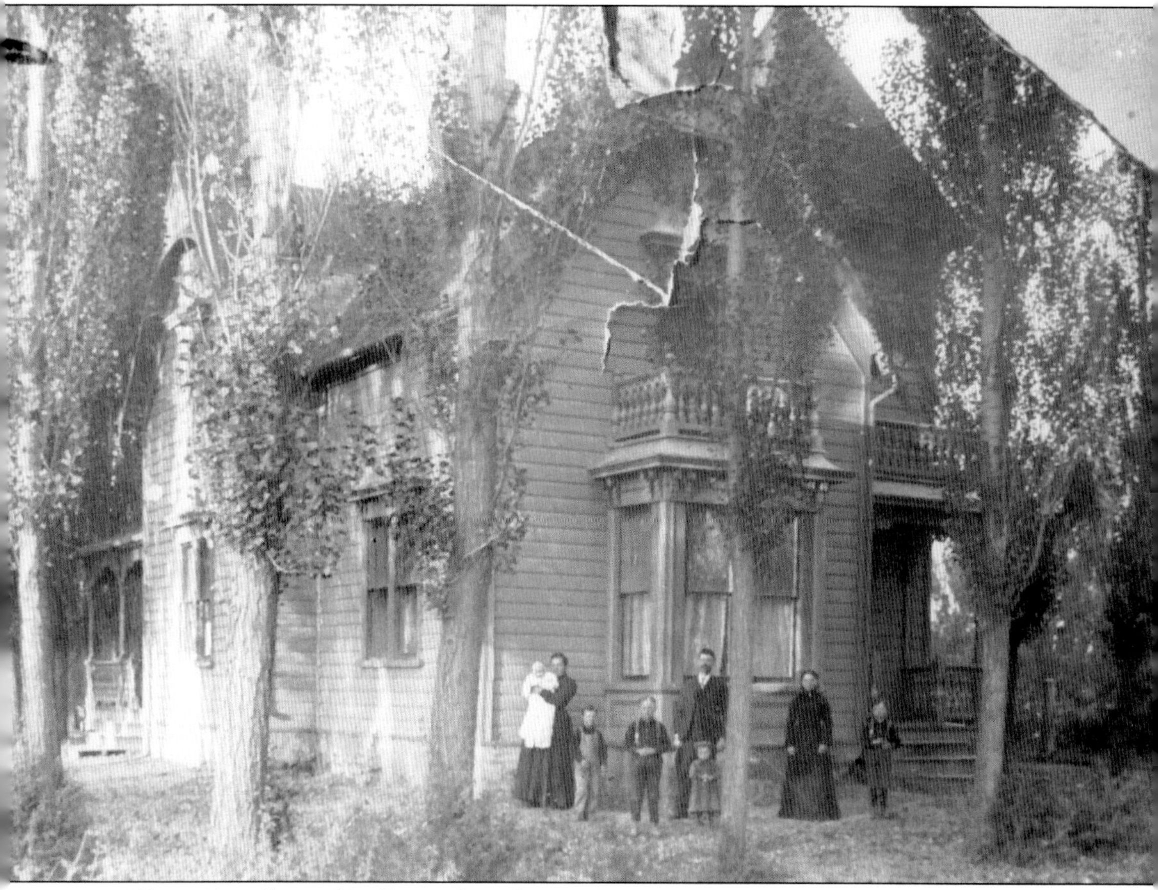

William Chandler and Nellie Nash Parkinson built this home in 1890 on the northeast corner of First East and Oneida Streets. Parkinson was a bishop as well as president of the Oneida, Hyrum, and Pocatello Stakes. Allen R. Cutler purchased the home in 1899. This photograph of his family was taken in 1903. From left to right are Lucy Hardy Cutler (holding Orvid), Charles, Allen, Elvin, Allen Sr., his second wife Malinda Ray Skidmore, and Karl. Cutler was a doctor in Preston; in 1899, he delivered Ezra Taft Benson, who grew up to became US secretary of agriculture under President Eisenhower, then president of the LDS Church. Cutler was also principal and superintendent for the Oneida School District. In 1927, Willis Hendricks bought the home, remodeling it into a mortuary. Sherwin Webb bought the place from Willis Hendricks in about 1945, continuing to use it as a mortuary. He and his family, including son and current resident Douglas Webb, continued to remodel the house into its current form.

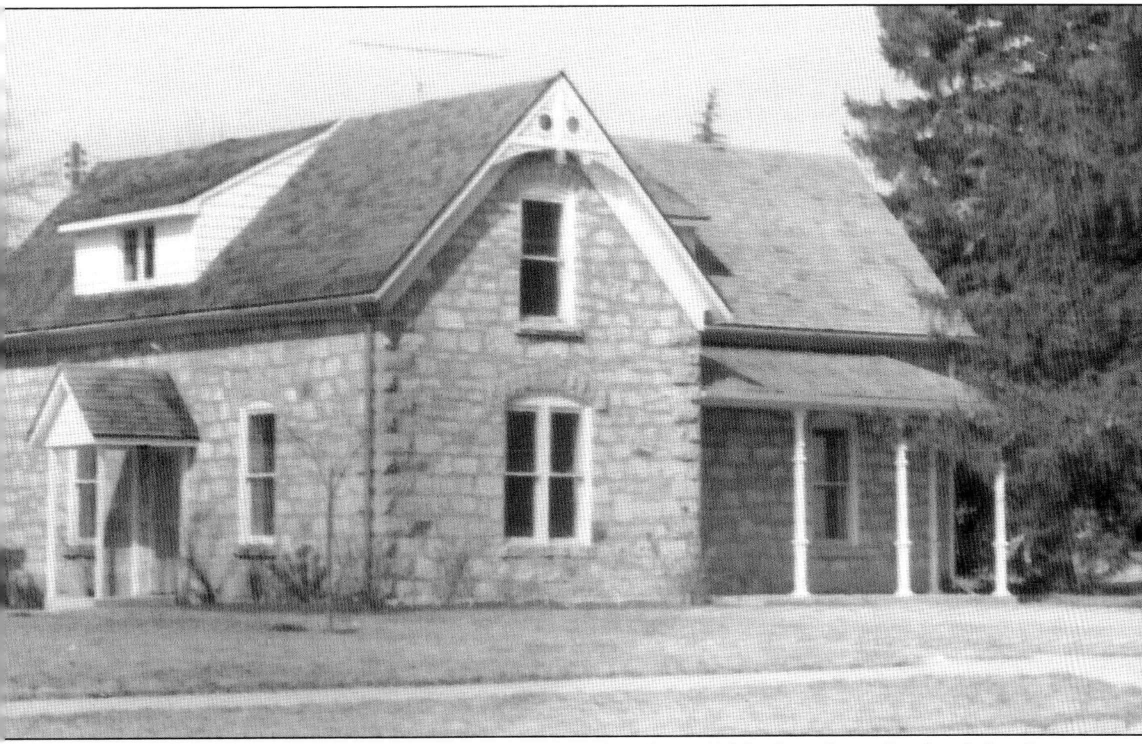

Located at 100 East 100 South, this home was completed in 1895 by Matthias Cowley. Like the Oneida Stake Academy, built one block to the north, it was constructed of sandstone quarried northeast of Franklin by John Nuffer, a German immigrant. It was listed in the National Register of Historic places in 1976 by then owners Edwin and Beula Hinckley. Matthias was a member of the Oneida Stake Presidency, which supervised construction of the OSA. According to son Matthew Cowley (1897–1953), visiting church authority Moses Thatcher prayed for "a prophet, seer, and revelator to be born under this roof." Matthew, the next child born in the home, was called to be an LDS apostle in 1945. Matthias sold the house to local bishop John Larson in 1898 and moved to Salt Lake City to fill his new position as an apostle. Another son, Samuel, was the first man inducted into the FBI Hall of Fame. He helped take down notorious mobster John Dillinger, then died in 1934 at the hands of another gangster, Baby Face Nelson.

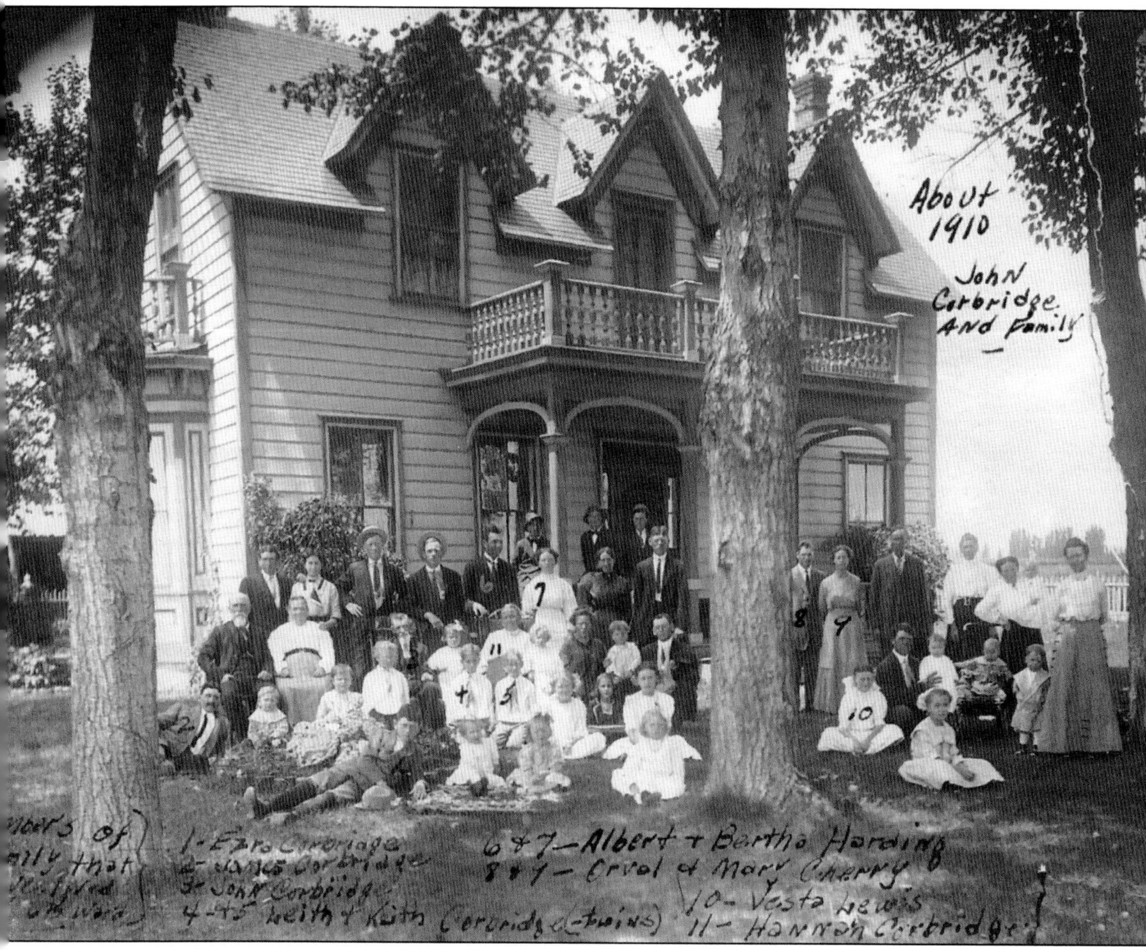

John and Hannah Lee Corbridge gathered their family at their home, two and a half miles south and a half mile west of Preston, for this c. 1910 photograph. They had 11 children, 10 of whom survived to adulthood. Apparently, the person who identified the people in this picture was only concerned with those who lived within the boundaries of the Preston Sixth Ward of the LDS Church, which comprised the southwest section of Preston at the time. They are (1) Ezra Corbridge, (2) James Corbridge, (3) John Corbridge (sitting by No. 11, Hannah), (4) Leith and (5) Keith Corbridge (twin sons of James Heber and Mary Ann Thomson Corbridge), (6) Albert and (7) Bertha Corbridge Harding, (8) Orvol and (9) Mary Corbridge Cherry, (10) Vesta Corbridge Lewis, and (11) Hannah Corbridge. Some of the other people in the image include Sarah and Will Corbridge, Elsie Corbridge, Cassie Hyde, Rosella Hyde, Florence Corbridge, Millie Corbridge, Fred Corbridge, and Ara (Ora) Hyde.

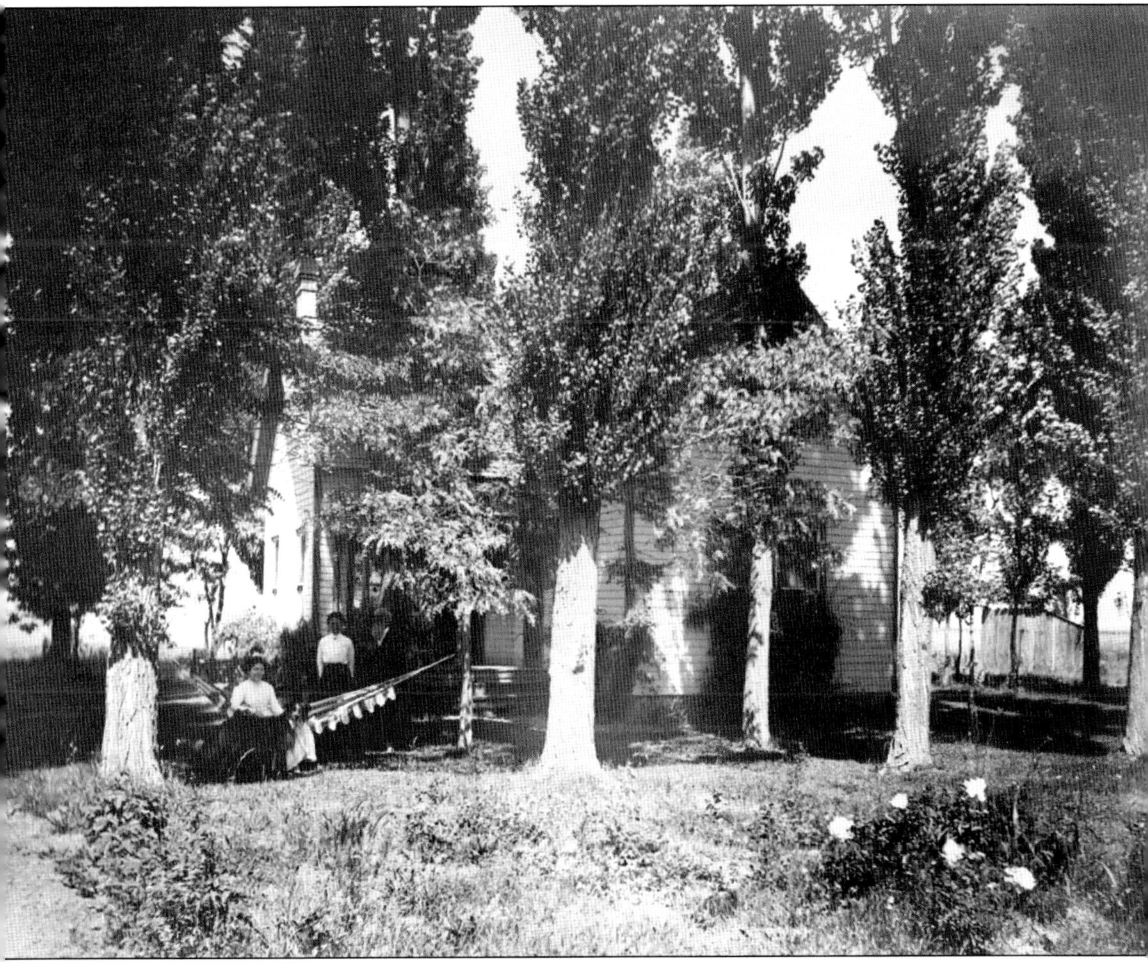

George H. and Lizzie Geddes Carver and their niece Edna Geddes (who later married Aerial Guy Eames) are pictured at the Carver home, one mile west and one-half mile north of the intersection of State Street and Oneida Street. This photograph was taken between 1906 and 1908, when George was in his 50s and Lizzie was in her 40s. Edna was born in Oregon in 1887 to William Stewart Geddes and English immigrant Margaret Ferguson Cullen Geddes. William was superintendent of the Oregon Lumber Company at North Powder, Oregon, a lumber camp. The 1910 census shows Edna living with George and Lizzie and going to school at the Oneida Stake Academy. George was farming at the time, but he was also president of the school board, with Nephi Larson, R.P. Stokes, Dr. A.R. Cutler, Joseph Johnson, and George D. Casto as board members.

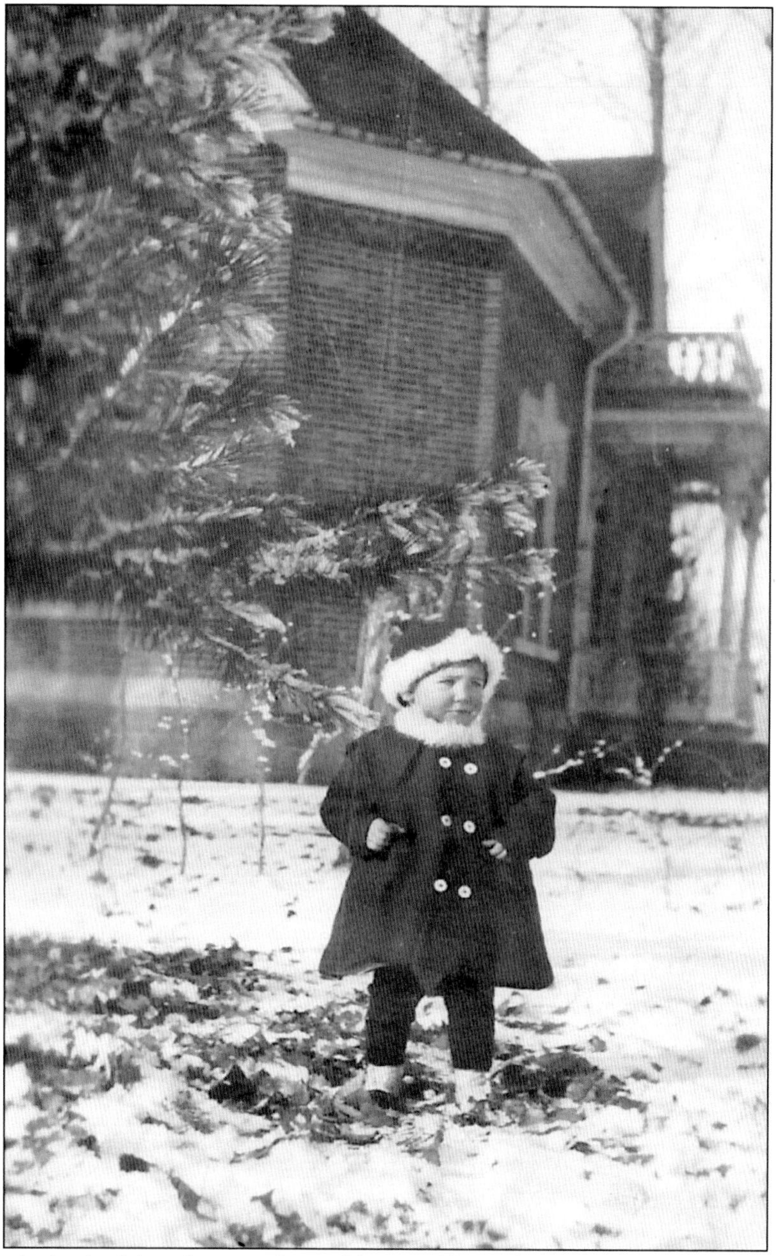

Written on the back of this photograph is: "Olive Geddes in front of old Parkinson House, which was Jim Geddes' home and not Eggett's." This home, built by Martin Johnson for George and Lucy Parkinson in 1895, was purchased by James Stewart and Dorothea Olive Nielson Geddes in 1913. According to Leo Geddes, the Geddeses' oldest daughter, Martha, never married and lived in the home throughout her life. She worked in the Carnegie Library. Her younger sister, Olive, was born on December 4, 1916. According to the 1940 census, Olive was living in Boise, where she was a stenographer for the State Department of Insurance, making $1,140 during the previous year. She had completed her first year of college and had a roommate, 27-year-old Dorothy Bingham. Olive married Edward P. Luhman in San Francisco in 1964. She died on February 20, 2001, in Salt Lake City, and is buried in the Preston Cemetery. This picture was likely taken in about 1918.

Nine

PEOPLE

The first white children born in Preston were Tessie Winn (August 3, 1869) and David Jensen (March 19, 1870). Tessie was the first child born on the west side of Worm Creek, and David was the first child born on the east side. Tessie was the daughter of Dennis and Margaret Winn. David's parents, David and Julia Konstanse Peterson Jensen, first settled that area about the time David was born. The first death recorded was that of five-year-old Dennis Evermont Winn, oldest child of Dennis Alma and Emma Lorena Bair Winn, in 1871. The couple eventually had 10 children, raising most of them in Vernal, Utah. Unfortunately, little Tessie was the second death, passing away in 1872. Both children were buried in Richmond. The first person buried in Preston was Ruth Hollingsworth, the baby daughter of Elam and Martha Mae Keetch, who died January 23, 1881. She was buried on her family's homestead on Worm Creek but was later relocated to the Sandhill Cemetery, southeast of Preston. Rose Green Porter, a young mother with two little children and wife of Nahum Boyd Porter, died in 1892. She was the first person buried in the cemetery located northeast of Preston, by the golf course.

The first newlyweds in Preston were residents James N. Winn and Angeline Thomas. They went to Richmond, Utah, on September 25, 1875, for the wedding ceremony, then returned to Preston to live. The first marriage performed in Preston was between Henry Myers and Elizabeth Winn on July 15, 1877.

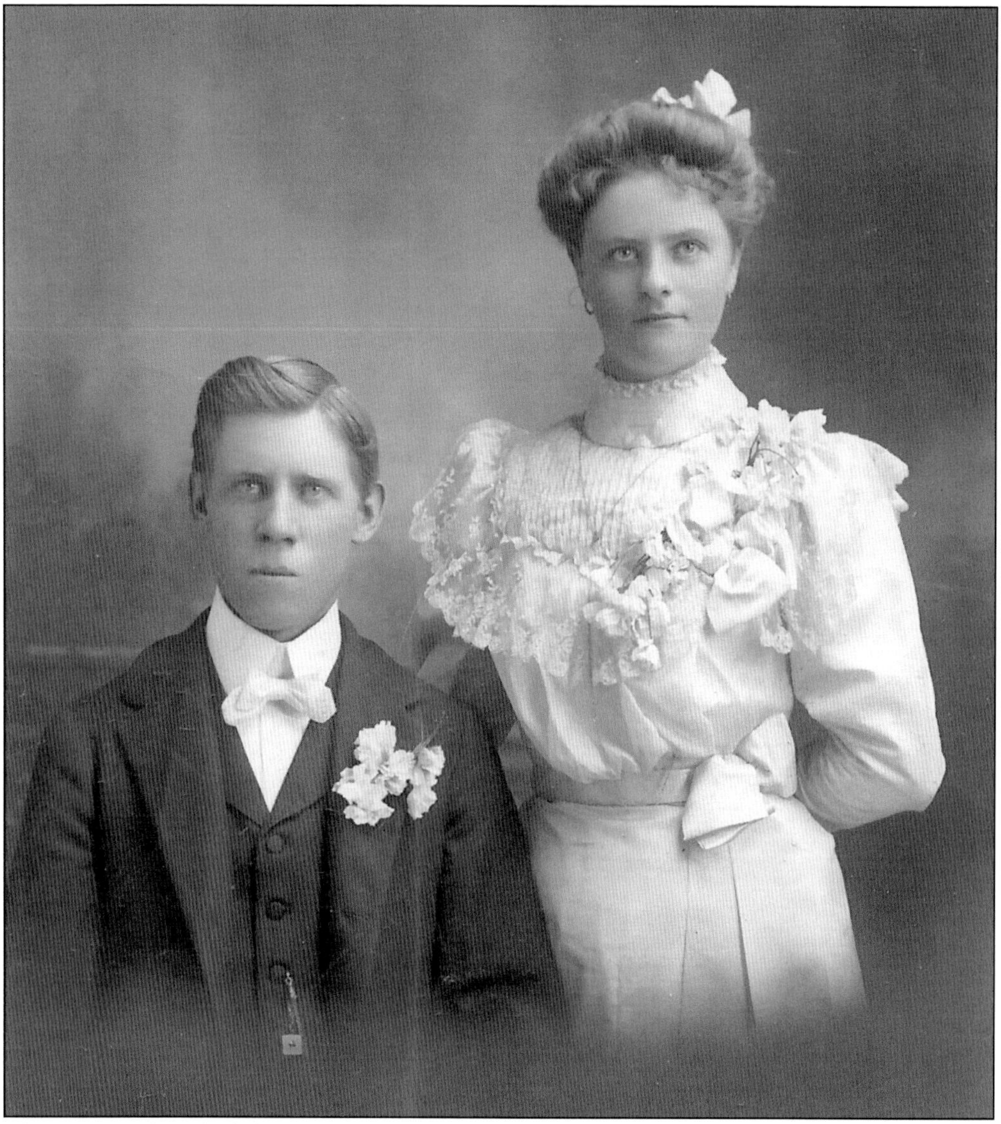

This picture of Emil Olaf Petterborg and Emma Rebecca Hanson was taken on their wedding day, November 14, 1900. He was 22 years old, and she was 21, and they were married in Logan, Utah. Emil was born in Preston in 1878 to Scandinavian immigrants Emil Olsen and Erika Eugenia Bjorkman Petterborg. Emily and her parents, Nels August Hanson and Mathilda Gustava Nilson, emigrated from Sweden in 1885. Emil and Emma remained in Preston, raising their children there. He drove wagons for a living. She died in 1964, and he in 1967. They are buried in the Preston Cemetery.

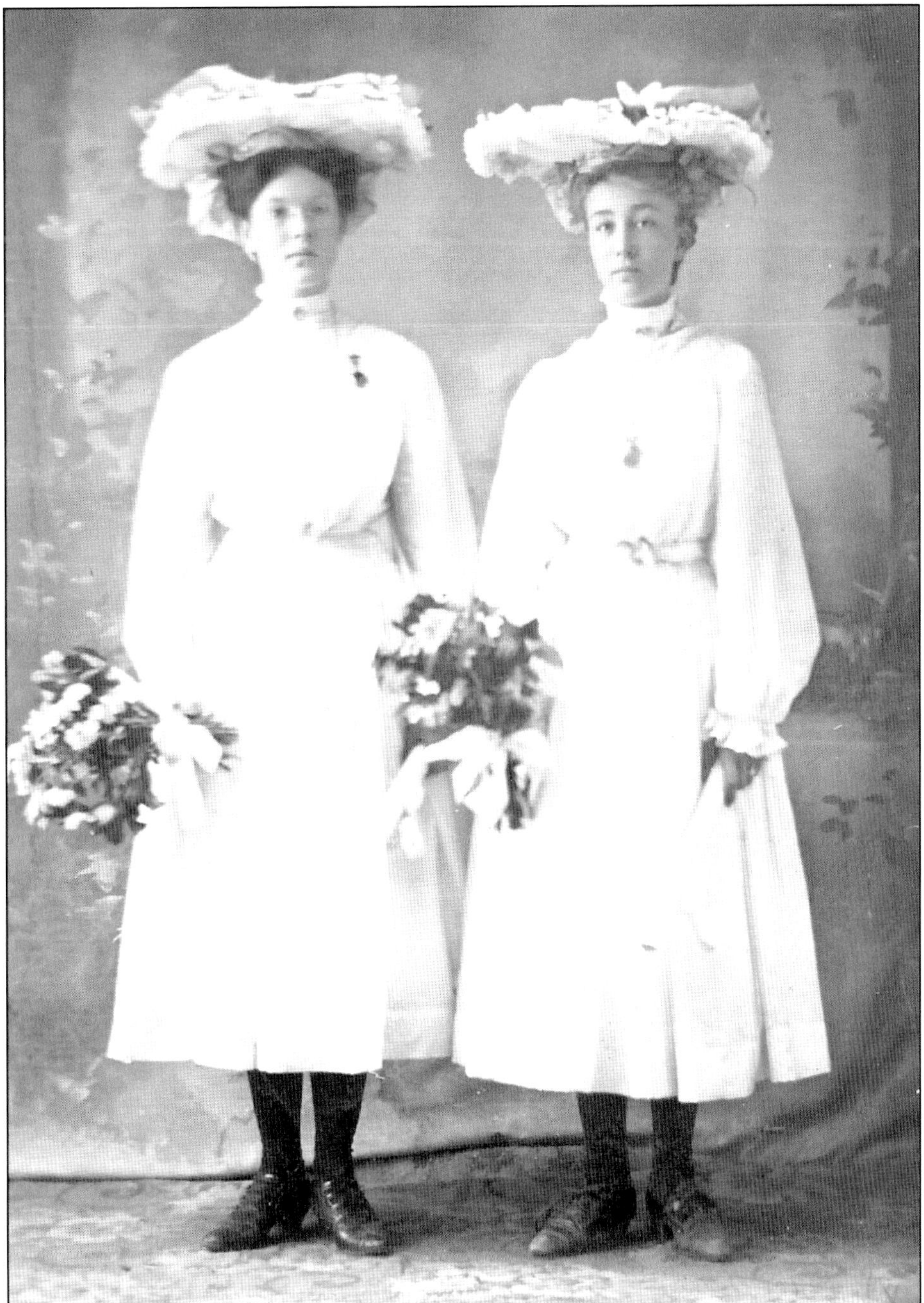

Flora Edna Geddes (left) and Vera Doney Parkinson (right) played a piano duet upstairs in the Oneida Stake Academy in 1903. They were performing for their eighth-grade graduation ceremonies. Edna was born in 1889 in Oregon to William Stewart and Margaret Ferguson Cullen Geddes. She married Aeriel Guy Eames, and they raised their family in Preston. Parkinson, the daughter of George Chandler Parkinson and Lucy Maria Doney, was also born in 1889, and married Brigham Young's great-grandson Richard Whitehead Young Jr. in 1915. They raised their family in Salt Lake City.

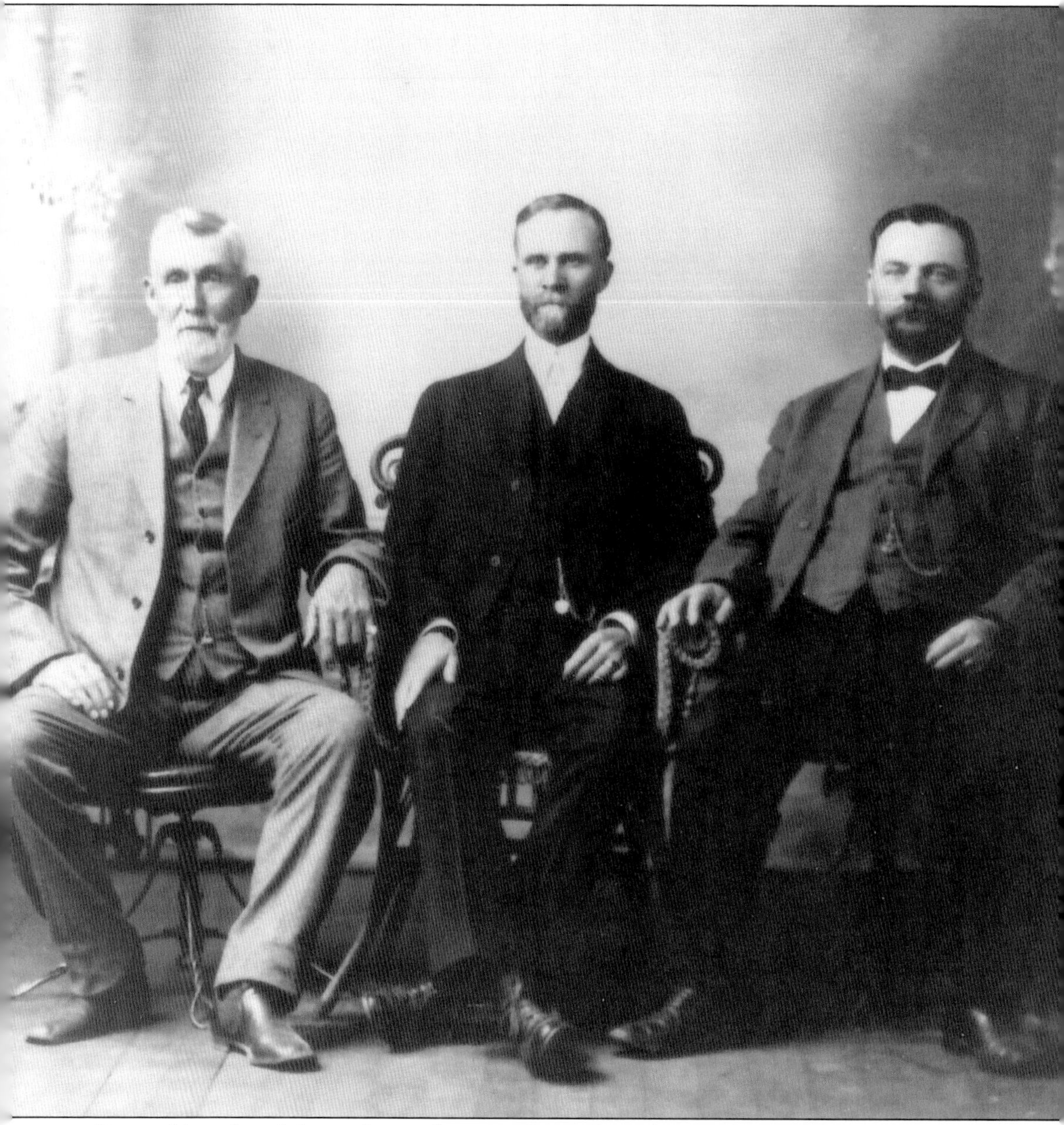

Pictured here from left to right are the men who made up the presidency of the Oneida Stake in 1890: Solomon Hale, George C. Parkinson, and Matthias Cowley. These men were responsible for implementing the directive of the Church of Jesus Christ of Latter-day Saints to build academies in each of the church's stakes. Solomon Hale was responsible for visiting each resident of the stake to invite them to donate toward the construction of the Oneida Stake Academy, which stands today at 90 East Oneida Street. It was built between 1890 and 1894 and was dedicated in 1895. Hale was also the first man to open up a livery business in Preston, in July 1900. It was located on West Oneida Street. Parkinson was just three years old when his parents moved from Kaysville, Utah, to become some of the original settlers of Franklin in 1860. He was the Oneida Stake president for 23 years, from 1887 to 1910. Matthias F. Cowley was called to be an apostle in the LDS Church in 1897. At that time, his family moved to Salt Lake City.

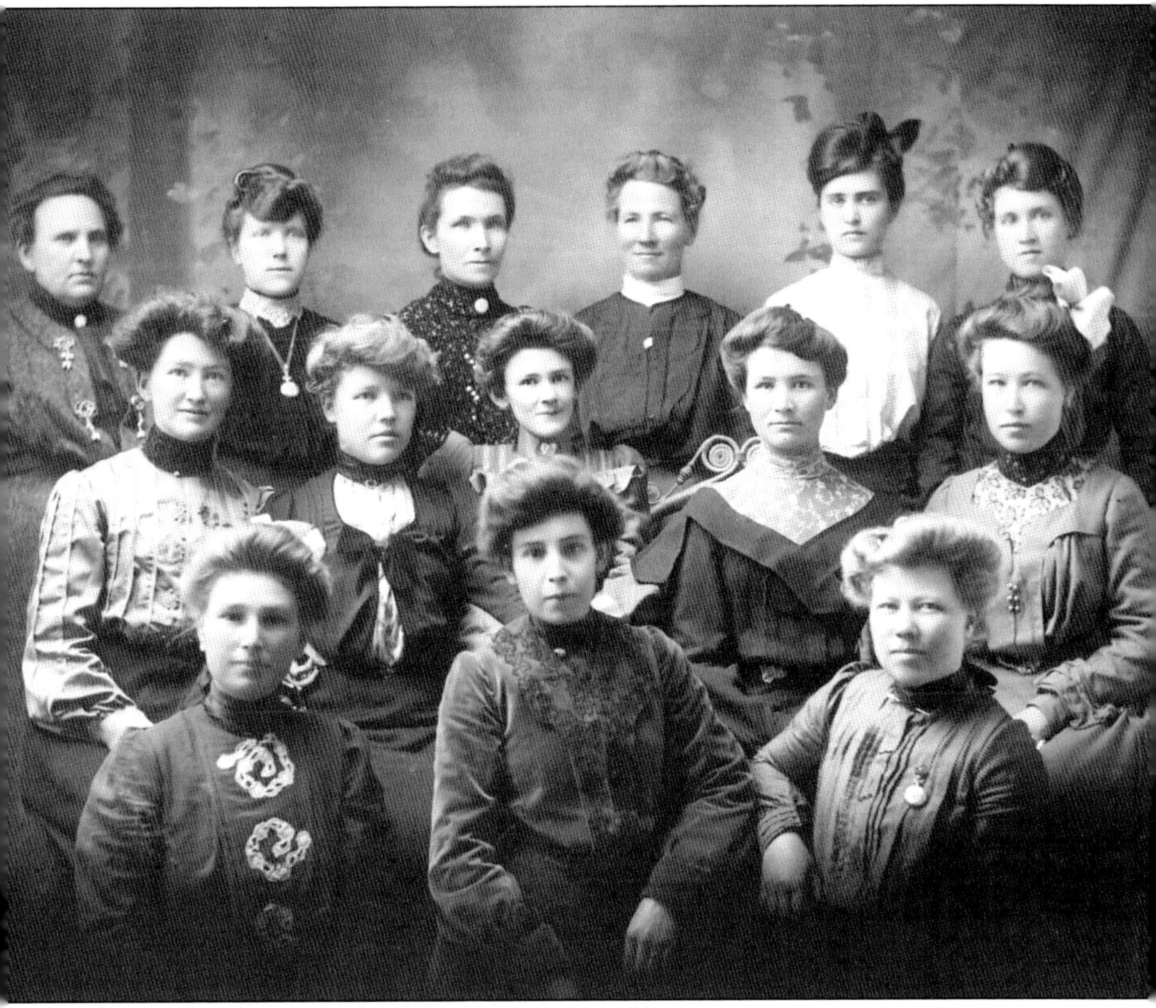

The ladies pictured above were the leaders of the Mutual Improvement Association of the Preston Third Ward of the LDS Church in 1905. The women were about to be released from this calling, so they decided to have their picture taken, according to the *Hometown Album*. They are, from left to right, (first row) Eldena Erickson Jensen (wife of Alma Jensen), Laura Hansen (plural wife of O.D. Merrill and daughter of Laura Hansen), and Sadie Eames (wife of Arthur Tippets); (second row) Annie Lewis Johnson (wife of James E. Johnson), Lillie Eames (wife of Frank Benson), Sadie Kidd, Anna Miller (wife of John A. Morrison), and Celia Hansen (wife of Abe Winward); (third row) Laura Hansen (wife of Pete Hansen), Ida Estella Bingham Roper (wife of Suel Roper), Susie Lamb Hawkes (wife of William Hawkes Sr.), Elizabeth G. Carver (wife of George Carver), Jane Stevenson, and Susie Hawkes Nelson (wife of Taylor Nelson).

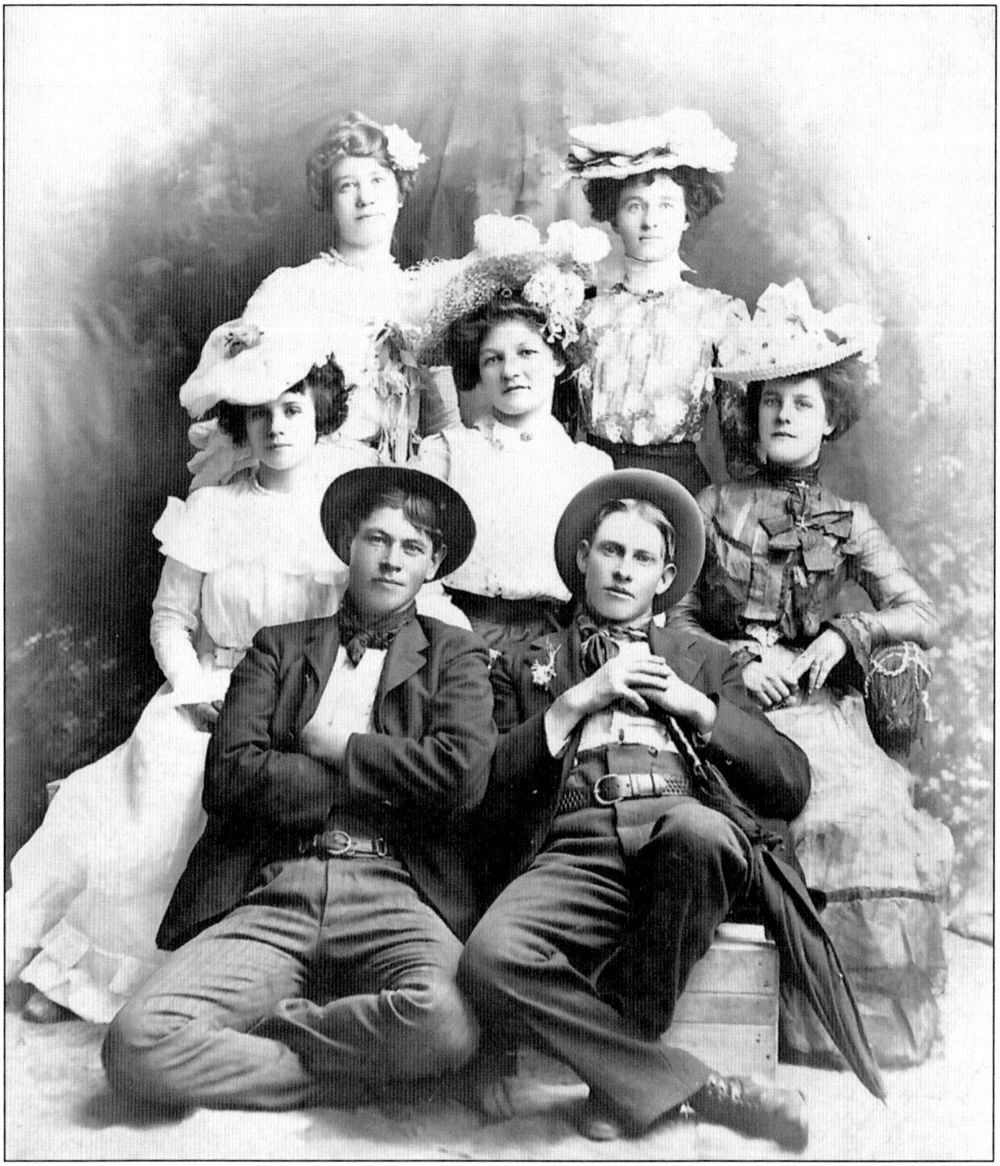

According to the *Hometown Album*, only three of these young people could be identified. At the top with the hat is the daughter of William Moroni and Elizabeth Hatch Daines of Hyde Park, Melva Daines, who married James Kearl in 1911. In the center is the daughter of Rasmus and Ann Caspersen of Preston, Elizabeth "Bessie" Ann Casperson, who married Burt Martin in 1905. To the left of Bessie is the daughter of John and Sarah Ellen Tippets of Preston, Sara Ellen "Nellie" Tippets, who married Robert Beckstead in about 1903. Hart noted that the young man on the left might have been Cal or Tom Jenkins or their uncle Owen. Cal married Eva Emma Stephens in 1905, and Tom married Sarah Agnes Hall in 1900. Tom was a farmer in Preston until his untimely death in 1914; the wagon he was pulling rolled, and he died about 12 hours later, leaving his wife with four boys to raise.

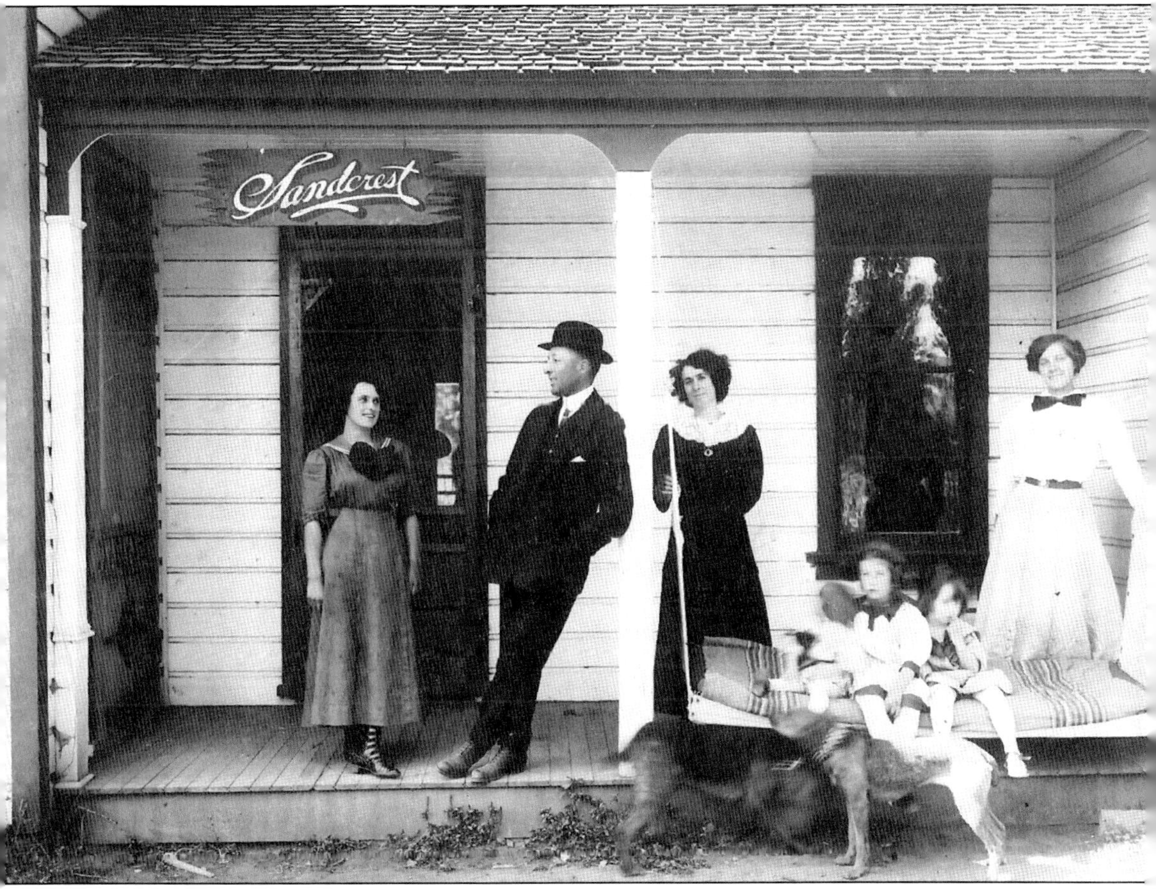

The back of this photograph identifies the adults as Fay Evans Edison, Simon Higginbotham, Daisy Fail, and Leah Higginbotham, and the children as Daisy Dean Fail, Louise Higginbotham, and Florence Fail. George Fail was a salesman in the flour industry. Simon and Leah Higginbotham moved to Preston sometime after 1910. Their daughter Louise was born about 1905, so this picture was probably taken around 1914. In 1920, Simon was in Bannock County, boarding with someone and working with the sugar beet company. Fay Evans, a popular young woman from Preston and daughter of Joseph J. and Margaret Davis Evans of Spanish Fork, married Louis M. Edison, a popular café proprietor of Preston who had recently sold the Franklin Cafe. Louis's family came from Norway. The couple was married in Salt Lake City in October 1913 and made their home in Preston. By 1920, census records have the Edisons in Hyrum, where he was an insurance salesman; the Higenbothams in Salt Lake City; and the Fails in Provo, Utah.

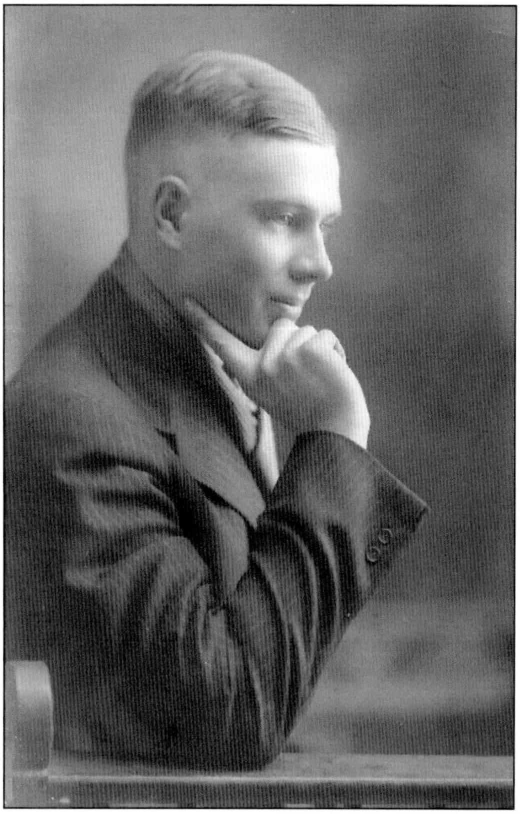

Lonsdale Roe (at left and below) was six years old when his father, Watkin Roe, moved his family from Utah to Preston in 1907 to publish the local paper. Watkin was responsible for changing the paper's name to the *Franklin County Citizen* when the county was formed in 1913. Lonsdale graduated from eighth grade in 1916. In 1921, he married Juanita Allen Heusser. By 1924, he was the newspaper publisher, running it with his brothers Watkin and Lewis. He also helped the youth of Preston High School print their newspaper, the *Beacon*, often winning bets with its editor, Scott Nelson, over the spelling and meanings of words. At that time, the newspaper was located on State Street, just north of the park entrance. Lonsdale was also a frequent participant in billiards at one of Preston's several local pool halls. The Roe brothers sold the newspaper in 1942 to William F. MacKnight. Lonsdale was living in Ogden at the time of his death in 1945, where he was working as a switchman for the Ogden Union Railroad & Depot Company.

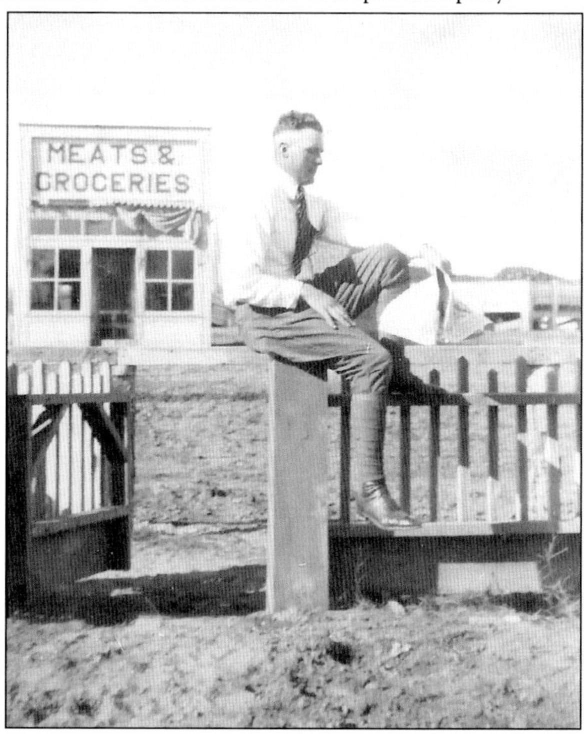

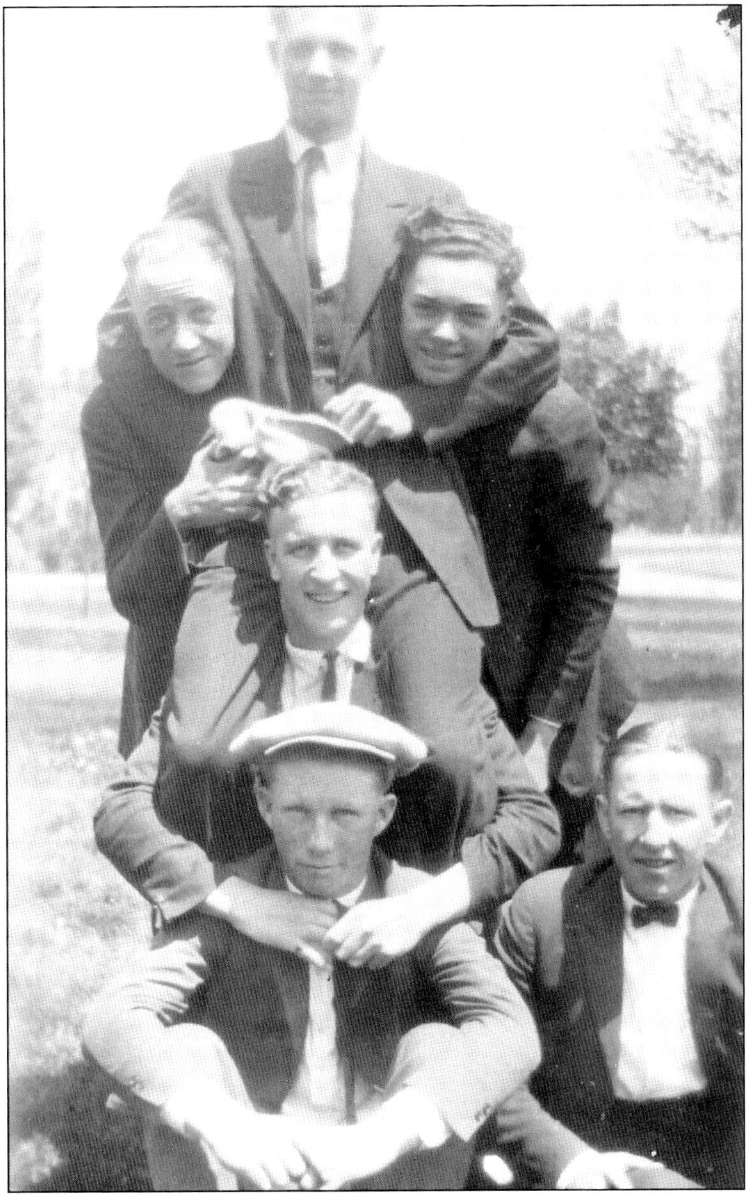

From the curved pathway, this picture appears to have been taken in City Park, known today as Benson Park. Although the occasion of the photograph is lost to time, it likely shows members of a party club masquerading as a parliamentary club, Hokhmah (a Hebrew word for "wisdom"). Pictured from the top down and left to right are Denzil Petterborg, Spud Geddes, Lee Packer, Jerry Weaver, Stan Hawker, and Joseph Thomas. Other club members were Blaine Larson, Maurice Brimhall, Leo Petterborg, Bruce Wallace, Lowell Smith, Tug White, Clair Merrill, Helmar Jorgensen, Harold Hawkes, and Scott Nelson. One year, school authorities told the club to cancel one of its fundraising dances, as it coincided with a pageant advertising Brigham Young University. The boys were incensed. They moved their dance from the Nelson Gymnasium to Franklin. Nelson recalled the chiding he received from English professor N.L. Nelson: " 'You were organized as a DEBATING society. Instead you were nothing but a bunch of good time Charlies.' He could have been right . . . but we had one consolation. We had won our only debate of the year."

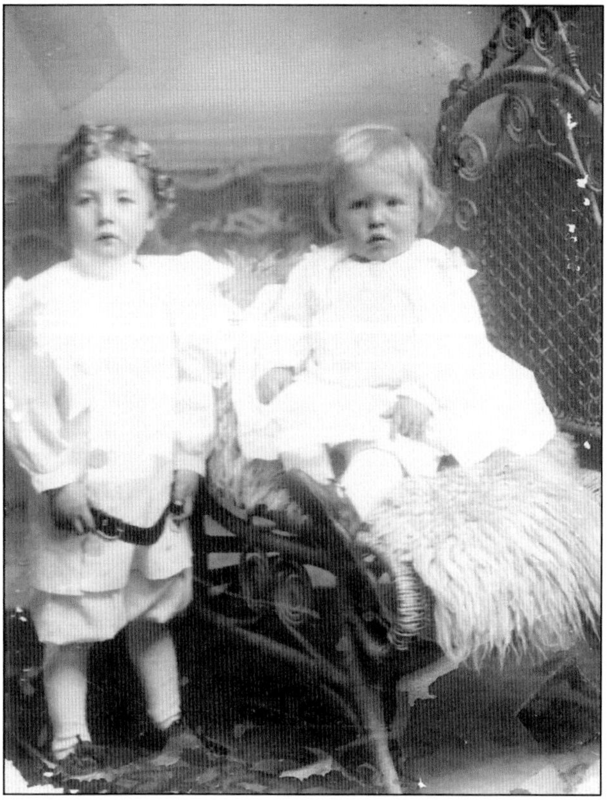

These darling children, Willard Deloss and Clarence Levon Hansen, are the children of Clarence Deloss Hansen and Clarabelle Benzon. Willard was born in 1904 and Levon in 1906, in Preston. (Kathy Griffin.)

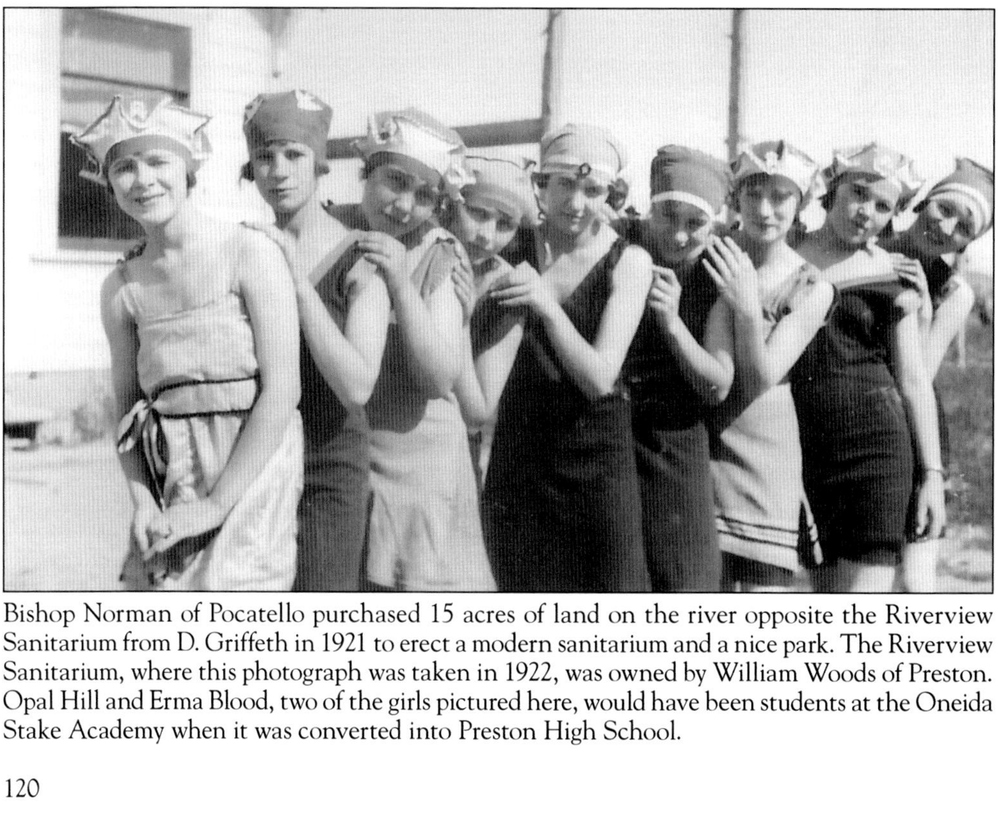

Bishop Norman of Pocatello purchased 15 acres of land on the river opposite the Riverview Sanitarium from D. Griffeth in 1921 to erect a modern sanitarium and a nice park. The Riverview Sanitarium, where this photograph was taken in 1922, was owned by William Woods of Preston. Opal Hill and Erma Blood, two of the girls pictured here, would have been students at the Oneida Stake Academy when it was converted into Preston High School.

Nada Morgan Merrill, pictured here in front of the Oneida Stake Academy, was the daughter of Samuel Perry Morgan and Jane Elizabeth Elwell. She was born in 1902 in Franklin and married Frank B. Merrill of Mapleton, Idaho, in 1925. In 1930, they were farming in Preston, and they had two little boys: Gerald and Frank. Anne and Samuel came along while they lived in Preston, too. The family moved to Ogden, Utah, in the 1950s.

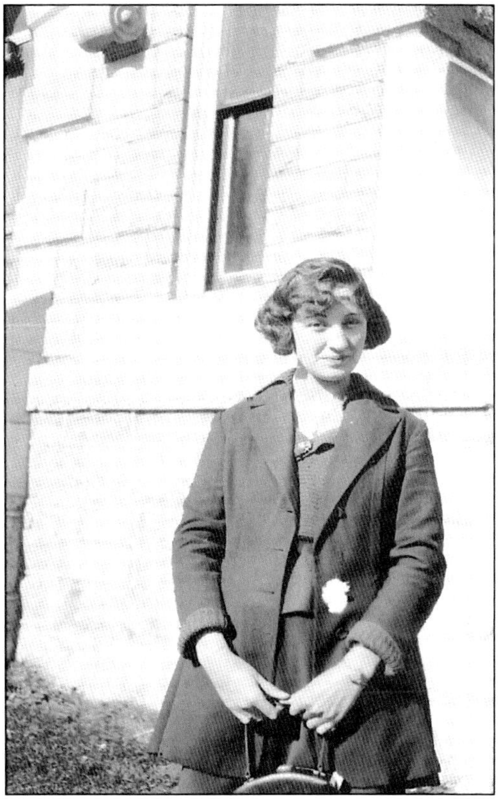

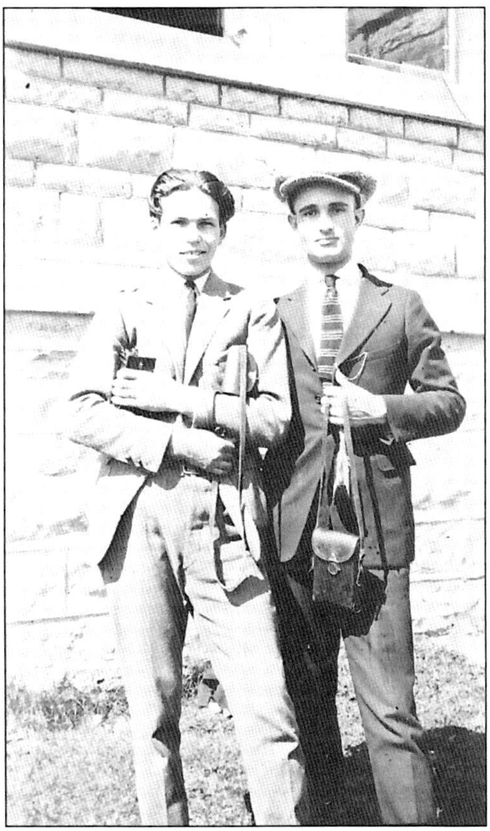

Owen Romney (left), the son of Thomas Cottam and Lydia Ann Naegle Romney, was about 22 years old when this picture was taken in 1920. Thomas taught at the OSA and was the last president of the academy, in front of which these boys are standing. Nelson Larsen (right) may be the 19-year-old Nelson B. Larsen, son of Jacob and Ellen Larsen, of Preston, according to 1920 census records.

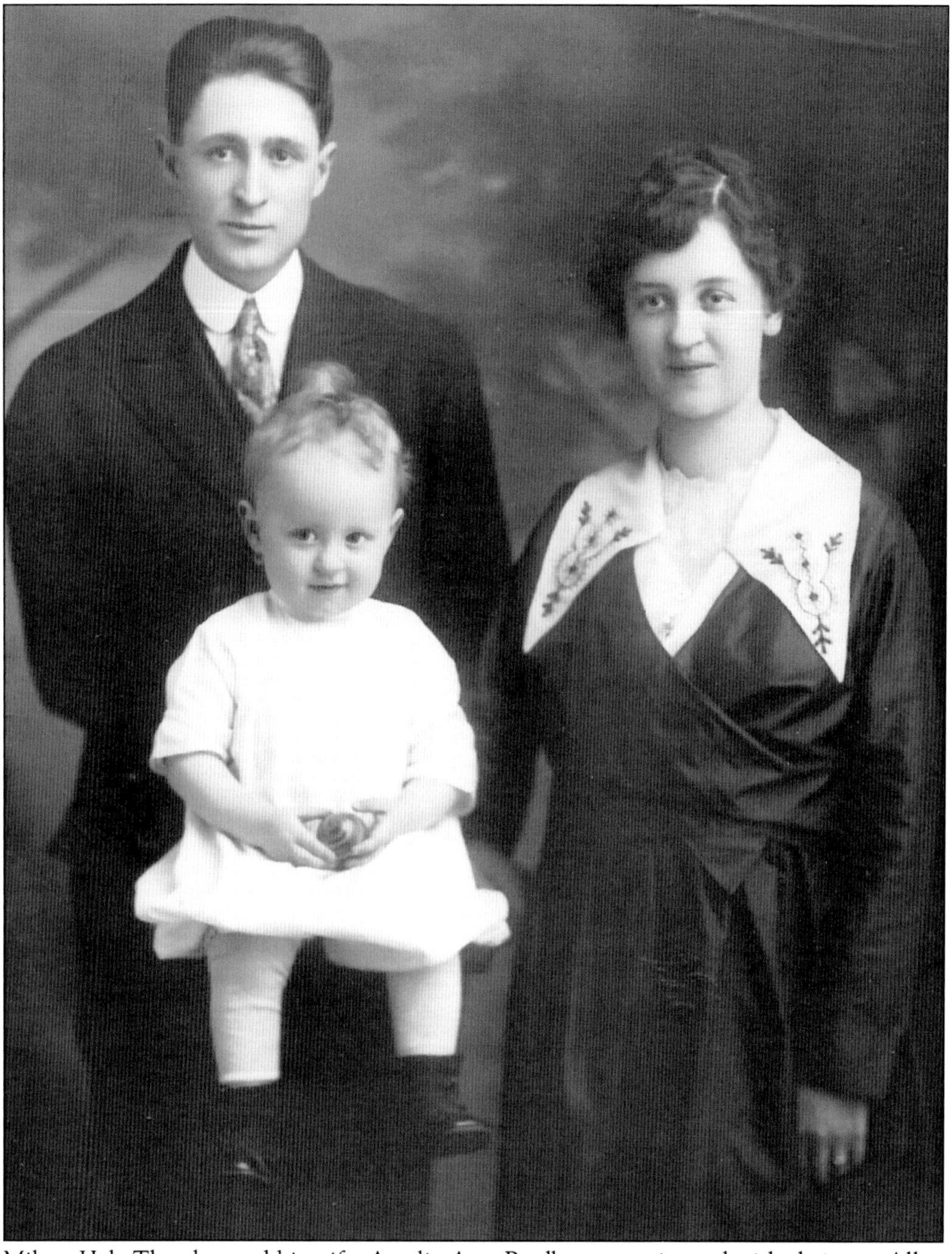

Milton Hale Thatcher and his wife, Amelia Ann Bradbury, are pictured with their son Allen Hale Thatcher, who was born in Boise in 1918. Milton, the son of Milton Herbert and Hattie Violate Hale Thatcher, was born in Preston in 1891. Amelia Ann Bradbury was born in 1895 to William and Mary J. Bradbury in Liberty, Idaho. She and Milton were married in 1915 in Boise, Idaho. They had a daughter, Kleo B. Thatcher, in 1919, and another baby girl in 1922, who died the day she was born. In 1930, Amelia's mother was living with the couple in Kuna. Amelia died in 1939 and is buried in Boise. Milton then married Preston native Vila Rose Beckstead in 1946. Milton and Vila died within days of each other in 1988 and are buried in Preston.

Arvilla "Billie" Thatcher (right) lived to be 101 years old. According to her obituary, she was born in 1904 to Milton Herbert and Hattie Vilate Hale Thatcher in Preston, and was the granddaughter of Solomon H. Hale. Milton died when she was four years old. Billie graduated from eighth grade, then worked at a bank to help provide for her family. In 1923, she married Elgin Stewart Campbell. They lived in Preston, Bancroft, Central, Treasureton, Weston, and Mink Creek, Idaho, and in Cove, Utah, with Elgin working as a schoolteacher in each community. They had six children and retired in Boise, where they operated a horseback-packing and guide service for big-game hunters and fishermen. She outlived three of her children and her husband. Below, a 1936 fishing party is made up of, from left to right, Clifford Warr, Lonsdale Roe, Allen Cutler, two unidentified, Dr. Evans, Erwin Spilsbury, unidentified, and Van Ness Hanson.

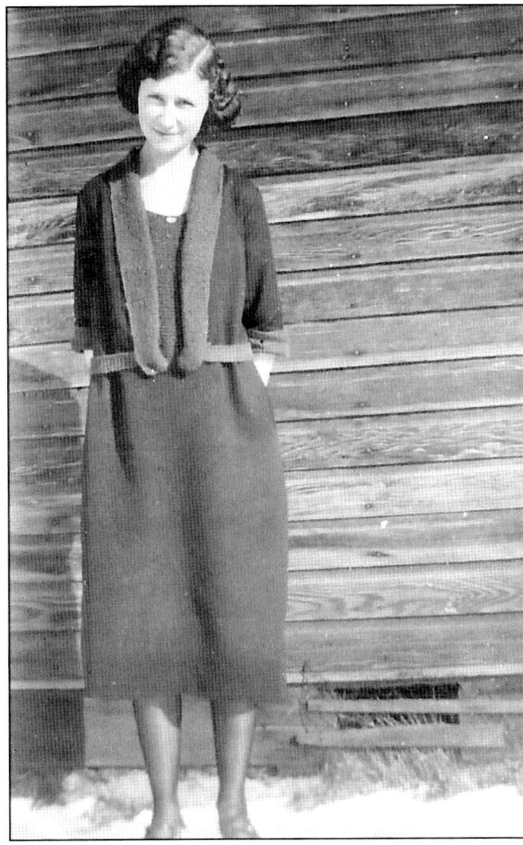

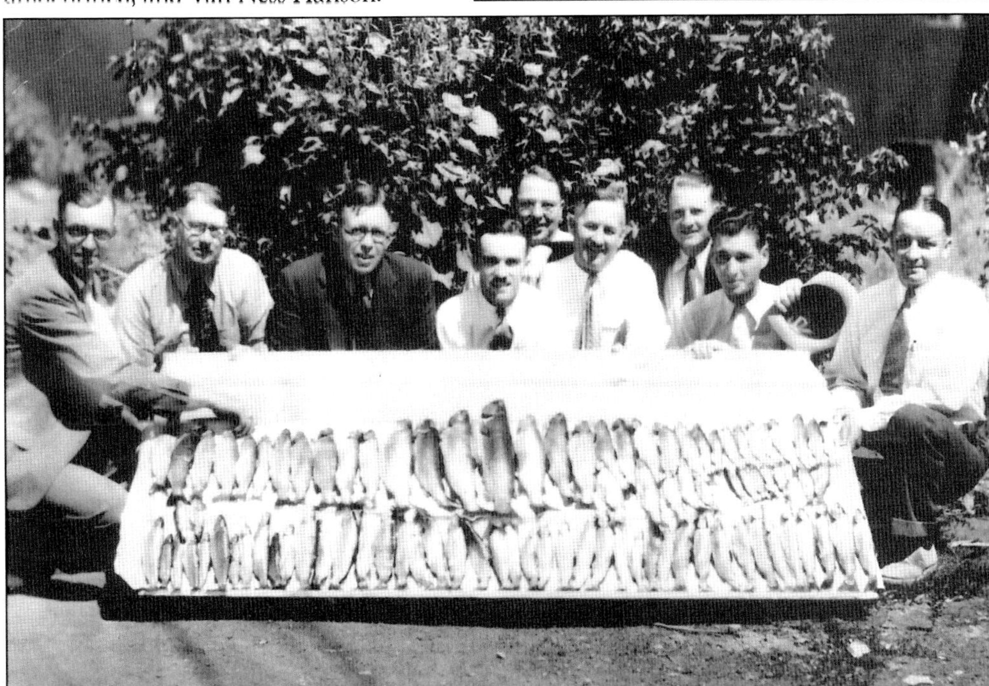

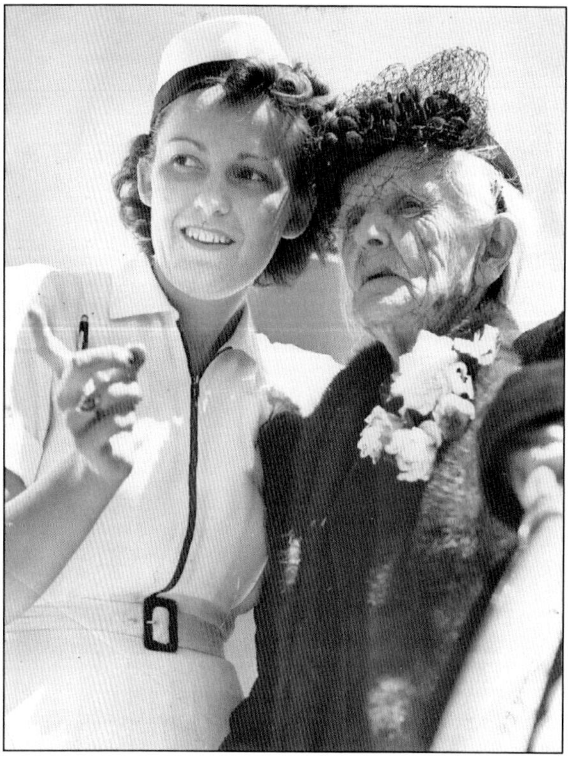

Millie Crockett (left) and her mother, Elizabeth Bird Howell, 94, went to San Francisco in 1940 for the unveiling of a plaque honoring pioneers who traveled to California from New York on the ship *Brooklyn* in 1846. Elizabeth Howell was the last person living who made that trip, which took three months by way of South America. Theo Petterborg and his wife took Howell and Crockett by car to the airport in Salt Lake City.

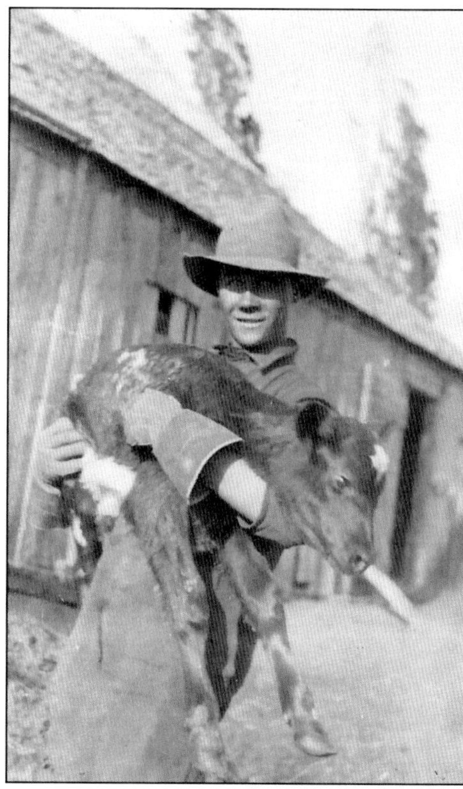

Cristen Lorris Miller, one of 13 children of Nicolai Christensen and Anne Christine Nielsen Miller, was born on February 6, 1894, in Preston. He registered for the draft between 1917 and 1918. In 1930, he married Annie Mildred Fletcher of Rock Springs. In 1940, they lived in Preston, where Cris farmed, and had three children. Cris died in Salt Lake City on July 5, 1966, and was buried in the Preston Cemetery. Annie followed in 1986.

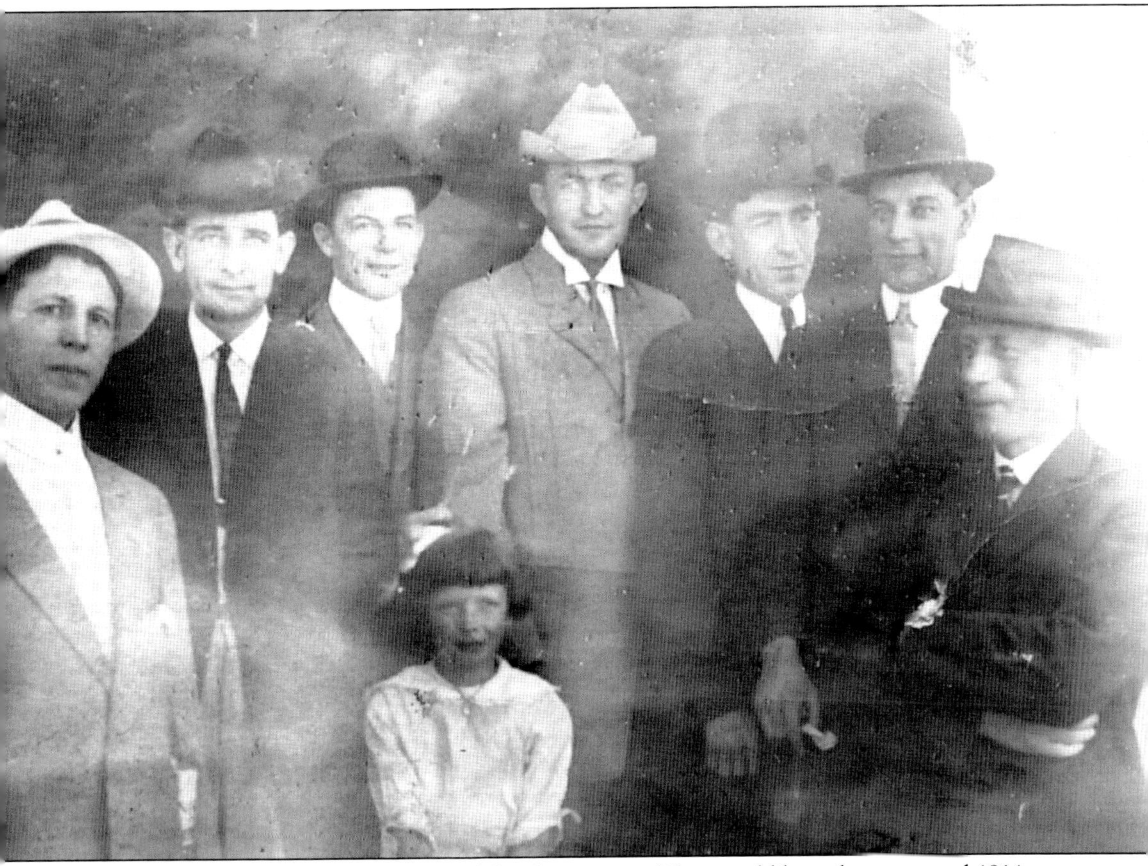

Several businessmen from Preston posed for this picture. This would have been around 1914, as the little girl, Rada Parkinson, was born in 1904 to Dr. George Taggart Parkinson and his wife, Florence Loretta Wilson. The second man on the left is Lew Edison. In the center, wearing the light hat, is Dr. Tylor, a dentist. Next to him on the right is Tom Boyle, born in 1883 in Logan. Boyle was a druggist, working at the Riter Brothers Drug Store on the corner of State and Oneida Streets. He and his wife, Jennie Ovida Lorentzen, had four children. Boyle was a charter member of the Rotary Club in Preston and was always on a committee. He helped organize dances for the elderly and the Elks Lodge. He suffered a nervous breakdown during the Great Depression, becoming a hypochondriac. He died in 1963 at the age of 80.

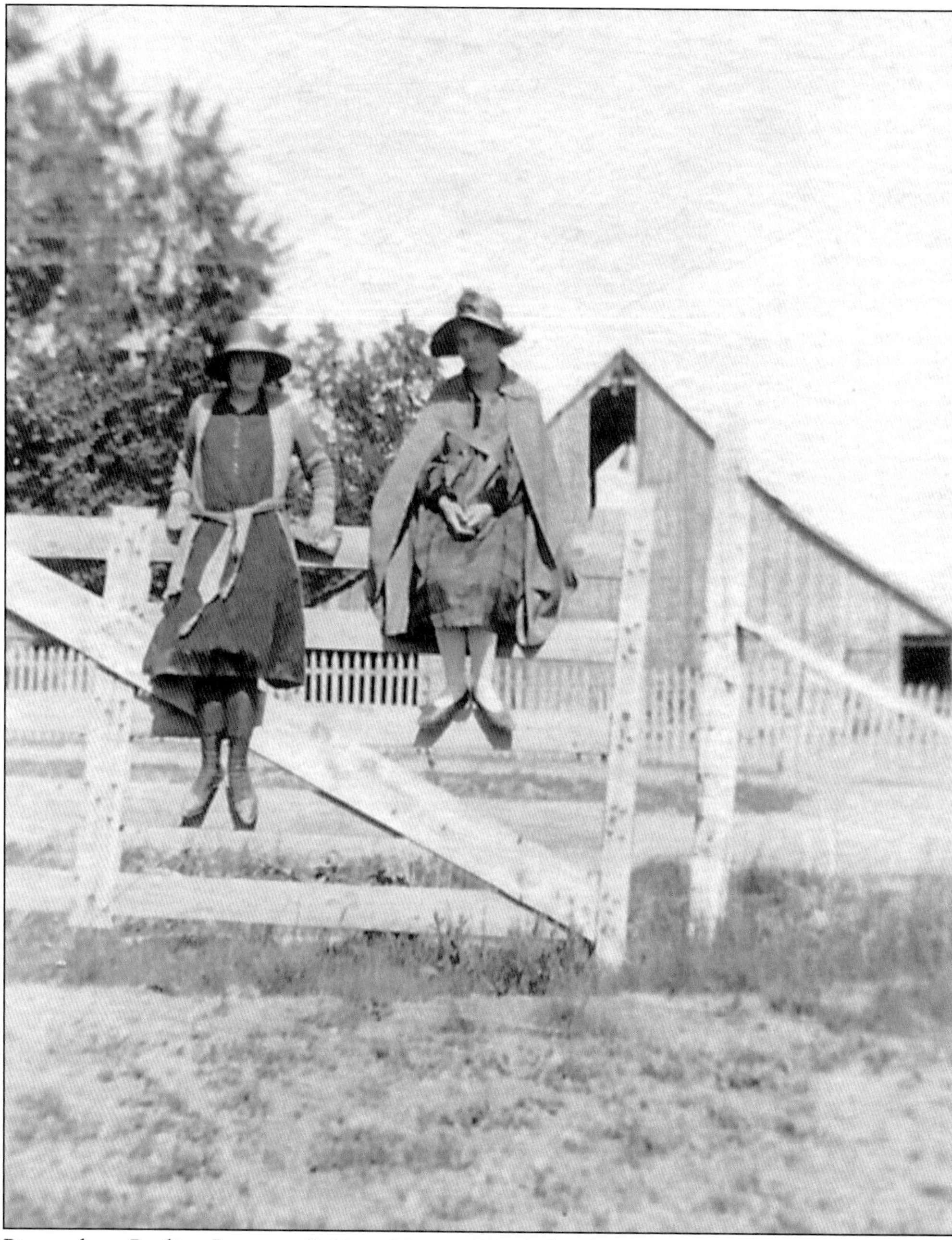

Pictured are Pauline Romney (left) and Lottie Ward, daughters of Thomas and Lydia Romney and Cyrus and Juliet Wade Ward. Pauline was born in Mexico in 1905; Pauline's cousin, W.W. Romney, started football at the OSA in 1919. Pauline married Vernon Samuel Thomander in 1927. She was a member of the first graduating class from Preston High School in 1923. Lottie married Karl Thomas Hickenlooper in 1925. They had four children and lived in the Ogden, Utah, area. Hickenlooper died in 1942, and Lottie remarried in 1966, to Briant Stringham. She taught school in Idaho and also taught for many years in Utah, eventually becoming supervisor for schools in North Sanpete County. Her sisters Harriet Peterson and Fawn Porter lived in Preston. She died in 1994 and is buried in the Ogden City Cemetery.

Sources

Cache Valley Clarion.

Cowley, Matthew. *Matthew Cowley Speaks.* Salt Lake City: Deseret Books, 1954.

Daughters of the Utah Pioneers and Newell Hart. *The Trail Blazer: History of S.E. Idaho.* Cache Valley Publishing, 1976.

Deseret News.

Durrant, Jill. " 'Next Year in Jerusalem:' The Trials and Triumphs of Music in the Schools of Preston, Idaho, 1888–1995." http://digitalcommons.usu.edu/gradreports/177. 2012.

Franklin County Citizen, 1913–1942

Hart, Newell. *Cache Valley Newsletter.* 1968–1983

———. *Hometown Album.* Cache Valley Publishing, 1973.

———. *Hometown Sketchbook.* 1981.

Oneida Stake, the Church of Jesus Christ of Latter-day Saints. *The Oneida Stake: 100 Years of LDS History in Southeast Idaho.* The *Preston Citizen.*

Polk's Pocatello City and Bannock County Directory, 1930.

Preston Citizen, 1943–1950.

Ricks, Joel. *The History of a Valley.* Logan, UT: Cache Valley Centennial Commission, 1957.

Simmonds, A.J. *In God's Lap.* Pediment Publishing, 2004.